Charles Allen was born in India ⟨...⟩ family served under the British Raj. During the early years of his childhood he lived in Assam, where his father was a Political Officer on the North-West Frontier until 1953. After being educated in England he returned to the Indian subcontinent in 1966 to work with Voluntary Service Overseas in Nepal. He ended his service with a long walk through the Himalayas that won him the *Sunday Telegraph* Traveller of the Year trophy in 1967. Since then he has trekked and climbed extensively in the Himalayas and in other corners of the world.

A writer and historian specialising in colonial and military subjects, Charles Allen is the author of several other books including *Soldier Sahibs, Plain Tales from the Raj, Tales from the Dark Continent, Tales from the South China Seas* and *The Search for Shangri-La*. He lives in Somerset.

CHARLES ALLEN

A Mountain in Tibet

The Search for Mount Kailas and the
Sources of the Great Rivers of India

An *Abacus* Book

First published in Great Britain in 1982 by
André Deutsch Limited
First Futura edition 1983
Reprinted 1984, 1986, 1991, 1993
First published in Abacus 1994
This Abacus edition published in 2003

A CIP catalogue for this book is
available from the British Library.

ISBN 0 349 10496 4

Printed and bound in Great Britain by
Clays Ltd, St Ives plc

Maps and additional material drawn by Colin Edwards and partners

Abacus
An imprint of
Time Warner Books (UK)
Brettenham House
Lancaster Place
London
WC2E 7EN

www.TimeWarnerBooks.co.uk

Contents

Preface

When I was four my father, Geoffrey St G. T. Allen, was appointed Assistant Political Officer on the Balipara Frontier Tract in Assam. For several years we lived in the APO's bungalow at Sadiya, on the banks of the Brahmaputra river and under the shadow of the Eastern Himalayas. Every morning there were visitors – exotic even to a child's eye – who gathered in the compound, squatting on their hunkers and smoking as they waited for the sahib to appear on the verandah. They were tribesmen from the hills, mostly Abor and Mishmi warriors, sturdy, wild-looking men in rudimentary loin cloths, with swords strapped across their shoulders. In the summer months their numbers were swelled by Tibetans, sweating, awkward giants with pigtails and flashing teeth who wore their thick, yak-hair coats rolled down to the waist to reveal pale, butter-coated skin. They had crossed the Himalayan barrier, bringing turquoise, amber and musk to trade in the plains.

Later I came to England and from my grandmother heard stories about her father, Colonel St G. C. Gore, Surveyor-General of India from 1899 to 1904, who in his time had spent months and even years on lonely surveys in the Himalayas. He had known Everest, Godwin-Austen and General Walker as well as Sven Hedin and the Pundit explorers, Nain Singh and Kishen Singh Rawat.

Later still I met Professor (and Colonel) Kenneth Mason, then almost ninety and probably the last of the players of the Great Game. He told me how once in his youth he had outsmarted a Russian adversary in the high Pamirs; the two men had swapped toasts all night and in the morning, while the Russian lay in a stupor in his tent, Mason had exchanged his own useless ponies for the other man's yaks and made off with them. Besides being a distinguished explorer and geographer, Kenneth Mason was also a keen historian. It was from him that I first heard the outline of the story that is told

7

here – the astonishing geographical properties of South-Western Tibet that are celebrated in Hindu and Buddhist sacred literature; the Indian surveyor-spies called the Pundits who explored it in disguise; and the controversy surrounding Sven Hedin's claims that was all the talk when Mason first came out to join the Survey of India in 1909.

I owe his memory a debt of gratitude for setting me on this particular journey – as I do my family and many others who helped me to complete this book. Among them I would like to thank especially Mrs Charmian Longstaff, who most kindly searched through her late husband's papers for me and found a crucial letter; Lord Perth, who helped me to find out more about his kinsman, Robert Drummond, and supplied the family photograph of the Drummond brothers taken in 1858; Sir Martin Lindsay, Bt, for allowing me to quote extensively from his father's letter written during the Abor Campaign of 1911–12; John Hearsey, who led me through the branches of his family tree and most kindly allowed me to borrow – and quote from – the manuscript Journal of his much maligned ancestor, Hyder Jung Hearsey; Lord Kilmorey and other members of the Needham family for their help in tracing the antecedents of Jack Needham; G. E. D. Walker (another distinguished Political Officer from the Assam Frontier) for his help and advice on the Assam chapters; Professor Adolf Gansser for his most valuable observations on the geology of the Kailas-Manasarovar region; Mrs Ken Saker for allowing me to see the film and photographs of that same area taken by her late husband in 1942; Michael Mason for his guidance on tantric philosophy; Hanna Yates for her German translations, Matthew Reisz for his Latin, Françoise Reisz and Alice Rockwell for their typing.

I am also greatly indebted to the Director and Secretary of the Royal Geographical Society for permission to quote from a number of unpublished letters in the Society's archives and from the *Geographical Journal*. I am particularly grateful to the Society's Archivist, Mrs Christine Kelly, for her help and advice and to the Librarian, G. S. Dugdale, and staff. I am similarly indebted to the Director of the Sven Hedin Foundation, Stockholm, for allowing me to quote from unpublished letters in the Foundation's archives and to publish a number of Sven Hedin's drawings and photographs, and to Peter Thunberg for his kindness. My thanks, too, to the following institutions: the Royal Society for Asian Affairs, the India Office Library and Records, the British Museum, the Victoria and Albert Museum, the National Army Museum, the School of Oriental and African Studies, the US Geological Survey and the Curator and staff of the Leeds Museum (who tracked down for me the stuffed Tibetan yak presented to the museum by Edmund Smyth in 1863).

Now to India and to the persons and institutions who assisted my research in the Garhwal Himalaya: in particular, I would like to thank Colonel J. A. F. Dalal (formerly Surveyor-General) and Mrs Nergis Dalal; the Surveyor-General, Survey of India; the Director, National Archive of India; Indra Singh Rawat (a descendant of Kishen Singh), Colonel Ranjit Singh Rawat (Nain Singh's grandson) and other members of that distinguished family; Kira Singh Fonia for his knowledgeable assistance on the culture of Garhwal and the Bhotias and his nephew Yashu Pal for guiding me through several Bhotia villages, and Richard Cooke, who came with me to the traditional source of the Ganga. My thanks, too, to Sally Thompson, the *Telegraph Magazine*, the Indian Tourist Board, Mountain Travel India and the Garhwal Mandal Vikas Nigam for making my travels possible – and to Air India, that most courteous and dependable of airlines.

A final expression of thanks to my editor, Faith Evans, whose patience and encouragement enabled me to complete this book.

Prologue

Death of a Bold and Most Ambitious Explorer

On 26 November 1952 Sven Anders Hedin died in Stockholm. Once honoured as the man who had done more, single-handed, than any other to colour the blank spaces of the map of the world, the eighty-seven-year-old Swedish explorer ended his days friendless and neglected. Among the newspapers that noted his death was *The Times*. It recalled how Dr Hedin had supported Kaiser Wilhelm II in the First World War and Adolf Hitler in the Second (despite being, as the writer put it, 'one-sixteenth non-Aryan'). As to his achievements, it recalled that Hedin was apt to dismiss the geographical fruits of all discoveries other than his own.

But these criticisms were mild by comparison with the obituary notice that was published three months later in the *Journal* of the Royal Geographical Society. For his contributions to geography and exploration the Society had awarded Hedin its Founder's Medal in 1898 and its Victoria Medal in 1903. Half a century later it took a rather different view. The writer of the notice was a Member of Council of the RGS, Sir Clement Skrine, one time HM Consul General at Kashgar in Chinese Turkestan (now Sinkiang). 'Dr Sven Hedin was a bold and most ambitious explorer,' wrote Skrine:

Once he had made up his mind to attain a particular object, no consideration of other people's feelings, convenience or even safety was ever allowed to deflect him. In his own words, the adventure and the 'conquest' of an unknown country, and the struggle against the impossible, all had a fascination which drew him with an irresistible force. But to him exploration in the field was only half the battle; its

11

results had to be recorded for all time to the glory of Sweden and Dr Sven Hedin. By temperament Hedin was a Nazi, to whom exploration was a *Kampf*, a struggle not only against the forces of nature but also on paper, against rival explorers. It is not surprising that he espoused in turn the causes of Kaiser Wilhelm II and Adolf Hitler.

In the 128 years of the history of the Royal Geographical Society no more bitter appraisal of an individual had ever appeared in the pages of its *Journal*.

It was not simply Hedin's manners or his politics that Skrine attacked. What British geography could not forgive, even after nearly half a century, were his claims; in particular, the discoveries so triumphantly revealed by the returned explorer at the Queen's Hall on the evening of 8 February 1909 – and so rapturously acclaimed by his audience. They marked an end to a century of exploration and dispute – or so Hedin declared – for he had brought back from the wastelands of Tibet an answer to 'the most important and magnificent geographical problem still left to solve on earth'. He offered nothing less than the final solution to a geographical mystery that had captured and held men's imaginations ever since the first Aryans penetrated the great Himalayan mountain barrier some three thousand years ago.

This mystery was centred on the belief shared by a large slice of humanity that somewhere between China and India there stood a sacred mountain, an Asian Olympus of cosmic proportions. This mountain was said to be the navel of the earth and the axis of the universe, and from its summit flowed a mighty river that fell into a lake and then divided to form four of the great rivers of Asia. It was the holiest of all mountains, revered by many millions of Hindus, Buddhists and Jains as the home of their gods. In metaphysical form it was called *Meru* or *Tisé*; in its earthly manifestation it was *Kailas*, the crystal, or *Kang Rinpoche*, jewel of snows, an isolated snow-peak on the Tibetan plateau.

Not a whisper of this belief, so ancient and powerful in Asia, reached the West before the seventeenth century. Even in our own day the legend of the holy mountain and its attendant waters is hardly known outside Asia, partly as a result of the dominance of the Western cultural viewpoint which until recent years tended to disparage all things oriental, partly because of the sheer size and inaccessibility of the area in question. Kailas, its lakes and all the sources of the major rivers of South Asia lie behind the greatest natural barriers on earth; by the Himalayan ranges to the south and west and the deserts of Takla Makan and the Gobi to the north and east. Even its outermost ring of defences appeared, in the view of a nineteenth-century surveyor, as 'a mighty maze without a plan'.

Forced to choose between highly improbable oriental beliefs and the solid cartographical reasoning of Ptolemy, European cartographers preferred to stay with Ptolemy until well into the eighteenth century. As late as 1800 Sir James Rennell, who has been described as the father of modern Indian geography and is generally acclaimed as the first man to put the Himalayas on the map, was still toeing the classical line when it came to setting down the supposed source of the river Sutlej on his charts.

Not until British power had actually begun to lap up against the walls of the Himalayan barrier in the first decade of the nineteenth century was there any serious attempt made to examine the mysteries that were said to lie beyond. In 1808 two British officers and an Anglo-Indian soldier of fortune entered the Nepalese-held mountain country of Garhwal to explore the headwaters of India's most sacred river, the Ganga. A century later, when Sven Hedin returned from the last of his great journeys through Central Asia in 1908, the process of discovery was all but complete. The last of the great white patches on the map of Tibet had been filled in – and the legend of Mount Kailas and the sources of the great rivers of Asia was shown to have its basis in solid geographical fact.

This century of Tibetan exploration coincided with Britain's rise as an imperial power, and it was largely through the window of British India that the world looked into Tibet. The Victorian appetite for expansion in the name of trade had given rise to that tough and enterprising breed, the Victorian traveller, to whom Tibet's historic inaccessibility proved an obvious and tantalizing lure. After Timbuctoo in the late eighteenth and early nineteenth centuries, Tibet's holy city

13

of Lhasa became one of the most sought after of far-off places, the Blue Riband of the exploring world. No less enticing were the sources of the four greatest rivers of India – the Indus, Sutlej, Ganga and Brahmaputra – whose upper courses all lay hidden behind the ramparts of the Himalayas.

Few of these trans-Himalayan travellers, doughty and courageous though they were, made a name for themselves. Apart from Sven Hedin there were no giants of Central Asian exploration to rival the Victorian and Edwardian public heroes of African and polar exploration. The unravelling of the mysteries of Western Tibet, intertwined as they were with the religious beliefs of several cultures, remained elusive to the popular imagination by comparison with, for example, the Nile and its sources in the mid-nineteenth century. Politics also played its part. The East India Company, and its successor, the British Raj, were jealous powers, opposing any attempts, even by such distinguished institutions as the Royal Geographical Society, to open up the Asian interior. Since Tibet offered no prospects for commercial advantage there was nothing to be gained by its annexation – while the Government of India had every reason to discourage interest, national or individual, in Tibet. That arid, inhospitable, table-land served its purpose as – in Lord Curzon's favourite phrase – a buffer state, and only when its neutrality was threatened, as Curzon believed it to be by Russia in 1903, did the Raj actively promote intervention.

The prospective Asian explorer had thus to contend not only with the Himalayas but with two hostile governments as well. If he was a foreigner there was every chance that he would not be allowed off the ship at Bombay; if he was a government servant he risked his career. It required nerve and a strong measure of rebelliousness to overcome such obstacles – and rebels, as a rule, did not prosper long under the British Raj. Only Sven Hedin learnt to play the system to his advantage, and he paid the price for his temerity.

After the jolt provided by Curzon's unwarranted invasion of Tibet the rival powers in Central Asia – Britain and Russia – agreed that Tibet was out of bounds. The way was cleared for China to strengthen a hold that had never been more than tenuous, and to intensify Tibet's seclusion from the outside

14

world. In recent years an uneasy peace on both sides of the Himalayan border has done little to diminish Tibet's extraordinary isolation. Even with the arrival of satellite photography it remains to this day the least known, least explored country on earth, rich in mysteries, still beckoning us with its secrets and still denying us the answer – a vacuum at the centre of the world.

Chapter 1

The Fountainhead
of Asia

As the dew is dried up by the morning sun so are the sins of men dried up by the sight of the Himalaya, where Shiva lived and where the Ganga falls from the foot of Vishnu like the slender thread of a lotus flower.

There are no mountains like the Himalaya, for in them are Kailas and Manasarovar.

From the Skanda Purana

Twenty million years ago Tibet lay at the bottom of the sea. The manner in which it was shaped into its present commanding position in Central Asia has been described as an epic in the long history of the formation of the earth's crust. Caught between two approaching land masses, the sea bed buckled into a series of long parallel folds. The tops of these folds were levelled down by rain-bearing winds blowing up from the Indian Ocean, while the intervening depressions were filled with alluvial silt, creating the Chang Tang, the vast northern plateau of Tibet that stands at an average elevation of sixteen thousand feet above sea level. As the squeeze continued so the remaining sea waters drained southward into one enormous river system, the Indo-Gangetic river, which acted as a gutter to this newly-raised roof of the world and allowed it to evolve into a relatively fertile land of alpine forests and grasslands.

These early stages in Tibet's prehistory took place without human witnesses but are celebrated in Tibetan mythology with stories of a time before the advent of man when the plateau lay submerged under a vast lake – until a compassionate *Bodhisattva* (one who delays Buddhahood in order to help mankind) cut an outlet through the Himalayas for Tibet's 'great river', the Tsangpo. In reality, the Himalayas succeeded the formation of the Tibetan plateau. They represent the last

17

and most dramatic phase of this extraordinary upheaval, a recent and rapid event in the geological time-scale, but one that added at least another mile to the general height of the Himalayas.

The outcome of this prodigious burst of activity was a twenty-thousand-foot wall that spans twenty-five degrees of meridian from Namche Barwa in the east to Nanga Parbat in the west; a fifteen-hundred-mile barrier that has blocked the monsoon winds from the south and turned much of Tibet and Central Asia into desert. A leading authority in Himalayan geomorphology has gone so far as to suggest that some sections of the Himalayas may have risen as much as nine thousand feet and more within the last half-million years – and that the rise may be continuing at the rate of some thirty inches a century. What is certain is that the rapid growth of the Himalayan ranges took place not so very long ago, and that it effectively put a stop to man's migrations to and fro across the steppes of Central Asia. Thus Tibet became the isolated and forbidding land that it is today, sealed off from the south and west, its lakes and rivers becoming increasingly desiccated as the Himalayan wall continues to capture more and more rainfall.

Anyone who has stood at dawn on the ridge of one of the lower foothills of the Himalayas and seen the first rays of the sun light up a seemingly endless succession of snowpeaks will know how the advance guards of the Aryans must have felt when they first crossed the Punjab in the second millennium BC and saw the Himalayan ranges rising tier upon tier before them. In Atkinson's *Himalayan Districts* – the *vade mecum* of the Victorian sportsman or administrator in the hills – the author speculates as to how these Aryan immigrants from the west might have reacted to the awesome spectacle:

> The rugged grandeur of the scene, the awful solitude and the trials and dangers of the way itself naturally suggested to an imaginative and simple people that they had at length rediscovered the golden land, the true homes of their gods whom they had worshipped when appearing under milder forms as storm and fire and rain.

18

Taking their inspiration from this 'abode of snow' – *Himavant*, *Himachala* or *Himalaya* – the Aryans developed a cosmography that established Meru, the mountain of 'blazing appearance', as the central core of the universe and navel of the earth. They sited it beyond and to the north of the Himalayan ranges – 'kissing the heavens by its height', according to the *Mahabharata*, greatest of the Hindu epics, 'shining like the morning sun and like a fire without smoke, immeasurable and unapproachable by men of manifold sins'. On Meru's summit stood Swarga, the heavenly city of Indra, the ancient Vedic god of rain and storm, a paradise 'furnished with heavenly flowers and fruit and covered everywhere with bright gold dwellings'. Here were to be found the gods and celestial spirits, headed by Brahma the Creator, with lesser deities and saints inhabiting a less exalted plane lower down the mountain. Leading up to Mount Meru was the pathway of the stars, a never-never land of fragrant trees and flowers where the souls of the dead awaited rebirth.

A white mountain named Kailas also makes several appearances both in the *Mahabharata* and in that order, stodgier epic, the *Ramayana*, but at this early stage of development – dated at about the middle of the first millennium BC – it is only one of a number of subordinate holy mountains, not yet linked to the celestial Meru. Similarly, a lake called Manasarovar also makes an appearance – in the form of a single, fleeting reference in the *Ramayana* to 'the lake Manasa ... swollen with water on the arrival of the rains'. Both mountain and lake have been visited and named, but not yet understood.

As the Aryans continued their push eastward down the Gangetic plain so grew their dependence on that constant central artery, the Ganga, the river that still nourishes a third of India's population to this day. It succeeded the Indus as the most vital – and therefore the most sacrosanct – of India's rivers. It served as a life-force and as a channel between the gods and men, and its divinity took the form of a mother goddess, Ganga Mai, daughter of the Himalayas. To die by Ganga's banks and to be cast into her muddy waters was to be delivered directly to heaven. Even to dip oneself three times under her surface was to be cleansed of all sins, to emerge reborn. So it became the ambition – as it still is today

19

– of every devout Hindu to make a pilgrimage to the Ganga and to bathe there at least once in his or her lifetime.

The formula has not altered for nearly three thousand years. Soon after dawn the bather immerses himself fully three times, then cups his hands and three times raises the water as an offering to the sun. As he does so he chants the prayer of the seven sacred rivers of India:

> Gange cha! Yamune chaiva! Godaveri!
> Saraswati! Namade! Sindhu! Kaveri!
> Jale asmin sannidhim kuru!

> O Ganga! O Jumna! Godaveri!
> Saraswati! Namade! Indus! Kaveri!
> May you all be pleased to be manifest in these waters!

Before the bather climbs out of the water he changes into a clean *dhoti* – or a clean *sari* – to emerge as a new person. He has, in a spiritual sense, completed a turn in the wheel of life, death and rebirth.

One of the oldest and most familiar legends in India concerns the birth of this most celebrated of rivers; how the goddess Ganga Mai was moved by the devotions of a saint named Bhagirath to come down to earth to purify the remains of the sixty thousand sons of King Sagar, blasted to ashes by an angered holy man. Mother Ganga descends from Mount Meru only to be caught up in the matted locks of the god Shiva, representing the Himalayan mountains. Bhagirath continues his prayers and the god Shiva relents and releases the goddess, whose waters flood across the land and touch the ashes of the sixty thousand sons of Sagar, so redeeming their souls.

Of the many sites along the river Ganga visited by pilgrims none bestow more merit than those associated with its origins. What adds greatly to their value is the fact that these holiest of holy places are buried so deep in the Himalayas as to be virtually inaccessible, so that to make a pilgrimage to some of these mountain shrines is to place oneself almost literally in the lap of the gods. Yet despite – or because of – the difficulties, pilgrimages into the mountains have always been an important feature of Hindu religious life. High-caste Hindus in the fourth and final stage of life are exhorted by their scriptures to free themselves from all family ties and responsibilities and to go in search of deliverance from the cycle of death and rebirth. They shave off their hair and beards, conduct their own funeral ceremonies and take on the pale ochre robes – symbolizing rebirth through the purifying flames of the funeral pyre – of the *sanyasi*, the ascetic who roams from one holy place to another seeking final absorption into the Absolute. Those who come to the Himalayas begin their pilgrimage at *Ganga-dwara*, the gateway of Ganga, the narrow break in the Siwalik foothills through which the river pours out into the Indian plains. Passing through this gateway they enter the holy land of the Hindus, sometimes called *Uttarakhand*, the north country, or *Kedarkhand*, Shiva's country, where every peak had its deity, every valley its temple and every spring its shrine.

This Himalayan holy land had been thoroughly explored by the time that the first of the sacred texts known as the *Puranas* came to be written. So, too, had at least part of the high plateau lying beond the Himalayas, allowing the basic cosmography of the *Mahabharata* to be expanded into a more solid and realistic Asian geography.

The eighteen texts that together make up the *Puranas* were compiled over a thousand-year period – from about 200 BC to AD 800 – and they concern themselves chiefly with the works of the Hindu gods. The oldest and the best-known of the *Puranas* is the *Vishnu Purana*, believed to date from the second century BC. Its main object is the glorification of Vishnu, but one of its chapters is given over to a description of the earth. It describes how the world is made up of seven continents ringed by seven oceans. The central island has Meru at its core, bounded by three mountain ranges to the north and three to the south, and lying between them 'like the pericarp of a lotus'. One of these ranges is the Himalayan barrier, interposed between Meru and the Indian subcontinent (*Bharatha*). The world-pillar itself stands eighty-four thousand leagues high, with four faces of crystal, ruby, gold and lapis lazuli. From the heavens – or, more precisely, from the nail in the great toe of Vishnu's left foot – falls 'the stream that

21

washes away all sin, the river, Ganga, embrowned with the unguents of the nymphs of heaven, who have sported in its waters.' After washing the 'lunar orb', the Ganga alights on the summit of Meru, circles the mountain and then divides into four mighty rivers which flow to the four quarters of the earth, 'for its purification'. These four rivers – 'four branches of but one river' – are named as the Sita, Alaknanda, Chaksu and Badra:

> The first, falling upon the tops of the inferior mountains on the east side of Meru, flows upon their crests and passes through the country of Bhàdrashva to the ocean: the Alaknanda flows south, to the country of Bharatha and, dividing into seven rivers on the way, falls into the sea: the Chaksu falls into the sea after traversing all the western mountains and passing through the country of Ketumala: and the Badra washes the country of the Uttara Kurus and empties itself into the northern ocean.

Here, in all its essentials, is the prototype of a legend that spread with only minor variations as far afield as Japan and Java; the archetypal image of a mountain at the hub of the world from which four mighty rivers take their source – an image powerful enough to be reflected not only in religious literature but also in the art and architecture of South Asia. It can be seen in the earliest Buddhist and Hindu structures to be laid out in stone: the Great Stupa at Sanchi in Central India (built in the third century BC), the central temple of Tibet's oldest monastery (built at Samye in the lower Tsangpo valley during the eighth century AD) and the temple mountain of Borobudur in Java (built a century later) – all are microcosms in stone, sharing a common form in the world-pillar rising above the four continents.

The same image forms the symbol known to Hindus as the *yantra* and to Buddhists as the *mandala*. Both are visual maps used to provide a focus during the act of meditation, guiding the practitioner towards the centre as he seeks to integrate his being with the Absolute. Both combine the circle (water) with the square (earth), superimposed upon a cross representing four paths or doors. It is a standard yogic exercise to place oneself mentally within such an image, imagining the spinal column to be at one with Mount Meru, so achieving a deepened sense of earth-consciousness. Underlying all such mystical exercises is the oriental concept of natural harmony, of union achieved through a balance of opposing forces, as between earth and water, male and female, light and dark; in the Taoist idiom, as between *yin* and *yang*; in the Tibetan tantric tradition, *yab* and *yum*; in Shaivite tantra, *Shiva-Shakti*.

The strength of the Meru image lay in this natural harmony, but what made it doubly potent was that it was rooted in geographical fact. The original Meru probably took its inspiration from the Himalayas in general; the later Meru of the *Puranas* was founded on the unique geographical properties of South-Western Tibet.

Though it presented a formidable obstacle to any large-scale migrations, the Himalayan barrier could always be crossed by enterprising travellers during the summer months. The series of longitudinal foothills and ranges that build up to the Great Himalaya Range are cut across at a number of points by deep transverse gorges – the old antecedent water-courses that pre-date the massive uplift and which, by continued erosion, have kept pace with the elevation of the Himalayas. In such gorges it is possible to look out across the valley and pick out on the opposite wall a complete cross-section of vegetation ranged by altitude from high alpine to subtropical, from the *bhojpatra* or silver birch that grows above ten thousand feet and whose soft bark provides the writing-material for religious texts, to the sturdy *sal* tree of the plains, the evergreen hardwood of the *terai* jungles.

By journeying up one such transverse gorge Hindu pilgrims could reach deep into the heart of their holy land, Uttarakhand. The river that made this possible was the Ganga's main Himalayan tributary, the Alaknanda. Of the four mighty rivers named in the *Vishnu Purana* – the Alaknanda, Sita, Chaksu and Badra – this river alone is immediately identifiable. It is the Ganga of our own times, with the same attributes then as those ascribed to it today:

The branch that is known as the Alaknanda was borne

affectionately by Mahadeva [the great god, Shiva] upon his head for more than a hundred years, and was the river which raised to heaven the sinful sons of Sagar, by washing their ashes. This sacred stream, heard of, desired, seen, touched, bathed in or hymned, day by day, sanctifies all beings; and those who, even at a distance of a hundred leagues, exclaim 'Ganga, Ganga', atone for the sins committed during three previous lives.

Having followed the Alaknanda upstream for two hundred miles through the Great Himalaya Range the pilgrim eventually arrives at a temple complex nestling in a side-valley, overshadowed by a score of sharply defined snowpeaks. This is the shrine of Vishnu, manifest in the form of Lord Badrivishal, and the place is Badrinath, most sacred of all the Vaisnava shrines in India. Some form of temple has stood on this site, beside a hot-spring, for at least two thousand years – but not always dedicated to Lord Vishnu. The weathered black stone idol that occupies the inner sanctum has the form and posture of a Buddhist Bodhisattva. Buddhists argue that it dates back to the golden years of Emperor Ashok in the third century BC, when the Way was preached throughout Northern India – only to be converted into a Hindu god in later centuries as Buddhism was suppressed. Hindus counterclaim that if there ever was a Buddhist shrine on this spot it was preceded by an even earlier Vedic one. Whatever its origins, for most pilgrims this distant shrine has been the limit of their aspirations.

North of Badrinath there rises another great mountain wall: the eastern half of what is now termed the Zaskar range. It presents an even more formidable barrier than the Great Himalaya, because here there is no transverse gorge; the Ganga's northern watershed has been reached. The pilgrim who hoped to proceed further – on to that central pivot where the Alaknanda and the other mighty rivers of Asia were said to have their common source – was now faced by such Himalayan giants as Kamet, Ibi Gamin, Rataban and Tirsuli. But between these massifs are a number of saddles, one as low as sixteen and a half thousand feet, another eighteen, which for three or four months every summer are free from snow. These are the passes – the *ghats* or, in Tibetan, *la* – that lead into Tibet. The summit of each is marked by a cairn of piled-up *mani*-stones incised with Tibetan prayers, signalling the end of one cultural boundary and the start of another. From here the pilgrim could look northwards, out across the Chang Tang, the great plateau of Tibet.

What he actually sees looks nothing like a plateau: immediately below the passes the land falls away into a deep depression, one of the sediment-filled longitudinal troughs formed after the Tibetan uplift. Beyond the depression, cutting across the skyline at a distance of some fifty miles, is yet another mountain wall; the Kailas range, dominated – even at this distance – by the mountain that provides the keystone to the drainage system of much of South and Central Asia. This is the high point of the Tibetan table-land; the south-western corner that has been given an extra tilt upwards by the nearby Himalayas to form a highly improbable complex of watersheds and river basins in which four major river systems take their rise.

At the centre of the complex stands a pyramid of rock and snow, towering above the surrounding mountains, as the Tibetans say, 'like the handle of a mill-stone'. This is Mount Kailas. Deep clefts on either side isolate it from the rest of the Kailas range, which makes it especially well-suited to the act of devotional circumambulation, known as the *parikarama*, practised by Hindus and Buddhists.

Even in the strictest geological terms Kailas stands alone, being the world's highest deposit of tertiary conglomerate – a vast pile of cemented gravel laid down in the period immediately preceding the arrival of early man and then thrown up into the sky. It has four clearly-defined walls that match the points of the compass, and on its southern face a deep gully runs down from the summit, cutting across an equally distinctive rock band of horizontal strata. This is the mark that has earned Kailas the title of 'swastika mountain', and it is this southern face, emblazoned with its talisman of spiritual strength, the *swastika*, that the pilgrim first sees as he climbs out of India; Kailas on the horizon and, occupying much of the depression in the middle distance, what was formerly one large circular lake with an island at its centre but is now two lakes divided by a narrow isthmus of high ground.

The larger of these two lakes, roughly circular in outline and about fifteen miles across, is the sacred lake Manasarovar – the lake 'formed in the mind |of God|'. In his *Himalayan Districts* Atkinson quotes an account of its creation from one of the later *Puranas*, the *Skanda Purana*:

The sons of Brahma proceeded to the north of Himachala and performed austerities on Kailas. There they saw Shiva and Parvati and there they remained for twelve years, absorbed in mortification and prayer. There was then very little rain and little water, and in their distress they went to Brahma and worshipped him. Then Brahma asked what their desire might be. The Rishis [sages] answered and said 'We are engaged in devotion on Kailas; make a place for us to bathe in.' Then Brahma by a mental effort formed the holy lake of Manasa and the Rishis again engaged in mortification and prayer on Kailas and worshipped the golden *ling* which rose from the midst of the waters of the lake.

By the time that this account came to be written lake Manasarovar had long been established as the queen of lakes. Among those who extolled its virtues was the great Hindu classical poet Kalidasa, writing in the third century AD, in his lyrical poem, *The Cloud-Messenger*. Since the days of the *Mahabharata*, Manasarovar had increased mightily in reputation and sanctity. Indeed, long before the time of Ptolemy it had become the holiest and the most famous lake in Asia, conferring great merit to those who reached its shores:

When the earth of Manasarovar touches anyone's body or when anyone bathes therein, he shall go to the paradise of Brahma, and he who drinks its waters shall go to the heaven of Shiva and shall be released from the sins of a hundred births. Even the beast that bears the name of Manasarovar shall go to the paradise of Brahma. Its waters are like pearls.

26

The pilgrim who succeeded in crossing the Himalayas was expected to follow the precepts laid down in the *Puranas*:

> He should bathe there and pour a libation of water to the shades of his forefathers and worship Mahadeva |the great god, Shiva| in the form of a royal swan. He should there make the parikarama of the holy Manasa lake, gaze at Kailas, and bathe in all the neighbouring rivers.

The lake's growth in status had also been matched by the nearby mountain: from being a mere acolyte to the world-pillar, Kailas had now risen to become its earthly avatar, a physical manifestation of a metaphysical phenomenon. Part of the impetus behind this dramatic promotion must have come from the realization that there really was something quite extraordinary about the hydrography of the Kailas-Manasarovar region. Increased movement by Indian travellers – emissaries, marauders, traders and wandering pilgrims – beyond the northern barriers, particularly during the years of the Ashokan empire in the third and second centuries BC, had led to greater contact with other peoples, and increased knowledge. The time came when enough evidence had been gathered to show that the four largest rivers on the subcontinent – the Indus, Sutlej, Ganga and Brahmaputra – even though they emerged from the mountains many hundreds of miles apart, all had their origins in one small corner of the distant plateaulands beyond the Himlayas. However, this increase of geographical knowledge could only detract from the majesty and mystery of the world-lotus. Without any formal announcement of the change, Meru assumed a purely abstract form – and Kailas took its place.

An equally important factor in the advancement of Mount Kailas was the elevation of Lord Shiva to the top division of the Hindu gods, to take his place beside Brahma and Vishnu in the Hindu holy trinity. Much of the writing in the *Puranas* is given over to promoting the virtues of one or other of Brahma's new partners, either Shiva or Vishnu. This rivalry ended in the triumph of the more popular, orthodox cult of Vishnu, the Preserver, over the older, more elemental cult of Shiva, Destroyer and Transformer. The vast majority of modern Hindus as worshippers of Vishnu or one of his more approachable avatars, such as Rama or Krishna. *Vaisnavas* – followers of Vishnu – are strongest in Northern and Central India; *Shaivas* are in a majority only in South India and in the Himalayan regions.

Shiva has always been a god of mountains; he is the great lord of yogis, mystics and wanderers, often portrayed seated in a lotus-position on a tiger-skin, ash-smeared and clad only in a deer-skin. He wears his hair piled up into a moon-shaped coil and the moon's crescent is drawn above the third eye in the centre of his forehead. In his hands he carries a trident and the universal instrument of the *shaman*, the small hourglass-shaped rattle-drum known as the *damaru*. As both destroyer and transformer of life he takes many forms. In destructive mood he is Bhairava the terrible, with serpents in his hair and threaded skulls about his neck; as transformer he is worshipped in the form of the phallic symbol, the *lingam*. From his Aryan predecessor, Rudra, god of the elements, Shiva inherited Kailas as his special abode.

Sharing Shiva's mountain with him is his *shakti*, the goddess Devi, who reflects and matches his qualities in female form. In her gentler aspects she is Uma, the light, and Parvati, the mountaineer; in her fiercer avatars she is Durga, the inaccessible, and the hideous Kali, the black one. Her elevation also represents a significant development in Hindu religion: recognition of the worship of the female principle that has always been present in the religion of the subcontinent. One of its more unorthodox manifestations was the growth in the sixth and seventh centuries AD of tantric cults which sought ecstatic enlightenment through the arousal and activation of the male principle by the female. In Hinduism it expressed itself in the tantric cult of *shakti*, in Buddhism in the tantric cult of the *tara* goddesses, representing the female creative energy that liberates the male. Thus Shiva acquired his *shakti*, the *lingsam* its *yoni*, the *yab* its *yum*.

The cult of tantra plays a key role in the devotional cults of Tibetan Buddhism. The Tibetan counterparts of Shiva and Devi are the four-faced demon Demchog, with his trident and drum, and his scarlet consort Dorje Phangmo – always depicted in paintings and sculptures locked together in

28

athletic sexual embrace. They also have their home on the mountain which they know as Tisé (the peak) or Kang Rinpoche (jewel of snows). But just as Shiva has his progenitor in the Vedic god Rudra, so Demchog has an earlier prototype who was also closely associated with the holy mountain. For not only is Kailas the Olympus of Hinduism and Buddhism; it is also the home of the 'black belief', the old shamanistic religion of Bon-Po that flourished in Tibet long before the arrival of Buddhism.

The traditional founder of the Bon religion is said to have looked down from heaven and seen that the Kailas region was well suited to be its stronghold. Old Bon-Po texts describe how the 'nine-story swastika mountain' at the heart of their religion had to be moved to its present site from North-Eastern Tibet, which may well refer to the westerly migration of Mongolian peoples across Tibet that took place about two thousand years ago.

The Bon-Po texts also contain the story of the four great rivers, although the Bon version varies in some details from the accounts given in the *Puranas*. The nearest Tibetan equivalent is found in a book of uncertain date called the *Kangri Karchhak* (Ice-Mountain Guide). Here it states that a stream flows down from Tisé into the lake Mapham Tso (unconquerable lake). From the lake emerge the four rivers, circling the lake seven times before taking their respective courses to north, south, east and west. The first of these rivers is the Senge-Khambab, the 'lion-mouth' river, rich in the sands of diamonds, whose waters flow north and make those who drink from it as brave as lions; flowing south is the 'peacock-mouth' river, the Mapchhu-Khambab, rich in silver sands, whose waters make those who drink from it as lovely as peacocks; flowing to the east is the 'horse-mouth' river, the Tamchok-Khambab, with sands of emerald and waters that make those who drink from it sturdy as horses; finally, flowing to the west is the Lanchen-Khambab, the 'elephant-mouth' river, with sands of gold and waters that make those who drink from it strong as elephants.

Looking further afield, towards China and early Chinese geographical texts, we can find elements from both Indian and Tibetan accounts. In some ways this combination pro-

vides the most satisfying account of the Meru-Kailas legends
– as in the following cosmography from *Ta-T'ang-Hsi-Yu-Chi*
(Records of the Western World), compiled during the T'ang
Dynasty (AD 618–907):

> The mountain called Sumeru stands up in the midst of the
> great sea firmly fixed on a circle of gold, around which
> mountain the sun and moon revolve. This mountain is
> perfected by four precious substances and is the abode of
> the Devas [gods]. Around this are seven mountain ranges
> and seven seas.
>
> In the middle of the Shan-pu-chao [the central continent]
> there is a lake called Wo-jo-nao-chih, to the south of the
> fragrant mountains and to the north of the great snowy
> mountains. It is 800 li and more in circuit, its sides are
> composed of gold, silver, lapis lazuli and crystal. Golden
> sands lie at the bottom and its waters are clear as a mirror.
> The great earth Bodhisattva transforms himself into a Naga-
> raja [snake divinity] and dwells therein; from his dwelling
> the cool waters proceed forth and enrich Shan-pu-chao.

As might be expected, there are four of these 'cool waters':
the *Kan-chieh* (Ganga) flowing from the mouth of a silver ox;
the *Hsin-tu* (Sindhu) from the mouth of a golden elephant;
the *Hsi-to* (Sita) from the mouth of a crystal lion and the *Fu-
chu* (Vakshu) from the mouth of a horse of lapis lazuli. The
first two can be readily identified as the Ganga and Indus and
the third, the Sita, is shown from the text to be associated
with the Tarim river, in Sinkiang, and (after travelling a great
distance underground) the Hwang Ho. The identity of the
last river, the Vakshu, became a favourite subject for academic
dispute in geographical circles in the nineteenth century: the
most popular view favoured the Oxus.

At the time of the T'ang Dynasty Buddhism had only just
begun to gain a foothold in Tibet, and another three or four
hundred years were to pass before it could claim to be the
predominant faith in the Bon country of Western Tibet. The
struggle between the two faiths, which eventually ended with
the supremacy of lamaistic Buddhism in the thirteenth
century, is nicely symbolized in a famous duel over the

possession of the holy mountain that is said to have been fought out between the yogi Milarepa, the champion of tantric Buddhism, and Naro-Bonchung, the champion of shamanism. It took the form of a contest in magic – very much in the manner of two wizards hurling spells at one another – with the contestants finally agreeing that whoever reached the summit of Kang Rinpoche first at dawn the next day should win the mountain. At sunrise Milarepa's disciples were greatly perturbed to see Naro-Bonchung flying up to the summit mounted on his shamanistic drum, while their own master remained deep in meditation. However, at the last moment Milarepa soared up into the air, overtook the Bon-Po and won the mountain for Buddhism. The vertical gash down the south face of Kailas is said to have been gouged out by Naro-Bonchung's *damaru* – dropped by him in his alarm at seeing the yogi overtake him.

Thus the old black gods of shamanism were expelled from Kailas and replaced by lamaistic Bodhisattvas, such as Cakrasamvara, God of Wisdom, or by such acceptable transmutations as Demchog and his consort. Indeed, even Naro-Bonchung was allowed to keep a nearby hill in the shadow of Kailas as his abode, symbolizing the eventual accommodation between the two rival beliefs that was finally arrived at. Yogi Milarepa himself is often portrayed in religious prints and paintings seated on the holy mountain. He is the first historical figure to be directly associated with Mount Kailas. He spent much of his life in Western Tibet and died in a cave just south of lake Manasarovar early in the twelfth century AD. It is to Milarepa's tantric school of Buddhism, Vajrayana or the 'thunderbolt path', that we owe the mystic, oft-repeated *mantra 'Om mani padme hum,'* the incantation that has been inscribed on countless *mani*-stones throughout Tibet, Ladakh and Nepal and spoken endlessly by countless millions of Buddhists. The phrase is usually translated as 'Hail, jewel in the lotus' but it has a far more profound meaning. The first syllable represents the sound of enlightenment, the most fundamental of all *mantras*, and the last represents the sound of fulfilment. Encapsulated between the two is the phrase *'mani padme'*, which does indeed translate as 'jewel in the lotus' but signifies *'lingam* in *yoni'*, the mystical

31

and sexual fusion of complementary opposites. It is *yab* and *yum* united; Shiva and *shakti* activated.

Enshrined in Kailas-Manasarovar are the elements of the ecstatic and the anti-orthodox in Indian and Tibetan religion. Its mountain and lakes belong to Shiva and Parvati, to Bon-Po, to Demchog and Dorje Phangmo, to yogi Milarepa. It is, in effect, the repository of the old, dark gods and their earth-goddesses; a mountain of magicians, thunderbolt-hurlers, trident-wielders and drum-shakers. And for more than two thousand years it has been the lodestone – the all but unattainable goal – that draws towards itself all the devotional cults that seek the attainment of bliss through self-sacrifice, austerity and penance. It is the greatest and hardest of all earthly pilgrimages.

Chapter 2

'Here Christians are said to live': the Jesuit Explorers of Tibet

The first foreigner to attempt a systematic inquiry into the sources of India's great rivers was the Emperor Akbar, the great Mogul who ruled most of Northern India from 1556 to 1605. One of Akbar's most attractive qualities was his religious tolerance and his interest in non-Islamic cultures. According to the Venetian adventurer turned court physician, Niccolo Manucci, the Emperor was curious to discover more about the Ganga and the legends surrounding it:

> Long before Akbar's time the peoples in the Indies were persuaded that the Ganges took its source in a high mountain range whose figure resembled that of a cow's head. In the days of Akbar its source was still unknown, as the source of the Nile was unknown not above an age ago. The Emperor therefore spared no cost to discover the head of a river that was the best jewel in his crown.

An expedition was assembled and dispatched with orders to follow the river northwards to its source. After forcing their way through narrow gorges and untrodden forests, they arrived at a mountain 'which seemed to be shaped by art into the form of a cow's head'. Out of it issued a vast quantity of water, which they took to be the source of the Ganga.

The fruits of this first Himalayan venture can be seen on the map used to illustrate Samuel Purchas's curious travel book, *Purchas His Pilgrimes*, published in 1625, which purported to be a 'History of the World in Sea Voyages and Land Travel by Englishmen and Others'. There on Purchas's map is the Ganga, sited on the edge of the plains at Hardwar rather

33

than in the mountains, but flowing through a cow's mouth into a lake.

By the time this map was published other foreigners besides Moguls were reaching into the Himalayas. Akbar's interests extended to Christianity, and in 1580 a Jesuit mission from the Portuguese trading enclave at Goa was invited to attend his court at Agra. These first missionaries at the court of the Great Mogul were greatly excited by stories they heard from wandering *sadhus* and yogis of a people living beyond the mountains who followed religious practices very similar to those of the Catholic Church. This led to intense speculation among the Jesuits that waiting to be discovered in Tibet was that long-lost Christian civilization, the legendary kingdom of Prester John.

In 1906 manuscript documents were discovered in St Paul's Cathedral Library in Calcutta which had been written more than three centuries earlier by Antonio de Monserrate, a Jesuit Father who had spent two and a half years at Akbar's court as tutor to one of his sons. From India, Monserrate had been transferred to Abyssinia, where he made use of six years in captivity to write a long narrative that in some mysterious way came into the collection of Jesuit papers at St Paul's, Calcutta – where it remains today, untranslated and unpublished. This Latin manuscript contains the first known European reference to lake Manasarovar, *incolis Mansaruor*:

If the yogis – who visit many territories but tell many lies and mix in legends with facts – are to be believed, there are still surviving Christians there. For many of the priests in the region of the Imae [Himalayas], when asked, spoke as follows: 'The mountains are steep and difficult to climb but flat on the summit [plateau] and suitable for habitation. On the banks of a certain lake there – which the local people call lake Mansaruor – a certain tribe inhabits a very old city.'

Accompanying the manuscript is a tiny sketch map, measuring five inches by four. Beyond the great arc of the 'Imaus' mountains is a large circular lake, marked in bold letters

34

'MANSARVOR Lacus' and accompanied by the inscription 'Hic dicunter Christiani habitare' (here Christians are said to live).

The lake itself held no particular interest for the Jesuits; it was the possibility of finding a surviving Christian community that drew them there. The first reconnaissance was dispatched from Agra in 1603 with the highest hopes, but ended in failure. Its leader, Benedict de Goes, died of exhaustion at the Chinese border, north of Koko Nor. Not only had he failed to reach lake Manasarovar, he had even failed to locate the country in which it lay.

Two decades later, in the spring of 1624, a second expedition set out from Delhi. It was led by the head of the Jesuit Mission to the Mogul court, Father Antonio de Andrade, a tough, battle-hardened veteran of the mission field, aged forty-four. Andrade took with him as his lieutenant a younger Portuguese lay brother named Manuel Marques, making up the rest of their party with two Christian servants and locally recruited porters. All we know about this first European expedition over the Himalayas is contained in two short letters from Andrade that were published in Lisbon in 1626 under the grandiose title of *Novo Descobrimento do Gram Cathay, ou Reinos de Tibet* (A New Discovery from Grand Cathay, or the Kingdom of Tibet). The letters reveal an extraordinary faith and stamina on the part of Andrade and Marques but are understandably vague on geographical details. The result was that their claims to have entered Tibet came to be regarded as exaggerated and unreliable. Later generations of European travellers, who crossed into Tibet by the same route, were quite unaware that the Jesuits had been there before them – nearly two centuries earlier.

Andrade and his companion left Delhi disguised as pilgrims and attached themselves to a large party of Hindus bound for the Himalayan shrine of Badrinath. They apparently had no scruples about passing themselves off as orthodox *yatris* or pilgrims and enthusiastically joined in the shouts of 'Ye, Badrinath! Ye, ye!' as their party entered Shiva's hills, the Siwaliks, through the Gangadwara gorge. This is where Hardwar now stands; the ugly, flyblown, pilgrim town which to the follower of Shiva represents the gateway to Har (Shiva) and to the follower of Vishnu, the

35

gateway to Hari (Vishnu). To Shaiva and Vaisnava equally, this is where every journey into the holy land to the north must begin and end.

From Hardwar the pilgrims travelled through the domains of the Rajah of Srinagar, following the Alaknanda tributary through the deep Himalayan gorges until they were north of the Great Himalaya Range. To get to the 'pagoda at Badrid', the famous Vaisnava temple at Badrinath, they had to cross the river again and again on rope-and-pulley bridges. At last they reached the most accessible of the three main Himalayan shrines associated with the Ganga's sources, sited in a region inhabited by a semi-nomadic hill people called the Bhotias. Beside the temple were some hot-springs, too hot to bathe in at their source but running through a series of rock pools where the pilgrims bathed 'to cleanse their souls, the hot water being tempered with the cold'.

Leaving the other pilgrims at this Vaisnava holy of holies, Andrade took his party on up the valley towards Tibet. Their departure was observed, however, and before they could begin the final climb that led out of the Rajah of Srinagar's territory and over the 17,900-foot Mana pass into Tibet, they were stopped by the Rajah's officials and ordered to return to Badrinath. Andrade decided to take a chance; leaving Marques to stall the Rajah's agents, he and the two Christian Indians made a dash for the summit of the pass, taking with them a guide from the nearby Bhotia village of Mana.

It was too early in the year for the pass to be open. For three days they struggled up through deep snow and blinding snowstorms, suffering increasingly from altitude sickness. Andrade was baffled by this sinister and unreasonable phenomenon that left a man breathless whenever he took a pace forward, but he was unwilling to accept the Bhotias' explanation that it was caused by poisoned air. 'According to the natives, many people die on account of the noxious vapours that rise,' he noted. 'It is a fact that people in good health are suddenly taken ill and die within a quarter of an hour.' He could only ascribe the ill-effects that he and his companion were suffering to 'the intense cold and the want of meat'.

The last stages of the first recorded climb in the Himalayas were appropriately dramatic. A blizzard hit the travellers as

36

they reached the saddle of the pass, accompanied by a biting wind: 'Our feet were frozen and swollen so much so that we did not feel it when later they touched a piece of red-hot iron.' They forced a passage through the snow, even though 'it was all one dazzling whiteness for our eyes, which had been weakened by snow-blindness and could make out no sign of the road we were to follow', until at last they stood on the saddle of the Mana pass and could look down into Tibet. 'The journey was continued to the summit of the mountains,' Andrade recorded, 'whence is born the river Ganga from a large pool, and from whence is born another stream that waters the lands of Tibet.'

Many years later this reference to a large pool was interpreted as proof that Andrade had reached the fabled lake Manasarovar. It seems much more likely that Andrade was describing a large glacial tarn known locally as the Deo Tal (lake of God) sited at the head of the Mana valley just below the pass. Since the lake feeds the headwaters of the Saraswati river, which in turn joins the Alaknanda just above Badrinath, Andrade's statement is correct; he had indeed reached the source of one of the principal tributaries of the Ganga. Going on a little further he reached the watershed at the head of the Mana pass – and saw another stream running northwards down into Tibet.

This was as far as Andrade got on his first attempt; seeing ahead of him 'an awful desert' without trees or human habitation, he turned back. A month later, when the snows had all but gone and relations with the Rajah of Srinagar were greatly improved, Andrade and Marques crossed the Mana La together and entered Tibet. They descended into a desolate country split into immense ravines and canyons, part of the ancient kingdom of Gugé. For nearly seven centuries its capital, Tsaparang, together with the nearby monastery of Totling, had been the political and religious centre of Western Tibet, exerting an influence that extended to the furthest corners of the plateau. Now it was on the verge of collapse. Andrade and his companion saw it in the last days of its glory; and, unwittingly, they contributed to its final downfall.

They found no Christians in Gugé, only a deeply religious people who welcomed them with every mark of kindness and respect for their faith and who showed a genuine interest in a religion that in its outward manifestations – its vestments, chants and expressions of worship – so closely resembled theirs. For his part Andrade was less attracted by the demonic aspects of lamaism, the use of human skulls for drinking vessels and drums and thighbones for trumpets. Yet he obviously made a great impression on the king and queen of Gugé. They were so struck by his religious zeal that they agreed to let him return the following summer and set up a mission – and before he left he was given a document bearing the king's seal that pronounced him to be 'Our Chief Lama', with full authority to preach the gospel throughout the kingdom: 'We shall not allow anyone to molest him in this and we shall issue orders that he be given a site and all the help needed to build a house of prayer.' It looked as though a great future for the conversion of pagan souls had been opened to the soldiers of Christ.

In the summer of 1625, Andrade returned to Tsaparang with more of his colleagues, and after spending the winter there witnessed the laying of the foundation-stone of the first Christian church in Tibet – a ceremony performed by the king himself. The letters that he and other Jesuits sent back to India over the next few years are full of optimism about the prospects for the mission. 'This country promises more than any other I have yet heard of,' wrote one of Andrade's colleagues in 1627, 'for they are a tractable and upright people.' Their confidence was based on the knowledge that the king's authority was still paramount throughout Western Tibet and extended as far as Rudok, a hundred and thirty miles away to the north, where Andrade was able to set up a second mission. Although he never quite managed to persuade the king to take the final plunge and the conversion rate among the Tibetans remained depressingly low, Andrade left Tsaparang in 1630 convinced that the mission could only prosper – and totally unaware that a revolution was about to break out. He took over the running of the Jesuits' main mission in Goa and died four years later – poisoned, it is said, by someone who objected to the enthusiasm with which he promoted the Inquisition.

Andrade's fellow-pioneer, Manuel Marques, met an even

more melancholy end. Within a few months of Andrade's departure from Tsaparang, the Jesuit mission had collapsed. The lamas had seen their authority gradually being whittled away by the king's enthusiasm for another faith and had finally come out in revolt, aided by soldiers from the neighbouring king of Ladakh. After a month's siege Tsaparang fell, the king was overthrown and the town sacked. The church and the mission buildings were pulled down and the five Jesuits in residence were imprisoned. They were soon released, but in the face of continuing harassment by the lamas they eventually decided to close down the mission and withdraw.

Six years after Andrade's death an attempt was made to reopen the mission. With Manuel Marques acting as their guide, a fresh group of Jesuits made their way over the Mana La. But as they entered Tibet they were set upon by Tibetan guards. There was a struggle in which Marques was captured; the others fled back across the border. A year later a despairing letter from Marques reached the Jesuit fathers in Agra. He wrote that he was being tortured by the Tibetans and had given up all hope of rescue. Efforts to secure his release through intermediaries in Ladakh met with no response, and no more was heard of him.

With the deposition of the king the power of the ancient dynasty of Gugé was broken. Its territories were absorbed briefly by Ladakh and then came under the dominion of Lhasa. Within twenty years Gugé had disappeared from the map of Tibet and its former capital lay in ruins. In 1912 an official of the Indian Civil Service visited Western Tibet as a member of a trade mission. At the request of the Jesuit authorities in Calcutta he made a detour to the long-abandoned capital. He found most of the buildings in ruins, mud brick houses which had long since crumbled into dust. However, there was one surviving relic of the mission: a weathered wooden cross lying on top of a large pile of stones.

In 1667 Father Athanasius Kircher of the Society of Jesus in Würzburg published his *China Documentis Illustrata*, in which he incorporated details of the latest journeys of the Jesuit fathers into a social geography of China and Central Asia. Accompanying this survey is a map of Asia showing

39

the supposed routes travelled by St Thomas the Apostle, Marco Polo, Benedict de Goes and two Jesuits named Grueber and d'Orville, who had crossed from China to India by way of Lhasa in 1661. There too is Andrade's route to 'Caparangue' (Tsaparang) and 'Radoc' (Rudok), set close beside two remarkable features: a lake from which four rivers flow southward across the Mogul Empire (*Imp. Magoris*) and a vast mountain with another lake from which flows the Ganga – but which is identified as the source of the Ganga *and* Indus ('*Origo Gangis et Indi*'). In the text Kircher explains how he came to put two apparently conflicting views on the sources of the great Indian rivers on the same map. The great mountain with the lake was drawn from Andrade's narrative, supported by the personal testimony of an eighty-six-year-old Indian named Joseph, one of the two Christian servants whom Andrade had taken with him over the Mana La. The lake with the four rivers, shown south of the mountains, had come from Hindu sources. It was the first appearance in the West of the old Puranic legend:

There is a great lake on the highest mountain of Tibet (which are always covered by snow) from which there take their birth the greatest rivers of India; thus the Indus, the Ganges, the Ravi, and the Athec come out from this basin.

Even before Kircher's time, maps had been appearing in Europe showing a great lake in Asia with four, five and even six rivers issuing from it. But this giant among lakes was nearly always sited north of Burma and Siam rather than Tibet and most often associated with the Brahmaputra, Salween, Irrawaddy and Mekong. It crept into European cartography in 1550 and there it stayed, growing bolder and larger with the years until Kircher shifted it out of South-East Asia and into the Indo-Tibetan sphere. Although it went by different names – the most enduring of which was 'Lake Chiamay' – its link with the holy lake of the *Puranas* is inescapable. It was lake Manasarovar as seen from a South-East Asia point of view, where the legend was well known but was quite reasonably associated with that more familiar group of rivers whose upper courses run close to each other through the mountains east of the Assam Himalayas.

Although Andrade's reputation soon faded into obscurity the memory of his brave venture across the Himalayas was kept alive among the Jesuits. In time it caught the imagination of a new recruit to the order, Ippolito Desideri, a young Italian from Pistoia in Northern Tuscany. While Desideri may have lacked the cold-hearted determination that was said to distinguish the true soldier of Christ, he was not short in other Jesuitical qualities, notably an insatiable intellectual curiosity and a passionate commitment to his cause. His desire to find out what had happened to the Christian population in Gugé in the years since the withdrawal of the Tsaparang mission became something of an obsession. In 1712, when he was twenty-eight years old, he managed to persuade the Pope to back a new mission to Western Tibet. He was ordained as priest in August of that year and within a month had set sail for the Indies.

It took Desideri a full year to reach Goa and another twelve months before he could get his expedition organized and on the road. Affairs in the Indian subcontinent were no longer so well ordered as they had been in Andrade's time. The last of the great Mogul emperors was dead and the empire that Akbar and his descendants had administered so ably was now well on the way to disintegration. It was not only Mogul power that was on the decline; the British and French trading companies had now seized the initiative from their Dutch and Portuguese rivals.

Even so, the Portuguese were not entirely without friends at court. At Agra Desideri found a powerful patron in Donna Juliana, a remarkable Portuguese noblewoman who exercised varying degrees of influence over no less than three successive Mogul emperors. Donna Juliana not only promoted his cause at court but funded Desideri's expedition out of her own purse. However, even she was unable to prevent the appointment by the local Jesuits of one of their men, a Portuguese named Emanoel Freyre, as its leader. Father Freyre was a missionary in the classic mould, devoted to his faith but with his zeal tempered and perhaps a little blunted by the rigours

41

and disappointments of more than twenty years' unbroken service in the field. Set in his ways and somewhat short on stamina, Freyre proved to be no match for Desideri's overriding enthusiasm.

Both men left vivid accounts of their travels. Desideri's version runs to four volumes and is a major work of scholarship – the first comprehensive study of Tibetan culture and religion to have been written. Freyre's narrative, in the form of a report written soon after his return to India in 1717, provides a lightweight counterpoint, gossipy and often revealing in its candid observations about the expedition.

The Jesuits had decided on a flanking rather than a direct approach to Tibet, going by way of Kashmir. Andrade's references to Srinagar in his reports may well have misled them, as they certainly misled others. Desideri and Freyre were probably unaware that there were *two* Srinagars: one the obscure little town in the Garhwal Himalayas that formed the capital of the hill-state of the Rajah of Srinagar, the other the capital city of the far grander kingdom of Kashmir. They made their way towards the latter, setting out rather late in the autumn of 1714 and finding the crossing over the Pir Panjal range that guards Kashmir from the south unexpectedly difficult. It was like climbing staircases 'piled one on top of another', wrote Desideri. He began coughing up blood, so instead of pressing on directly into Baltistan and Ladakh – then known as Little Tibet and Second Tibet – the two Jesuits decided to winter in Kashmir. Like many Europeans in years to come, Desideri was greatly taken by the vale of Kashmir and its lakes and water-gardens. Where Freyre saw only 'stagnant water' and 'abundant refuse', the enchanted Desideri observed 'a most ornamental garland round the city'.

In the early summer of the following year the expedition moved westwards into Ladakh – 'mountainous, sterile and altogether horrible' – crossing the notoriously treacherous Zoji pass only with the greatest difficulty. By Himalayan standards it was not a high pass but its extensive snowfields made the crossing a slow and exhausting business. Snowblindness was another unexpected hazard. Freyre describes how he woke one morning after sheltering in a cave to find that Desideri had temporarily gone blind: 'When we were standing looking at the first rays of the dawn Father Hyppolitus and one of our Christian servants found that they could not distinguish them; and we saw then that their eyes were running with water from the glare of the snow.' The porters went on strike – the first recorded occurrence of what was to become a familiar and time-honoured feature of all the best Himalayan expeditions. It was resolved in an equally traditional way: Father Freyre slipped the leader some money and 'soothed them with soft words'. Before going on, however, the porters improvised goggles to cut down the glare of the sun: 'Each tore a piece from his tunic which he rubbed in the charcoal of the spent fire and stretched it across his eyes like a veil.'

On 20 June the party finally stumbled into Leh, the capital of Ladakh. As they fly into Leh airport, modern visitors to this long inaccessible corner of India will find Desideri's description of Leh in 1715 familiar in almost every detail:

> It is situated in a wide plain entirely surrounded by mountains and studded with villages. The city extends up the slope of a mountain to the residence of the Chief Lama and the palace of the King, both large and fine buildings. The whole is crowned with a large fort close to the summit and another fort on the summit. Below and on its flanks the town is surrounded by walls and defended by gates.

Although the land itself was 'altogether horrible', Desideri found the Lamaist inhabitants to be 'kindly, cheerful and courteous'. They met with the same warmth and friendship that Andrade had found in Gugé a century earlier – so warm in fact that Desideri was greatly tempted to abandon his search for Gugé and its Christian community and stay in Ladakh to evangelize. His companion had very different ideas. Freyre now regarded their quest as fruitless, but at the same time he deeply distrusted the rulers of Ladakh. His only concern was to get out of this benighted country and back to India – but not by way of the dreadful pass over which they had come. However, there was no easy way out of Ladakh; Desideri put it over to him that if he was determined to return

43

to India without recrossing the Zoji La, then it would have to be done via Tibet. 'After praying together to God for guidance,' wrote Desideri, 'we consulted together and decided to continue our journey to Third and Principal Tibet, as being the head and centre of that false sect, and also because Father Antonio de Andrade and other missionaries of our Society after him had once been there.' Freyre may have been the official leader of the expedition but from this point on it was Desideri who was effectively in command.

In August the travellers set out again, riding on horseback along the ancient trade-route that runs alongside the river Indus and then climbs up and out onto the great Tibetan plateau. After three weeks' journey they came to the Tibetan monastery of Tashigang, on the border between Ladakh and Tibet. Beyond lay a 'vast, sterile, and terrible desert', too cold and too arid to provide more than the meanest of existences; an unexplored wilderness of thin scrub and salt flats broken by mountain ranges, grazed over by yak and antelope and herds of wild asses – and occasionally by *dokpa*, nomadic 'dwellers of black tents', with their herds of domesticated yak, sheep and long-haired goats.

Across this wilderness ran the Tasam highway, the trade-route that led from Ladakh up the Indus valley to the trading centre of Gartok and then on eastwards down the Tsangpo valley to Lhasa. Those who travelled unarmed along the Tasam highroad provided an easy prey for the chief predators of the Chang Tang, fast-moving posses of armed bandits mounted on shaggy ponies and even shaggier yaks. The Jesuits were warned that to go any further without an escort was to risk death: they should stay in Tashigang until they could attach themselves to a caravan. This was the accepted and, indeed, the only safe way to travel in Tibet for vulnerable travellers. The land itself and its hostility to natural life – where every little comfort and every means of existence had to be fought for – brutalized and bred violence, and the philosophy of Buddha offered a means of keeping the violence at bay. It was a fact of Tibetan life with which every visitor from the outside world had to come to terms, that a people committed to a religion of peace and compassion lived permanently on the brink of chaos and strife.

44

The Jesuits, too, had their philosophy. They prayed, and 'God who never abandons those who put their trust in Him provided us with the best escort that could be imagined.' Their supplications were answered in the beguiling form of a Tartar princess, who was about to start from Tashigang with a large caravan and an escort bound for Lhasa:

Standing before her with hands uplifted in a worshipping attitude, we presented her with a piece of Bengal cloth embroidered and red in colour (for the Tartars have a great liking for stuffs in red) and with ten crowns in the bargain. The lady, whose pretty face was radiant at receiving our gifts, raised her eyes to ours and asked us with womanly curiosity: 'To what do we owe your presence and where is fate leading you?'

Speaking through their Moslem interpreter, Desideri and Freyre told the princess that they were 'well-meaning pilgrims' heading for Lhasa and asked to join her caravan. She replied that it would be an honour to be able to help two lamas from a far-off land and their presence would be very welcome. She was also able to give them some sound advice as to how best to prepare for what lay ahead:

For three whole months the traveller finds no village nor any living creature; he must therefore take with him all provisions, such as tea, butter, flour or parched barley and meat, which becomes so frozen that it will keep for a long time. Not only must one carry provisions for the men, but barley and flour for the horses, the ground being generally so covered with snow that they can find no food. Water is frozen hard and for cooking you have to thaw snow or ice over a fire. Now wood is not to be found in the desert, save here and there a few prickly bushes, and to make a fire one has to search for the dry dung of horses and cattle. Your bed at night is the earth, off which you have to scrape the snow, and your roof is the sky, from which falls snow and sleet.

Helped by their princess the Jesuits bought further provisions for themselves and for their three Christian servants and Moslem interpreter, as well as knee-length sheepskin *poshteens*, sheepskin boots and sheepskin hats. At first these luxuries – 'suggested partly by self-love and partly to protect our servants against frost-bite' – troubled Desideri greatly, but his doubts vanished when the full rigours of a winter crossing of the Chang Tang became apparent.

The caravan set out in mid-October, leaving Tashigang in great pomp and style:

> At the head of our caravan rode a number of the Princess's servants and some squadrons of Tartar cavalry, followed by the Princess and her Tartar ladies, all on horseback; her ministers and the officers of her army. Then came more Tartar cavalry with whom we generally rode. The rear guard was also composed of cavalry, and a crowd of men on foot and led horses.

Once they were on the exposed plateau it soon became clear that the risk of 'losing nose, fingers, toes and even your life' was never going to be far away. The linen tents that the Jesuits had brought with them from India proved to be hopelessly inadequate: accumulated snow and ice made them heavy and unmanageable and when a strong wind was blowing it was almost impossible to peg them down. 'The night was rather a cessation of fatigue than real repose,' noted Freyre, 'the intense cold and the intolerable annoyance of the insects harboured in our clothes prevented any real sleep.' Like the Tibetans the Jesuits had decided that warmth was preferable to cleanliness, which meant putting up with three months of accumulated dirt and playing host to a rich assortment of insects. Freyre reveals that Desideri stopped washing after the water he was lifting in his cupped hands froze to his beard – 'and a fine sight he looked with his face stuck round with icicles!' Whenever the opportunity occurred, they held de-lousing sessions: 'Now and then, seated in the sun, we would remove some clothes, and were saved the trouble of picking the lice off one by one – for we could simply sweep them off!'

The progress of every caravan in Tibet is extremely slow.

The pack animals move forward at their own pace and where there is a patch of grazing they are allowed to spend several days resting and building up their reserves. These enforced delays gave the members of the Tartar princess's caravan ample time to get to know each other. Desideri and the princess soon became close friends – a relationship that Desideri looked back on nostalgically in later years: 'As I had learnt a little of the language from our interpreter, she would invite me to her tent and order my horse to be cared for.' Here the young Jesuit would sit down on a rug by his hostess and sip salt-butter tea and do his best to answer her questions about Europe and its customs, as well as all sorts of inquiries about 'Our Holy Law, the images of saints in my breviary, my manner of praying and the meaning of my prayers'.

One evening after sunset Desideri left his princess and began to look round the camp for his own tents, which were being brought up by Emanoel Freyre and the rest of their party. It soon became apparent that they had failed to arrive:

> Much troubled I waited until the third hour of the night, when at last our three Christian servants arrived with the baggage horse. I anxiously asked about the Father [Freyre] and the interpreter. They said that by his orders they had left them behind. The Father's horse having fallen exhausted in the snow, he had decided to wait until the poor beast recovered a little.

Greatly alarmed, Desideri sent a message to the princess asking for her help. A search party was quickly assembled and sent back along their trail until eventually Father Freyre and the interpreter were found half-buried and half-frozen in the snow. They were brought to the princess's tent and thawed out in front of a large fire, where Father Freyre explained that his horse had dropped dead from hunger and exhaustion: 'When daylight vanished I lost trace of the others. All I could do was to lie against the horse's belly for the sake of warmth and wait for the morning.' As Desideri and Freyre were considering how best to overcome the loss of one of their seven horses, their hostess again came to their rescue by offering Freyre one of her own.

47

This is only one of many acts of kindness towards the Jesuits and their servants shown by this engaging and courageous woman. Although Freyre had less opportunity to get to know her intimately, he too was greatly impressed by her. Again and again in his narrative he cites instances of her solicitude:

Often when the terrible wind and cold would chafe my face so severely as to make me exclaim (I confess it): 'A curse on this cold!' she would comfort us with hot tea and some meat. Through the mouth of her interpreter she would tell us to have courage, for no dangers from the mountains nor avalanches had power to harm us if we kept to her side. Once when she saw me frozen to a state of inertness, she said to me: 'Hand me your coat,' and ordered one of her servants to line the sleeves with goat skins, the fur to the inside, and to place them in such a way that the hands should always be protected.

It took the caravan more than a month to journey up the valley of the Gartong Chhu, the southern tributary of the Indus. Early in November they crossed over the Jerko La, the 16,300-foot pass over the watershed between the Indus and Sutlej river systems. At this point they were as close as they ever came to Desideri's original goal. Directly below them to the south lay the headwaters of the Sutlej with the northern slopes of the Himalayan peaks beyond; only fifty miles downstream was Tsaparang and its ruined church. But Gugé and its seven centuries of ascendancy had already passed out of Tibetan history and there was no one to point Desideri in its direction.

The caravan continued its journey eastwards and away from Tsaparang. Had Freyre been told of its fate, he would have heaved a sigh of relief and demanded to be directed without delay towards the nearest pass into India. Desideri would have wanted to go on. His original interest in Andrade and his Christian outpost had been overtaken by a stronger urge: a passionate desire to get to know Tibet and to come to terms with its religion – and if this meant journeying on to

Lhasa and studying all that Lhasa had to offer, then it had to be done.

They had now entered the holy land of Kailas-Manasarovar, a region venerated by the Tibetans, so Desideri learned, 'on account of a certain Urghien [Padmasambava], who is the founder of the religion professed in Tibet'. As the caravan descended from the Jerko pass, Desideri was shown where Urghien was said to have his abode, in a high peak called Ngari Niongar. It was among the mountains close at hand to the north-east – where Kailas stood veiled in clouds:

Away from the road there stands an enormously high mountain, very wide in circumference, its summit hidden among the clouds, covered with perpetual snow and ice, and most terrible on account of the icy cold. In a cave of that mountain, according to legend, there lived the above-mentioned Urghien in absolute retirement and uninterrupted meditation. Not only do the Tibetans visit the cave, where they invariably leave some presents, but with very great inconvenience to themselves they make the round of the whole mountain, an occupation of some days, by which they gain what I might call great indulgences.

A few days later, in late November 1715, the tents of the Tartar princess's caravan were raised on the meadows beside a large lake, 'some days' march in circumference, from which the Ganges is supposed to take its source'. It was the fabled Manasarovar of the *Puranas*. Desideri was told that the lake's name was Retoa, but he had no difficulty in associating it with the traditional source of India's holy river. He observed that it was 'held in high veneration by the superstitious people' and that the pilgrims walked round it 'with great devotion'. He and Freyre had approached the lake from the north-west, first moving up what Desideri had assumed to be the main branch of the Indus to its supposed source. Then they had dropped down from the Jerko La to the headwaters of another river, flowing westwards, which appeared to have its source in one large lake. All this suggested to Desideri that he had arrived at the *Origi Gangis et Indi* of Athanasius Kircher

49

and Antonio de Andrade, the place where the two great rivers of Mogul India had their beginnings:

> I think that this mountain of Ngari Niongar [Kailas] should be recognized as the true origin and source not only of the Ganges but also of the Indus. For as this is the highest point from which the land sinks down on both sides, the waters which descend from there on the western side flow into Second Tibet, as experience shows, and from there into Little Tibet. Then, breaking through the mountains of Kashmir, they at last reach Little Guzzarrat, there to form the wide and navigable Indus. In the same way, the waters that descend from Ngari Niongar on the eastern side first flow into lake Retoa [Manasarovar] then take their course downwards and so gradually become the Ganges.

So true is this description of the drainage of the Kailas region and the course of the Indus that it is hard to believe that Desideri had nothing to go on but his own observations. He was wrong only in thinking that the second river was the Ganga, but in the circumstances he could not have known otherwise. Some days later he stood on the watershed of a third great river system, and again his conclusions, drawn from his own experience and from information gathered from the Tibetans, were uncannily accurate.

The caravan had toiled eastwards from the lake onto the 16,900-foot Maryum La, the divide between the Sutlej and the Tsangpo. Here it was Desideri's turn to have a horse die under him, and have a fresh one given him by the Tartar princess. But now the great desert plateau lay behind them and their course would run for five hundred miles alongside a river known simply as 'great river' or Tsang-Po, a river that Desideri soon realized was Tibet's main artery:

> Flowing from west to east it traverses the centre of Third Tibet [Tibet proper] and then turning to the south-east enters the country of Lhoba, whence it descends to Rongmati [Assam] a province of Mogor [Mogul India] beyond the Ganges, into which this principal river of Tibet at last flows.

This single paragraph contained the essential facts about the Tsangpo-Brahmaputra connection, over which geographers and map-makers were to dispute and quarrel for another century and a half. For the whole of that period it remained, along with the rest of Desideri's work on Tibet, unnoticed and unread on the bookshelves of an Italian country villa.

Eventually the Jesuits and their companions reached Lhasa. They were not the first Europeans to get there; two Jesuit fathers had reached Lhasa from Peking in 1661. But Desideri was well aware that it was a prize that few travellers would ever hope to attain, and he later recorded his achievement with a certain flourish: 'Finally, two years and four months after I left Goa, and one year and a half since our departure from Delli, and ten whole months since leaving Kascimir, we arrived by the grace of God, on the eighteenth day of March 1716, at the city of Lhasa, capital of this Tibet.'

The city stood at the centre of a plain surrounded on all sides by mountains. Just inside the city gates, on their left as they rode through the outskirts, was the 'residence of the Grand Lama of Tibet', the famous Potala Palace. It was built on a huge rock and dominated the city:

To the south is a handsome square surrounded by high walls with great gates and bulwarks like a fortress. From here a wide, well-planned and easy staircase leads up to the summit of the rock, where stands a sumptuous palace five storeys high. The riches contained therein are inestimable, especially in the apartment of the Grand Lama.

Lhasa itself was not particularly extensive – Freyre was disappointed to find that it was 'only the size of three parishes' – but it was densely populated, both by Tibetans and by traders from all over Asia. Here the Jesuit fathers parted from their escort and their benefactress. Both men were very conscious of the enormous debt they owed her and Desideri, in particular, sorely missed her company. 'The Princess stayed a short time at the Court,' he wrote later:

She soon went elsewhere into a convent of their sect where

51

she became a nun. So that when I had really mastered the language I could not, as I so heartily wished, see her again and have the opportunity to initiate her into our holy faith. But I pray to God constantly and fervently to recompense her for all the benefits bestowed on us, to illuminate her, convert her, and grant her eternal salvation.

Another parting in Lhasa took place without much regret on either side. After less than a month in the city, Desideri's travelling companion of two and a half years left for India:

My companion had always lived in hot climates and feared the intense cold and thin air, so after staying a few days in Lhasa to recuperate, he left by the more frequented road through Nepal and returned to Hindustan. Thus I remained for some time alone, the only Missionary, indeed the only European in this immense country of the Three Tibets.

In less than three weeks Emanoel Freyre was in Nepal, where he stayed for five months at the Capuchin mission in Kathmandu. After an eventful stay punctuated by outbreaks of plague, civil insurrection and an attempt to burn down the mission, he moved down into the Indian plains. Eventually he returned to the Jesuit mission at Agra where, in April 1717, he sat down to write his *Report on Tibet* for his Vicar-General. Yet Freyre seems to have been unable to settle down once more to ordinary mission work; two years later he left the Jesuits and moved down to join the large Indo-Portuguese community in Goa. A petition for his readmission to the Society which appears on Jesuit records for 1724 was apparently unsuccessful. Perhaps Freyre was too prone to human weakness to make either a good Jesuit or a good explorer.

Ippolito Desideri stayed on in Tibet for five years. At his first royal audience, he made a powerful impression on the 'King' of Tibet (the sixth Dalai Lama) and his chief minister and was given permission to speak and proselytize freely. Desideri records how: 'From that day until I left Tibet I made it a rule to study from early morning to sundown, and for nearly six years took nothing during the day save *cia* [tea] to drink.'

First he set himself to learn the Tibetan language and later, after presenting the Dalai Lama with a book written in Tibetan, 'to explain our faith and to refute their false religion', began a major study of Tibetan Buddhism as it was set out in its canonical texts. This work was interrupted by the Tartar invasion of Tibet, during which Lhasa was sacked, the great Potala Palace stormed and the King and his chief minister killed. Desideri took refuge in a monastery eight days' march from Lhasa, where he was able to continue with his studies without isolating himself from the historic events that were taking place nearby.

The disorders ended with the arrival of a vast and utterly invincible Chinese army which effectively brought Tibet into the dominion of the Manchu Emperors. Those who enjoy historical ironies may ponder on the fact that Andrade's mission to Tsaparang marked the fall of the kingdom of Gugé, while Desideri's stay in Lhasa coincided with the end of Tibet's independence from China.

In 1719 it was decided in Rome that the task of converting the heathen of Tibet should be transferred from the Jesuits to the Capuchins. It took time for the order of withdrawal to be transmitted to Desideri and for Desideri to respond, but finally he could delay his departure no longer. In April 1721 he left Lhasa. He managed to spend the winter in Tibet and Nepal, so it was not until April 1722 that he arrived at the Jesuit College in Agra – seven years and seven months since he and Father Freyre had first set out for Tibet. He never found any trace of a Christian community in Tibet, nor did he make much effort to establish one. His was a quest of a different order, a search for knowledge partly in order to refute it and partly for its own sake. He had the kind of lust that Kipling describes in *Kim*:

From time to time God causes men to be born – and thou art one of them – who have a lust to go abroad at the risk of their lives and discover news – today it may be of a far-off thing, tomorrow of some hidden mountains . . .

Desideri spent another five years in general mission work in India before he was ordered to return to Rome, where he

53

set to work on his comprehensive study of Tibet's religion, history, geography and culture. He fully intended this *Historical Sketch of Tibet* to be published, but on 14 April 1733, at the age of forty-eight, he died suddenly of inflammation of the lungs.

With his death, all traces of his work were lost. All that was known about his journey was contained in a single letter written to a friend from Lhasa in 1716 – until 1875, when a manuscript copy of Desideri's *Historical Sketch of Tibet* was found among the papers of a deceased Italian *cavaliere* of Pistoia. The find received wide publicity at the time and it was announced that an Italian edition would soon be published. In fact, it was another thirty years before it appeared in print and sixty years before a heavily-edited version was published in English. Emanoel Freyre's *Report on Tibet* also vanished: it was only discovered in the Vittorio Emanuele Library in Rome in 1924. By this quirk of fate the unveiling of the many mysteries hidden in Tibet was postponed for another century, and the holy mountain and lake preserved their secrets for an eccentric Englishman and fugitive Anglo-Indian to reveal in 1812.

Chapter 3

'A Mighty Maze Without a Plan': Hyder Jung Hearsey and the Sources of the Ganga

Soon after the middle of the eighteenth century the first pink splotches begin to appear on maps of the Indian sub-continent. By the end of the century a great wedge of British territory had been marked out from Bengal deep into Upper India, its thin end tapering to a point just short of the Himalayan foothills north of Delhi and the land of the Punjab.

For the time being the young thrusters of the British East India Company saw no reason to drive that particular wedge any deeper. The lands beyond were securely held and presented no immediate threat to the commercial interests and sound commercial principles upon which this extraordinary empire was being built. Along the north ran a thick belt of *terai* jungle and swamp backed by range upon range of seemingly impassable mountains; and west of the river Sutlej the young one-eyed 'Lion of the Punjab', Ranjit Singh, was carving out his own little empire that was to hold out against the British for another half century.

This was the great age of the *condottiere*, when all the more successful Indian leaders employed European mercenaries. Ever since the modern sepoy armies of Clive and Stringer Lawrence had shown the strength of European-trained militia, the services of such soldiers of fortune had been greatly in demand. One of the most successful of these freebooters was Pierre Cuiller, a deserter from the French navy. As General Perron, he rose to become leader of the confederate forces of the Marathas, the warrior peoples of the Deccan and Western Ghats, whose chiefs were intent on filling the vacuum left by the Moguls in Northern India.

In 1799 a seventeen-year-old cadet named Hyder Jung Hearsey joined Perron's army. Hyder Jung's paternal grandfather had fought on the wrong side at the battle of Culloden and by doing so had forfeited his family estates in Cumberland. His father had been forced to take the course then followed by many younger sons of the manse and joined the East India Company's Madras Army. In India he had fathered two sets of children: one wholly British and one 'country-born', by a 'Jat lady'. Liaisons between servants of the Company and Indian women were then regarded as perfectly respectable, so this was quite in keeping with the relaxed attitudes of the day, but it did not follow that the fortunes of the two sides of the family remained on a par.

Hyder Jung's legitimate half-brother joined the Bengal cavalry and rose to become a fine old sepoy general, one of the few to act decisively in the early days of the 1857 Mutiny. Hyder Jung himself was debarred by the circumstances of his birth from following his father and half-brother into the Company's service and so became a mercenary. After training with the army of the Nawab of Oude, he signed on with General Perron and the Marathas. When war with France broke out he transferred his allegiance to Perron's rival, General George Thomas, and when 'George Bahadur' was defeated by the Frenchman, Hearsey made off at the head of five thousand men to set himself up as an independent freebooter. Although poorly educated and regarded as a rough diamond by those who knew him only slightly, Hearsey was no fool. He soon learned to look after himself and while he was still a teenager won the affection of a young princess of Cambay, Zuhur-ul-Missa, whom he married. She was the adopted daughter of the Mogul Emperor himself and brought with her a dowry of estates that included property at Bareilly.

Like his more famous fellow-mercenaries, James Skinner and William Linnaeus Gardner, Hearsey placed his Irregular Horse at the disposal of General Lake when the Company finally went to war against the Marathas in 1803. He had a good war, led his light cavalry with distinction and survived a severe wound to the head. His only reward from an ungrateful and suspicious Governor-General was to have his body of irregulars called in and discharged. So it was that in

1807 this seasoned young veteran of nine years of war found himself without employment.

Unwelcome though it may have been for freebooters like Hearsey, the ending of the Maratha war allowed the military engineers and draughtsmen who made up the Company's mapping department, the Survey of India, to begin mapping the conquered and ceded provinces of Upper Hindustan. The first surveys of the Company's Bengal Province had been started by Major James Rennell, appointed Surveyor-General at the age of twenty-four by Lord Clive. Under his painstaking direction a small band of surveyors and draughtsmen had started to assemble the first accurate and detailed maps of the subcontinent. Although he left India in 1777, worn down by malaria and the enervating climate of Bengal, he continued to play a leading role in its geographical affairs for another forty years, fully justifying the title of 'father of Indian geography' that was later bestowed on him.

Rennell had been greatly impressed by his first sight of the Himalayan ranges and was the first European geographer to recognize their importance. 'I was not able to determine their height,' he wrote in 1788, 'but it may in some measure be guessed by the circumstance of their rising considerably above the horizon when viewed in the plains of Bengal, at a distance of 150 miles.' As to the upper courses of the three great Indian rivers – the Indus, Ganga and Brahmaputra – that disappeared into this mountain barrier so many hundreds of miles apart, Rennell could only admit to 'our ignorance'.

Rennell's first map of Hindustan, published in 1782, contains a striking innovation in the way that the 'Burrum-pooter' of Assam is linked for the first time with the Tsangpo of Tibet, but as far as the Ganga was concerned he was content to follow the Hindu belief that it had its fountain-head beyond the Himalayas at the sacred lake of Manasarovar. He was even prepared to interpret rather than dismiss out of hand the old story that it flowed out of the mouth of a cow. His theory was that the Ganga flowed south from the lake until it came to the Himalayas:

57

When meeting the great chain of mount Himmaleh this great body of water now forces a passage through the ridge of Mount Himmaleh and, sapping its very foundations, rushes through a cavern and precipitates itself into a vast basin which it has worn in the rock, at the hither foot of the mountains. The Ganges thus appears to incurious spectators to derive its original springs from this chain of mountains. And the mind of superstition has given to the mouth of the cavern the form of the head of a cow, an animal held by the Hindus in a degree of veneration almost equal to that in which the Egyptians of old held their god Apis.

Absurd as this notion of a trans-Himalayan tunnel now appears, Rennell's theories were no more fanciful than others of the time: a contemporary French map places lake Manasarovar in Kashmir and at the head of the Indus; another, apparently drawing its inspiration from the Hindu *Puranas*, provides the holy lake with three separate outlets. The fact was that as late as the start of the nineteenth century European geographers and cartographers simply had no clear idea where any of the larger South Asian rivers came from. The mystery was as great as it had ever been.

In 1807 the challenge was taken up by two cousins, Henry and Robert Colebrooke. Henry, the older of the two, was the son of a former Chairman of the East India Company. He had joined the Bengal Civil Service in 1780 and while acting as Assistant Commissioner in Purnea in the 1790s had come up with the first rough calculations of the height of the distant Himalayan range. His figure of 26,000 feet above sea level for one of the higher peaks was long regarded as quite absurdly exaggerated. Besides being an administrator, he was also a Sanskrit scholar and in 1807 became the first President of the Bengal Asiatic Society, assembling a wide range of material for the Society's journal. *Asiatick Researches*. It was this journal that provided the main notice-board for a great deal of the geographical exploration and research into India's past that took place during the next three decades. One of its principal contributors was Robert Colebrooke, appointed Surveyor-General of Bengal in 1794.

If Henry was the scholar and the intellectual, it was his cousin Robert who did much of the fieldwork and provided the more practical side of the partnership. He also came from a less privileged side of the Colebrooke family, as the eldest of three illegitimate brothers then soldiering with the Company's armies. They were part of what was accurately described by a contemporary historian, James Mill, as 'a vast system of outdoor relief for Britain's upper classes', whereby India serves as a dumping-ground for British gentlemen who were either without means or without recognized parentage. In the case of Robert Colebrooke this system most decidedly worked to India's advantage.

The two cousins had a common interest in the Ganga: while Henry devoted many hours of his leisure time to studying the river's place in Hindu culture and the myths surrounding it, Robert spent most of his working life either on the river itself or by its banks. After more than twenty years of survey work along its lower courses and channels, no European and few Indians could claim to know the river and its ways better than he – and none had a better reason for wishing to explore it to its source. Encouraged by his cousin, Robert Colebrooke applied for permission to extend his survey upstream:

Having long doubted the account which is given by Major Rennell of the origin of the Ganges at Munsaroar Lake, I determined; as soon as the opportunity should be afforded to me, to attempt myself to proceed to the celebrated spot where the Ganges is said to force a passage through the Hymalia Mountains.

The opportunity came in the spring of 1807, when the Governor-General authorized the Survey of India to start work upriver. Robert Colebrooke immediately set sail up the Ganga in a country boat, leaving the Survey offices in Calcutta in the charge of his subordinate, John Garstin, another close relative and soon to be his successor. There was nothing particularly unusual about a Surveyor-General doing his own fieldwork. His department was desperately understaffed and underpaid; the sickness and mortality rate was probably

59

higher in the Survey of India than in any other government department and it was always a struggle to get hold of good officers. None could be spared to accompany Colebrooke, so he sailed without an assistant.

The country boat took him as far as Cawnpore, bordering on the domains of the Nawab of Oude to the east and the newly-won British territories to the north. Here he disembarked and strengthened his little party with an escort of fifty sepoys under the command of Lieutenant Webb of the 10th Bengal Native Infantry (BNI). William Webb was then a comparatively inexperienced young officer of twenty-two, but he had picked up some surveying skills while on the line of march with his regiment during the Maratha wars and this made him particularly useful to Colebrooke.

The escort, however, proved to be inadequate and, 'as a necessary precaution to avoid being attacked and plundered by the Rebels', Robert Colebrooke secured the services of a local man who knew the style of the country better than any European and could supply his own arms: Captain Hyder Jung Hearsey.

Protected by Hearsey and some of his mounted irregulars, Colebrooke and Webb spent the cold weather of 1807–8 surveying the notoriously unhealthy *terai* jungle bordering on Nepalese Kumaon. Here the Surveyor-General contracted an intermittent fever that eventually forced him to revise his plans. He himself could not go on but he was determined that the survey should be continued to its goal. He gave Webb instructions that he was to explore the Ganga 'from Hurdwar to Gungoutri (or the Cow's Mouth), where the river is stated by Major Rennell to force its way through the Hymalaia Mountains by a Subterraneous passage' and determine 'whether this (should there be such a place) be actually the Source of the Ganges, or whether, as Major Rennell has stated in his memoir, it rises from the Lake of Munsaroar.'

Leaving the Surveyor-General camped in the *terai*, Webb and Hearsey set out for the foothills in mid-March 1808, taking with them a reduced escort and a considerable number of servants and baggage-carriers. While on the march they were joined by a friend of Webb's from his old regiment, Captain Felix Raper. Of the three officers, only Webb had a formal position on the expedition. Nevertheless, Raper made it his business to keep the official log, which was later forwarded to Henry Colebrooke and published by him in his *Asiatick Researches*.

Their party arrived at Hardwar, on the edge of the plains, just as the great religious gathering known as the *Kumbh Mela* was getting under way. Every year a spring festival or *Mela* is celebrated in Hardwar by the banks of the Ganga, and every twelfth year a vast multitude of pilgrims gathers for the *Kumbh* (Aquarius) *Mela*, all attempting to bathe during the course of a single day at one small *ghat*, a tier of steps leading down into the water. Today over ten million people attend these *Kumbh Melas*, and even in the early nineteenth century the numbers must have been considerable; at the festival in 1820, over four hundred pilgrims and countless sepoys were reported to have been drowned or trampled to death as the pilgrims struggled down to the water's edge.

By a great stroke of luck Webb and his expedition encountered among the pilgrims at the *Kumbh Mela* of 1808 a party of Gurkhas from Srinagar. These invaders from neighbouring Nepal had overrun the former territories of the Rajahs of Srinagar a decade earlier and were the new rulers of the hills. At the head of their party was the Gurkha Governor of Srinagar himself, whose permission was required before they could enter the hills. He professed at first to be extremely unwilling to allow any foreigners other than genuine pilgrims into his province, let alone map-makers from a foreign power, but finally, with the right sort of inducements, allowed himself to be won over. Indeed, once he had accepted the idea he went on to offer a guide, an escort of twelve Nepalese sepoys and a large number of coolies to carry their tents and baggage. Scarcely able to believe their luck, the travellers made their way through the Gangadwara gorge into the hills. It was the start of what a later recruit to the Survey of India, John Hodgson, was to call 'a mighty maze without a plan', a vast, formless jumble of sharp ridges, often snow-topped, intercut by deep, shadowed valleys – all of it *terra incognita*.

They avoided the pilgrim trail, which leads northwards alongside the river through the first ranges to the confluence of the Bhagirathi and Alaknanda rivers, where the two major tributaries of the Ganga come together below the cliffs of Deoprayag. Instead, they took a short-cut that led them north-west across the fertile valley of the Dun and over the site of the future cantonments of Dehra Dun. Then they climbed out of the vale some miles to the east of what would in another twenty years become the hill station of Mussoorie – and from a knoll on the Landour ridge they had their first uninterrupted view of the giants of the Garhwal Himalayas: an awesome, jagged banner of rock and ice that the eye could follow for well over a hundred miles to left and right.

Directly in front was the solid cluster of peaks that made up the Gangotri-Kedarnath-Badrinath group – and somewhere in its centre a sacred mountain that the travellers knew only as *Mahadeo-ka-Linga*, the lingam of the great god (Shiva). For Raper it was 'a sight the most sublime and aweful that can be pictured to the imagination'. From where they stood they could see seven or eight successive ranges, one rising above another, until the view was finally cut off by the snows:

> The depth of the valley below, the progressive elevation of the intermediate hills, and the majestic splendor of the 'cloud-capt' *Himalaya*, formed so grand a picture, that the mind was impressed with a sensation of dread rather than of pleasure.

Hyder Jung Hearsey took a less romantic view of the scene. 'We had a good and extensive view of the Himalea Mountains,' he noted in his own journal. 'The most remarkable peaks I delineated and took correct bearings of them with a theodolite.' A prosaic response, perhaps, but one that provides firm evidence of Hearsey's technical expertise, and gives the lie to later charges that he was no surveyor.

After two days of travelling through hills and valleys abundantly stocked with forests of deodar, oak and rhododendron they dropped down into the Bhagirathi and rejoined the pilgrim trail as it followed this western tributary of the Ganga to its source. It was this branch, named after the sage whose meditation brought the goddess Ganga Mai down to earth, that was popularly acknowledged to be the Ganga's true source. For several more days they were able to follow the river as it curved round to the north into an ever-deepening gorge, past fields where 'the rich flourishing crops seemed to exhult in the advantage of their situation.' Raper noted that here both the hill-men and hill-women shared the labour:

> The women even do not show that bashfulness and reserve which females in *Hindostan* in general exhibit, but made their comments with the greatest freedom. We could not help remarking that the female mountaineers exhibited the general failings of their sex, having their necks, ears and noses ornamented with rings and beads.

As succeeding generations of visitors to the Himalayas have found, these attractive characteristics are common to nearly all hill-women. It seems to be part of the nature of the *paharis*, the people of the hills, that they should be more open and less hidebound than the people of the plains, the *biharis*. The deeper into the hills one goes – and the further to the north and east – the more tolerant become the inhabitants, freed from inhibitions of caste and Islamic fundamentalism.

On 27 April 1808 the party reached the village of Batwari, at the lower end of the deep thirty-mile cleft down which the Bhagirathi forces its way through the Great Himalaya Range. Now they found themselves having to follow the narrowest of paths that had been cut across the steep walls of the gorge far above the river. 'A tremendous precipice was open on the outer side,' wrote Raper. 'For the greater part of the way we found it necessary to avail ourselves of the assistance of the bearers, to conduct us by the hand.' On the evening of the next day Hearsey noted in his journal that their day's march had been the hardest so far: 'To preserve a footing on the slippery rocks we had to ascend, we were obliged to pull off our shoes; the consequence was that our feet got very sore and we were obliged to halt.' The next morning they tried to press on for a few more miles; Webb called a conference and after a few minutes' discussion they decided to turn back, less than forty miles from their goal.

Though Webb was later to provide the Surveyor-General with a lengthy explanation as to why they had given up, his irresolution has never satisfactorily been explained. The most curious factor of all was that in order to make up for 'the deficiency occasioned by my abandoning the Tour', he dispatched 'an intelligent native, furnished with a compass, and instructed in the use of it, with directions to visit Gangotri'. Both Webb's letter to Colebrooke and Raper's published account leave us with the blurred impression of some anonymous but faithful hill-man struggling to reach Gangotri. But this was far from the truth – as Hearsey's journal makes clear. The 'intelligent native' was Hearsey's own Hindu *munshi* or interpreter, who reached Gangotri without particular difficulty in the company of six of the Gurkha sepoys as well as a number of Hindu pilgrims. Indeed, he even penetrated some miles beyond the temple, following the river until it was 'entirely concealed under heaps of snow'.

Although it was still too early in the year for much pilgrim traffic the *munshi*'s journey showed that the road to Gangotri itself was open; so it would not have been impossibly arduous for the *sahibs*. Part of the explanation for their puzzling behaviour can be found tucked away in a passage from Captain Raper's official account: 'Although we had provided ourselves with *Dandis* [open sedan chairs] as substitutes for the *Jampuans* [large covered litters], we found them equally useless; for we were forced to walk the greatest part of the way.' So totally unprepared to meet Himalayan conditions were these young and intrepid explorers that they had expected to be carried in litters to the source of the Ganga.

Much chastened by their failure but certainly with a more realistic appreciation of the scale of their undertaking, Webb, Raper and Hearsey turned their attentions to their next objective – 'visiting the source of the Alaknanda river at Badrinath before the setting of the periodical rains'. Without waiting for Hearsey's *munshi* to return they made their way downstream to the temples and shrines of Deoprayag, perched high on a promontory above the confluence of the two Ganga tributaries. Here they quickly established that the eastern branch, the Alaknanda, carried a far greater volume of water than the other, so that even if the Bhagirathi was regarded as the traditional source, it was nevertheless the Alaknanda that actually had the best claim to be the major source of the Ganga. Cheered by this discovery they proceeded northwards again, passing through the Alaknanda gorge and eventually arriving at the temple of Badrinath, never realizing that they had come through the main Himalayan barrier.

Here, at last, Webb was able to find what he regarded as a satisfactory source for the river. A few miles up the valley they came to the large Bhotia village of Mana, where Andrade and Marques had found their guide before setting out for the Mana pass two centuries earlier. But instead of following the main stream, the Saraswati, northwards as the Jesuits had done, Webb chose to take the party westwards – to the Alaknanda's *traditional* source, which lies in a narrow valley at the foot of the Badrinath massif. 'Proceed near one mile of snow – the river lost – no vestige remaining of its channels,' Hearsey jotted down:

We halted opposite a cascade of about 200 feet high – two streams fall from the mountain which by force of the wind is scattered with spray and freezes as it falls. Not a shrub or blade of grass in the vicinity of this place, nothing but snow and shivered black rocks. It is the most solemn appearance of winter I ever beheld.

It was against this dramatic background that Webb chose to site his 'visible Source' of the Alaknanda. He was now satisfied that he had carried out Colebrooke's original instructions as far as it had been possible; he wrote to the Surveyor-General to say that Hearsey's *munshi* had returned with 'convincing testimony' that the Cow's Mouth was 'entirely fabulous', while their own explorations had shown that the Alaknanda had no connection with the fabulous lake Manasarovar, whether by tunnel or any other means. Hearsey suggests in his journal that he would have liked to continue, having heard stories of a city built by the gods that was said to lie higher in the mountains, but his guides refused to go any further, saying that 'if we wished to be turned into stones (I suppose alluding to our being frozen) then we might make the attempt ourselves.' In the event, they decided it was time to return to the plains.

65

Rather than head back along the pilgrim route that had brought them up the Alaknanda valley, they chose a parallel route over the mountains further to the east, which took them out of the territory of Garhwal and into neighbouring Kumaon. They soon became aware of an increasingly 'unfriendly disposition' on the part of the Nepalese. Messengers appeared with contradictory orders, threats of decapitation or dismemberment by *kukri* began to be made against anyone who offered them assistance, and Gurkha sepoys began shadowing their trail. Finally all their porters decamped overnight, forcing them to abandon most of the baggage and supplies. To add to their misery the rains now set in; paths became watercourses, clothes stayed permanently sodden and leeches clustered by the score on every leaf and branch that overhung the trail, working their way into the most sensitive areas of the human anatomy. Very soon 'every puncture festered and turned to large sores, what with the flies and walking through the water.' Hearsey was not so badly afflicted as the other two officers, which he put down to the fact that 'instead of knocking the leeches when they attacked, I let them have their fill and drop off.'

The expedition was finally brought to a halt when it was within a day or two's march from the Gurkha fort at Almora, the provincial capital of Kumaon. Since their funds and their stock of gifts were now exhausted, they were no longer able to buy their way out of trouble. It took a week of delicate negotiations, coupled with promises to send gifts up from the plains, before the Governor of Kumaon would allow them to go on their way.

For some time Robert Colebrooke had been waiting anxiously at the new frontier station of Bareilly, ninety miles due south of Almora, for news of the expedition from which illness had forced him to withdraw three months earlier. Finally, at the end of June, four bearers carrying a single palanquin were sighted approaching the station. In it lay William Webb, seriously ill with 'jungle fever'. The other two *sahibs* and the rest of the party straggled in several days later.

Even if he was disappointed at Webb's failure to get to the source of the Bhagirathi, the Surveyor-General still had good cause for satisfaction. The expedition had swept away many

66

of the mysteries that had surrounded the river – including, so it seemed, the old story of the cow's mouth – and had reduced the Ganga to intelligible geographical dimensions. Colebrooke now felt free to take the home leave that had long been due to him; his own health was deteriorating and he was convinced that a sea voyage and a long spell in England were the only answer. Early in August he left Bareilly and set off for Calcutta, taking with him Raper's journal.

It was the worst time of the year for travelling as well as for sickness and disease. A month after Colebrooke's departure Webb received a letter from him in Cawnpore. He was suffering from dysentery and had decided to complete the rest of his journey by boat: 'I have determined to leave Cawnpore the day after tomorrow, being convinced that the river air is less favourable for my disorder than that of the Cantonments. It is most likely that I shall take my passage for Europe this year.' But Robert Colebrooke never lived to take his passage home. He sailed on down his beloved Ganga – now in full flood – growing weaker every day, until he died at Bhagalpur on 19 September. He had lived in India for thirty years without a break and he left two widows to mourn his passing; an English wife with nine small children, and an Indian *bibi* with a fourteen-year-old son, to whom he left a pension of fifty rupees a month. He also left behind a nasty scandal over a map.

The map in question now lies in the Map Record and Issue Office of the Survey of India at Hathibarkala, on the outskirts of Dehra Dun (an estate that once belonged, by a curious coincidence, to the Hearsey family), and it is clearly identified as having been drawn by Hyder Jung Hearsey. It carries two pencilled comments in the margin, written by another of Webb's brother-officers from the 10th BNI, Captain John Hodgson: 'This map was pirated from Captain Webb's documents' and 'Webb fell sick at Bareilly.' Also among the records of the Survey of India is a letter written in 1813 by John Garstin, the new Surveyor-General of Bengal. Garstin had been asked to explain why he had refused to employ a 'half-caste' named de Crux in the Survey of India. In his reply he cited a curious precedent:

When Lieutenant Webb was sent to the Gangoutri, or source of the Ganges, he was accompanied, among others, by Mr Hearsay, a pensioner of the Mahratta Horse, who, when the survey was over, surreptitiously obtained a copy of the Survey, and had the impudence to send it to the Court of Directors, as if he had been the discoverer of this Holy Fountain's head. On Lieut. Webb's laying the case before Government, they took the affair up very warmly . . . with these examples before me I could not possibly take upon me to recommend De Crux.

Strange, to say the least, that a man should be judged as unfit for employment on the basis of another man's alleged misdeeds, stranger still that so senior an officer in the Company's service as the Surveyor-General of Bengal should make such allegations. Yet the charges against Hearsey stuck, and to this day they remain the official version of events: that a half-caste stole a map from a sick man's bedside and called it his own.

The surviving evidence suggests a very different interpretation of events. Two accounts of the expedition are available. The first is Raper's Journal, which was discovered among his cousin's effects by Henry Colebrooke and published in *Asiatick Researches* in 1810. The other is the shorter, less formal account from Hearsey, which fell into the hands of a director of the East India Company in London and has been more or less neglected ever since. There is evidence of the close relationship that existed between the two Company men, William Webb and Felix Raper: in 1809 Webb was asking that Raper be allowed to join him on a second Himalayan expedition 'as our long acquaintance and friendship will render me most happy in his company.' But nothing in Raper's Journal or from Webb indicates that either man enjoyed the company of their fellow-traveller, which is not surprising when we consider that this hardened, country-bred mercenary of twenty-five was supposed to take his orders from an overcautious twenty-two-year-old. Indeed, Hearsey's name scarcely appears at all in Raper's account, where he is referred to as 'Captain Hearsey formerly in the service of the Madhaji Sendiah' – which is not only factually incorrect but implies unfairly that Hearsey fought for the Marathas against the British, rather than the other way round.

Hearsey's journal provides a more solid account of his part in the expedition and makes it clear that he saw his role as something more than just an escort. His technical references to surveying show that he was already well versed in the mapping skills that he used to good effect in later years. He would have had plenty of opportunity to pick up these skills from Colebrooke or even from Webb during their months together surveying in the *terai* – if he had not already acquired them earlier, for his father, Colonel Andrew Wilson Hearsey, was certainly capable of teaching him: among the Hearsey family papers are some neatly-executed route surveys drawn by him while campaigning in South India in the 1780s. There is no doubt that Hyder Jung was a good draughtsman; indeed, his gifts as an amateur artist were widely recognized. Emily Eden, who met him in Dehra Dun during her privileged travels *Up the Country*, admired his drawings while deploring his rough manners, and enough of his watercolours have survived to show that he had genuine talent.

Against this it has to be said that Hyder Jung Hearsey's manuscript account of his first Himalayan journey conceals, not at all skilfully, what seems to be a deliberate deception. An examination of the document, now in the British Library, will show that in quite a number of places the word 'we' has been erased, as in the following passage:

> We proceeded up the mountains a little above Rehoul, from whence |we| had a view of the Mahadeo's Ling – which |we| took the bearing of, with the Theodolite, from hence |we| perceived that we had entered the snowy range of mountains, many of the Peaks being S. of us.

If Hearsey doctored these passages – and no one else would have had cause to do so – it can only have been to show his role in a more positive light. Yet, if it was an attempt to deceive, it was a very clumsy one that was bound to have been spotted and could only have discredited Hearsey still further. Just the sort of thing, in fact, to expect from a half-caste who stole another man's map. But did Hearsey steal that map or draw his own? Whatever happened, it could only have taken place at Bareilly.

From the British point of view Bareilly in 1808 was a new and still insignificant station a few miles south of Nepalese Kumaon. Formerly it had been the capital of Rohilkhand but had been ceded to the Company by the Nawab of Oude to cancel a debt. Although Hearsey had his property there, few Europeans had established themselves, so it was most likely that the other *sahibs* – Colebrooke, Webb and Raper – would have stayed at his house while they were in Bareilly.

That is supposition. What is known for certain is that Robert Colebrooke left the station early in August 1808 and Webb's old chum from the 10th BNI soon afterwards, when he was recalled to regimental duty in Delhi. We know also that Webb resumed his survey work in December 1808, when he was ordered to map the Oude *terai*, and that Hearsey followed him to the same area at the start of the new year, when he was hired by the British Resident in Lucknow to stop Nepalese settlers from invading Oude. This suggests that the convalescent Webb was alone in Bareilly with his host for not less than four months – ample time, in fact, for Hearsey either to have 'pirated' his map from William Webb's documents while he lay sick (if we are to believe John Hodgson) or to have 'surreptitiously obtained a copy' of it (as John Garstin claimed).

But whether it was his own or copied, Hyder Jung Hearsey's map was certainly finished by 13 December 1808, when it was handed over, together with Hearsey's own journal and an accompanying letter, to a Captain Williams in Cawnpore. Captain Williams had instructions to deliver it to Sir James Rennell, the retired Surveyor-General, in London. 'By the earliest opportunity that occured I have the pleasure to transmit the accompanying sketch of a late Tour to the Sources of the River Ganges,' Hearsey wrote in his letter. All three officers had suffered financially from the confiscation of their belongings by the Nepalese, but since he was not a Company man, and had lost his patron with the death of Robert Colebrooke, Hearsey could not look forward to receiving any compensation. 'As this Tour was undertaken at our individual expense, may I beg you to present the sketch to the Hon. the Court of Directors, should they deem it worthy a remuneration, whatever their liberality may award, or permit private publication.'

Hearsey's attempt to get something for himself misfired badly. His map was beautifully drawn, covered entirely new ground and presented solutions to a particular geographical problem to which Rennell had been seeking answers for several decades. Small wonder that he was both captivated by it and deeply suspicious: 'The map is certainly a very curious one and bears the stamp of Truth, as far as *Internal* evidence goes.' Although he passed it on to the Court of Directors of the East India Company in Leadenhall Street, he also wrote at once to the Surveyor-General in Calcutta asking for an explanation – and the end result was that Hearsey was branded as a liar and a cheat.

John Garstin's chief concern was to protect the standing of his department. When he received Rennell's letter of inquiry he knew very well that his own man, William Webb, had still not completed his map – and he was desperately keen to see it finished. 'I understand Major Hearsey has sent one Home,' he wrote to Webb in January 1810, a full thirteen months after Hearsey's map had left Cawnpore. 'I much wished to have been able, by the last despatch, to have sent a General Map . . . from your hand, as well, as the twelve sheets of the Survey, and still hope to have them in time for the March Fleet.'

The unfortunate Webb finally sent in his completed map on 8 February 1810, together with his apologies:

The plan sent is certainly, in point of execution, a most wretched daub, *for I have lost the Draughtsman who used to assist me*, and although I have always acknowledged my incapacity in this way, I think the necessity I have been under to work when fatigued and at night, has either increased my natural want of ability, or that I grow worse and worse. [My italics.]

With all doubts removed as to which man drew his map first, we can go on to consider the identity of Webb's lost draughtsman. The meticulous and detailed Survey records

71

show that no qualified draughtsman or assistant was on Webb's staff during this period. From December 1808 to December 1809 he was surveying the Nepalese frontier of Oude – without assistants. The only man of proven ability as a draughtsman known to have been working in that same remote area is Hyder Jung Hearsey. Thus we have the intriguing possibility that, far from pirating the other's map, Hearsey not only surveyed, reduced and drew his own map but may even have helped the incapable Webb to draw *his*, until the latter was transferred in December 1809, so that Webb 'lost the Draughtsman who used to assist me.'

Whatever the justice of Hearsey's case, as soon as Garstin had received Webb's map he was able to send it on to Rennell and explain that this was the genuine one and the other merely a copy – and Rennell at once informed the Court of Directors:

A Mr or Major Hearsey thought proper to transmit it to me as *his own Production* (as he left me to understand), setting forth that the Expedition was undertaken by a Party at their own Expense, and requested that I would endeavour to obtain remuneration for him from the Hon. the Court of Directors. Thus informed I readily undertook what I thought a Meritorious Act; but I have since been informed that the Person who sent it to me only copied another Man's work, with a view to obtaining something for himself.

Once the father of Indian geography had spoken, Hearsey's reputation was damaged beyond recovery. It was an age in which patronage both in Indian and British circles was an essential prerequisite to advancement; those who lacked means or advocates to support their cause, irrespective of its merits, rarely found success. Hearsey was without champions either in Calcutta or in Leadenhall Street, whereas Webb had loyal friends and a Surveyor-General who was quite prepared to blacken another man's name for the sake of his department.

Webb himself seems to have had no hand in this character assassination. He remains throughout a curiously silent and uninvolved figure, at the very centre of the controversy yet never committing himself – so far as we know – to any sort of statement on a matter which must have affected him quite as much as it affected Hearsey. What we know of him suggests that he was a weak and unambitious man who could be manipulated, both by Hearsey and Garstin; weak enough, perhaps, to let Hearsey see his documents while he lay sick at Bareilly – and certainly weak enough to go along with Garstin's claim that his map was copied by Hearsey.

Webb's superiors claimed for him the title of 'discoverer of the Holy Fountain's Head', but this too was more than he deserved. For if the Ganga had any recognized head it was at Gaumukh, the source of the Bhagirathi. The first European to get close to it was James Baillie Fraser, a traveller and author who had an influential brother in the Indian Political Service. In June 1815 Fraser reached the shrine of the Mother Goddess, Ganga Mai, at Gangotri. He found a modest little temple, surrounded by tall deodars, which he sketched and embroidered in the Gothic manner. While he was there he asked the temple priest about 'the old popular idea that the Ganges issues from a rock shaped like a cow's mouth'. To his surprise the *pundit* laughed and 'observed that most of those pilgrims who came from the plains put the same question.'

Satisfied with this answer, Fraser made no attempt to explore the headstream any further. He retraced his route and at the end of the summer returned to the plains with an attractive set of watercolours that he turned into aquatints. They were later published together with his Journal and became immensely popular.

Yet there was, if not exactly a Cow's Mouth, certainly a mouth of a kind waiting to be discovered – and the first European to do so, treading in the footsteps of the many thousands of pilgrims who had been there before him, was Captain John Hodgson of the Survey of India, together with his assistant, Captain James Herbert. They came to Gangotri in June 1817 and on the night of their arrival narrowly avoided being crushed to death by falling rocks during an earthquake. Next morning they followed the river eastwards through a narrow gorge and then south-east, climbing until they found themselves at the entrance to a vast cul-de-sac, ringed by snowpeaks. Scrambling over a mass of boulders they at last arrived at the traditional source of the Ganga, the place that they marked on their map as Gaumukh, the cow's mouth. It was the snout of an enormous glacier, a glistening, hump-backed wedge of ice that ran back into the mountains for a distance of more than twenty miles. 'A most wonderful scene', was how Hodgson described it in his report:

The river here is bounded to the right and left by high snow and rocks; but in front the mass of snow is perfectly perpendicular, and from the bed of the stream to the summit we estimate the thickness at little less than 300 feet of solid frozen snow. The Bhagirathi, or Ganges, issues from under a very low arch at the foot of the grand snow bed!

Overlooking the glacier were four prominent peaks which Hodgson and Herbert, in a fit of patriotism, named St George, St Andrew, St Patrick and St David. But towering over the mouth of the glacier itself was a far more striking peak. Seen from the north it was shaped like a trident or, with a further stretch of imagination, like a cow's head with horns, formed by two ridges projecting from either side of the summit. When seen from the east, however, it was gloriously, unmistakably phallic. The British called it Mount Moira, in honour of the new Governor-General, Lord Moira. But to the Indians it was *Mahadeo-ka-Linga*, now known more simply as the Shivling mountain. It was not the god's main residence, which stands another hundred and thirty miles away beyond the last of the Himalayan ranges, but it was certainly the most splendid of his lesser abodes.

Chapter 4

'A Tour to Eastern Tatary': the British Discovery of Lake Manasarovar

Although the sources of the Ganga had now been identified, the mystery of what lay beyond the Himalayas in Western Tibet remained. Almost as soon as he had recovered from his sickness William Webb was writing to Garstin in Bengal proposing a second expedition. Webb had talked with an 'intelligent native' who had visited the Tibetan borderland and had been told that there were 'two great lakes, only one of which is laid down in any map extant, viz lake Mansurwar. The other, by far the largest and most important, named Rown Rudh, remains unnoticed. It has several considerable Islands in it, whose lofty Hills are covered with Woods; both lakes are surrounded by Mountains through which several large streams flow.' Webb declared that it was high time that these lakes and rivers were correctly identified and mapped. His former companion, Felix Raper, was kicking his heels in Delhi, and would be very willing to accompany him.

Garstin supported the idea and put it up to the Governor-General's office. But he was now familiar with Webb's deficiencies as a draughtsman and he proposed a third member for the expedition. He had just returned from the newly-acquired territory of Ludhiana with two new recruits to his department, both of whom were 'capable of making the drawings that will be required'. One of them was another of Webb's former brother-officers from the 10th BNI, John Hodgson. The other remains unidentified – but we can be sure it was not Captain H. J. Hearsey.

As it turned out, Webb's hopes were dashed by the government's refusal to allow a second expedition to enter Nepalese territory. In the two years since the Ganga recon-

75

naissance John Company had grown thoroughly disenchanted with its Nepalese neighbours. Having already expanded westwards along the Himalayan foothills through Garhwal and Kumaon the Gurkhas were now encroaching southwards into what the British regarded as their territory. The attitude of the Nepalese towards intruders had already been shown to be unfriendly, and a second expedition could only exacerbate an already strained situation.

No one knew more about the problems of Nepalese incursions than Hyder Jung Hearsey, part of whose property, in the form of a *jagir* or leased holding from which he could draw rent, bordered on Nepalese territory. Towards the end of 1811 encroachments onto his lands became so serious that Hearsey decided to take drastic action; in January 1812 he was reported to be 'raising troops and collecting arms with a view to the invasion of Nepalese territories adjacent to his *jagir*'. This was swiftly followed by an order from the Agent to the Governor-General, in Bareilly, for the immediate confiscation of Hearsey's *jagir*, on the grounds that he was 'conspiring to attack and take possession of the Doon, or vale, lying between the Ganges and the Sutledge, at present in the occupation of the Government of Nepal'.

Hearsey did indeed lay claim to the entire Dun valley – but not until *after* the Nepalese had been cleared out in the wake of the Anglo-Nepalese war of 1815. He did so on the not unreasonable grounds that he had bought this very desirable piece of real estate from its owner, the deposed Rajah of Srinagar. The Company (and later the Crown) took a different view and dismissed his claim, resulting in a lawsuit that was continued by his descendants and fought over for another seventy years before being finally thrown out of the courts.

In 1812, however, the invasion of the Dun valley would have been quite beyond Hearsey's resources – but perhaps that was not the point at issue. In the eyes of a government anxious – for the time being – to avoid open conflict with the Nepalese, the removal of a known gadfly like Hearsey from their flanks would have been distinctly convenient. There must, therefore, have been great relief in official circles when it was learned that Hearsey had abandoned all thoughts of offensive action. It seems he had other plans.

He had applied to the Agent of the Governor-General for permission to accompany the Superintendent of the Company's Stud, a veterinary surgeon named William Moorcroft, on what he referred to as a 'Tour of the Hills'. To the distracted Governor-General's Agent this evidently sounded like an answer to a prayer; it was a way of getting shot of the troublesome Captain Hearsey and another notorious nuisance, Dr Moorcroft, at the same time. He agreed – much to the horror of the authorities in Calcutta who, as soon as they got to hear of his decision, issued an immediate order countermanding it and stating that on no account should Hearsey be allowed to enter Nepalese territory. By that time it was too late, of course: Moorcroft and Hearsey had already disappeared into the foothills of Garhwal. Their precipitate departure also won Hearsey a stay of execution on his eviction from his *jagir*; the eviction order came through on 22 May, just two weeks after he and Dr Moorcroft had left for the hills.

Hyder Jung's partner on this second Himalayan adventure was of a very different calibre from his earlier companions. William Moorcroft was among the first of a new breed of travellers, men whose chief pleasure lay in the journey itself. The only known portrait of him does him scant justice: drawn by an Indian artist, it shows him perched uneasily on a rickety chair, a trim, slight man with the face of a spiv – small eyes, long nose, hairline moustache. It reveals nothing of the eccentric genius, the man possessed by curiosity, whose mania for gathering information made it quite impossible for him to restrict his interests to his own profession.

Moorcroft had started out to be a doctor, but while studying at Liverpool Infirmary in the 1780s a local outbreak of cattle plague had diverted his attentions towards what was then an entirely new branch of medical science. He decided to become a veterinarian instead, and after studying in France for a number of years set himself up in what soon became an extremely lucrative practice in Oxford Street. Having built up a considerable fortune, he then lost it all in a mad scheme to mass-produce horseshoes. It was at this low point in his life that he heard that the East India Company was looking for a vet; a man was wanted to run its new stud farm at Pusa, a small up-country station not far from Patna, with the aim of improving the quality of the Company's cavalry chargers.

Had Dr Moorcroft decided to stay on in England he would have had no difficulty in restoring his fortunes. But India presented new challenges; it was very much England's new frontier, where restless young men could still go out and risk everything on a venture. Moorcroft was then already over forty but his vigorous approach to life soon singled him out even in a land of young men; contemporary accounts make much of his 'energetic disposition' and his often misplaced enthusiasm. He became Veterinary Surgeon to the Government in Bengal and Superintendent of the Company's Stud in December 1808, and within a short space of time was greatly irritating his employers by putting the broadest possible interpretation on his job. The standard of veterinary care did indeed improve dramatically under his direction, but his search for the ideal horse for breeding purposes soon had him 'running over the country in quest of phantoms'.

At the beginning of the cold weather in 1811 Moorcroft was up at Saharanpore, not very far from the Dun country, where he met up with Hyder Jung Hearsey, then preparing – if we are to swallow the official version of events – to invade the Dun. Whether it was Moorcroft or Hearsey who came up with the proposal 'to penetrate into Tartary', both quickly perceived that they had common interests. Soon afterwards Moorcroft was badgering the Agent to the Governor-General with innocuous-sounding plans for a 'journey into the Hills' to find 'new blood from the Hill strains' for his horses as well as 'goats bred for the sake of their Long Hair'.

In spite of their hurried departure Moorcroft and Hearsey had gone to a lot of trouble in their preparations. They had decided that the safest course was to go disguised as Hindu pilgrims, so they set off wearing turbans and white linen robes and calling themselves Mayapori and Haragiri. Both men were anxious – for rather different reasons – to bring back as accurate a record of their journey as possible. Hearsey's role was that of map-maker: he lacked a theodolite but he had a compass and a thermometer with him and kept a survey notebook, and he was assisted by two Indian surveyors, Harballabh, whom Moorcroft refers to in his journel as the 'old *pundit*' and who may well have been Hearsey's *munshi* – the 'intelligent native' who went on to Gaumukh on the first expedition – and a younger *pundit* named Hurruck Dao, his nephew. A measuring perambulator would have been too conspicuous, so Hurruck Dao was given the unpleasant duty of keeping a tally of the number of steps he took, being 'directed to stride the whole of the road at paces equal to 4 feet each'. This last phrase of Moorcroft's led to some confusion when reports of the expedition were later published in Henry Colebrooke's *Asiatick Researches*, but in fact Moorcroft's direction was quite correct, since the Indian pace is recorded each time the left foot touches the ground – in other words every *two* steps. In addition to the *pundits* there was an Afghan warrior named Gholam Hyder Khan, who had been with Hearsey since his days as a soldier of fortune, as well as some fifty servants and coolies to carry the baggage and supplies, which included goods that they hoped to trade or sell in Tibet.

For the first two weeks of their journey the travellers were crossing old ground that Hearsey had covered either while escorting Colonel Colebrooke or with Webb and Raper. But on 24 May 1812 they came to the junction of the Alaknanda and Dauli rivers (see Map A), where they left the pilgrim route to Badrinath and began to make their way eastwards into unknown country. 'Here the horrors of the road were very great,' Dr Moorcroft was to write later. At one point Hearsey narrowly avoided being swept into the river by a rock avalanche set off by a family of bears crossing the hillside above them, and elsewhere there were many sections of the trail that had been torn away by landslides, forcing them into an unattractive choice between a long detour or a hair-raising traverse across cliffs that fell away steeply down to the river below.

The worst moment of all came when they found their way blocked by a huge rock that 'overhung the river at a great height'. William Moorcroft watched the leading members of the party inch their way out onto this horribly exposed rock face and decided to force a path for himself through the thick undergrowth above:

79

By clinging with their hands to the stones on the face of the mountains, Mr Hearsey and a large portion of the carriers went over the rock without accident, but at one point the courage of my *khansama* |cook| failed; on missing his footing with one leg he shrieked violently and shrank down almost senseless with one leg hanging over the abyss, calling out that he was lost. Mr Hearsey was at hand and assisted him most opportunely, along with the pundit.

The porters now included a number of hill-women drawn from the surrounding Bhotia villages, one of whom shamed her more faint-hearted male colleagues by making several journeys across the exposed rock face, carrying not only her own load but theirs as well.

Despite their usefulness Hearsey had a low opinion of these open and generous-minded hill-people, part Indian and part Tibetan in their antecedents and their culture. However, he managed to spare a few kind words in his journal for the younger women on the expedition; they had 'some claims to beauty, but credit must be allowed to their Chastity, as offers were made very liberally, which either want of language or management on our part prevented having the desired effect.' Hearsey returns to this theme later in his journal with the remark that 'although tempted very much |they| would not swerve from their Duty to their Husbands – from being constantly employed, their inclinations to venery are much curbed.' Hearsey's partner also seems to have had a healthy regard for the opposite sex. He was to gain a widespread – and not entirely unearned – reputation as a ladies' man thanks to the French traveller Victor Jacquement, who wrote that 'Moorcroft's principal occupation was making love'. But on this journey neither Moorcroft nor Hearsey appears to have made many conquests.

Like Webb three years earlier, Moorcroft and Hearsey failed to appreciate at first that they had broken through the main Himalayan barrier. They emerged from the Dauli gorge onto a broad glaciated valley covered in tall deodars and flowering scarlet rhododendrons. This was the Niti valley, which runs parallel to the Mana valley, twenty miles to the west, and had replaced it as the main thoroughfare to and from Western

Tibet. Here the Bhotia people had their summer village of Niti, a few miles south of the 16,630-foot Niti pass into Tibet. On the far side lay Daba, which had replaced Tsaparang as the district capital of that part of Western Tibet. The name of Gugé had long since ceased to be used and Moorcroft and Hearsey knew of the area only as Hundes (or Undes), inhabited by Hunyias and part of Eastern Tartary.

Moorcroft had sent a gift forward to the Tibetan Governor at Daba, on the far side of the pass, but on arrival at Niti he found that it had been returned together with a warning that, 'to prevent the entrance of white people', troops had been sent from Daba to guard all the main passes leading into Tibet. He refused to take this warning seriously: it was simply not in his nature to accept defeat. 'My obstinacy is almost equal to my enthusiasm,' he was later to write of himself. A new messenger was found and ordered to tell the Tibetan authorities at Daba that the pilgrims Mayapori and Haragiri were no more than 'men of character really intending to go to lake Mansarowar, having merchandise to dispose of and not harbouring any evil design against the general welfare of the country.' But the messenger was evidently none too happy at having to take such a message; Moorcroft and Hearsey watched in dismay as he was carried dead drunk to his yak. Before he and the yak passed out of sight at the head of the valley he was seen to fall off four times.

They now had to spend three tedious weeks at Niti, using the local Bhotias as middle-men in their negotiations with the Tibetans. The Bhotias were the traditional go-betweens of the Western Himalayas but Moorcroft and Hearsey seriously misjudged the extent to which they were prepared to risk upsetting their neighbours. Much of the Bhotias' livelihood came from trade with Tibet and they saw no advantage in offering assistance to two extremely dubious characters from the Indian plains. Hearsey found this attitude intolerable. 'To such a degradation has human nature fallen,' he wrote furiously in his journal when it became apparent that their negotiations were getting nowhere. 'Although I have been in various parts of India, I have never met with such a mean, cunning, low race and Cowards to an extreme.'

Dr Moorcroft reacted with some low cunning of his own.

He brought out his medical kit and doctored anyone who cared to come to him for attention, including a young Bhotia boy whom he successfully tapped for dropsy. It was a relatively simple operation but a spectacular one and it won him the gratitude of the boy's father, a trader from the neighbouring valley of Johar named Deb Singh Rawat. By a happy chance, Deb Singh Rawat and his brother, Bir Singh, were among the wealthiest and most influential Bhotias in the region – and by winning their confidence, Moorcroft set the seal on a remarkable alliance between the Bhotias and the British that still survives today.

The first practical effect was a sudden end to all local obstruction; after a final round of negotiations – greatly sweetened by a bottle of brandy broached and turned into a punch – the travellers were told they could continue, together with a guide, new porters and two yaks, known to the Bhotias as *chowhurs*. 'Surer footed animals do not exist in the Creation than these *Chowhurs*,' wrote Hearsey admiringly as he and Moorcroft proceeded on their new mounts slowly but very surely towards the crest of the Niti La. The firs and rhododendron gave way, first to 'gooseberry and wild rose-bushes', then to small alpine flowers and finally to bare rock and snowfields.

As night fell on 29 June 1812 they camped just short of the pass under 'mountains like spires, fracturing with cold', and looking back down the Niti valley saw the – then unidentified – peaks of Nanda Devi and Trisul catching the last rays of the setting sun.

Before dawn next morning Moorcroft woke with 'a great oppression about the heart' and breathlessness. He was now in his forty-seventh year, which was old by Indian standards and ancient by Himalayan ones. From this point onwards scarcely a day passed without Hearsey making some reference to his companion's poor health in his journal. However, on this morning both men were up and astride their shaggy transport by 6 am. It was a bright sunny day with few clouds in the sky and very little wind, and when they reached the saddle of the Niti La they found themselves looking out, somewhat apprehensively, over the seemingly limitless vista of the Tibetan plateau. 'The prospect was awfully grand,' wrote Hearsey. 'The country immediately below us to the N & E appeared a plain intersected by immense ravines – rounded on the horizon by the Kylass Mountains, many of whom were tipt with Snow.' Moreover, to their great relief there was no reception committee of armed Tibetans waiting for them. They rode on until they came to the first sign that they had entered Buddhist territory, a *lapcha* or cairn of white stones topped by prayer flags on long poles. Here every member of the party halted to add a stone to the cairn. 'This ceremony was observed very punctually by our Marchas,' Hearsey recorded, referring to their Bhotia guides from Niti. 'The success of an enterprise is dependent on this custom.' Soon afterwards they camped and Dr Moorcroft bled himself of 16 ounces of blood to ease a headache. Hearsey, who was also feeling in poor spirits, dosed himself with 'Black Salt and Aniseed'.

Next day they met their first Tibetans, two pipe-smoking traders on ponies carrying salt destined for Niti. Afraid that once out of sight they might secretly double back and inform the authorities of their presence, Moorcroft persuaded them to turn their horses round and accompany him to Daba. These are the two Tibetans who appear in Hearsey's well-known painting at the India Office Library, recording the moment when they crossed a second rise and saw the holy mountain rearing up ahead of them. Moorcroft watched the Tibetans dismount and prostrate themselves, bowing seven times before the mountain. On the same day their *shikari*, a professional hunter who had been conspicuously unsuccessful up till now, shot a *burrhel* (Blue Wild Sheep), a goat-like creature with long curved horns. Moorcroft was greatly intrigued by its physical characteristics and noted perceptively that 'were it not fanciful to suppose a chain between the works of nature, I should say that this animal was the link between the deer and the sheep.'

Two days later they reached Daba, a collection of flat-roofed houses and cave-dwellings built round a high promonotory of rock jutting out over the river Sutlej. As soon as their tents were up they received a visitor sent by the Deba, the town's head lama. He came ostensibly to inquire after their health but at the same time gave their temporary living-quarters a very thorough going-over. 'He looked about my small tent with much curiosity,' wrote Moorcroft, 'and observed that my friend's [Hearsey's] half-boots were like those of a *feringi* [European]. I had taken the precaution of having my English shoes furnished with long turned up toes and tags at the necks and his not being done excited his suspicion.' But while Moorcroft was still congratulating himself on his foresight the Tibetan began to ask why the doctor should have such a strange complexion: 'The redness of my face, which from being exposed to a hot sun and a cold wind was almost wholly deprived of skin, particularly attracted his attention.'

Next came a meeting with the Deba himself and a more direct cross-examination. But after accepting gifts of scarlet broadcloth, sugar and spice, the Deba pronounced himself satisfied that 'the first representation of their being Gorkalis or Feringis was a mistake.' He had already sent a messenger on horseback to the Military Governor at the trading post of Gartok informing him of the arrival of two foreigners at Daba; now he sent a second horseman with a fresh message that was intended to supersede the first.

The Governor cannot have been greatly impressed by the Deba's judgment, since Mayapori and Haragiri were at once summoned to appear before him at Gartok. There had been a scare four years earlier when it had seemed that foreigners were about to invade the country – almost certainly a reverberation from the Ganga expedition of 1808 – and the Governor was not prepared to take chances.

For William Moorcroft, this deviation from his original plan to go straight to lake Manasarovar suited him very nicely. As well as being a staging-post on the Ladakh-Lhasa highway, Gartok was the most important trading centre in Western Tibet and the possibility of opening up or diverting some of this trade down into India had been one of Moorcroft's principal reasons for coming to Tibet. The party left Daba and crossed the Sutlej a day's march upstream of Tsaparang. They climbed up into the mountains that Moorcroft had named the 'Kylass range' and soon afterwards crossed into the area drained by the Indus. Crossing a plain on which they saw some wild asses and a 'prodigious number' of hares they reached the bed of a 'clear, broad and rapid, but not deep river' which (like Desideri before them) they took to be the upper course of the Indus. Had they been allowed the opportunity to continue downstream past Gartok for another sixty-five miles to the confluence of the Gartang and Senge-Khambag rivers, they might well have had second thoughts. As it was, they felt sufficiently confident to claim on their return to India that they had established the source of the Indus.

Gartok itself was something of a disappointment; it turned out to be no more than a few stone huts surrounded by traders' tents. However, the meeting with the Governor went off very well from Dr Moorcroft's point of view. During the next few days he spent many happy hours sipping Tibetan tea with the Governor and the agent of the Rajah of Ladakh and discussing various possibilities for future trading ventures. His chronic weakness for commercial transactions soon had him deeply involved in the Gartok livestock market. The goods they had brought up from India were traded in and Moorcroft and Hearsey left Gartok with a large flock of sheep as well as fifty *pashmina* goats, whose soft undercoats provided the *pasham* wool from which the shawls and woollens of Kashmir were made.

Moorcroft envisaged a great future for this *pasham* wool in India. The goats themselves could only live at high altitudes but he foresaw that if their wool could be brought south through Garhwal a very substantial trade could be developed. This is exactly what happened: *pasham* wool became the mainstay of trans-Himalayan trade and within half a century it was the proud boast of the Bhotias that the shawls woven by their womenfolk were gracing the shoulders of the greatest monarch of them all, *Bilayat ki maharani*, Victoria, queen of the British.

The Governor had given Dr Moorcroft permission to take his party back by way of Manasarovar, provided they kept to the traditional pilgrim routes. They hung on to their Indian identities but no longer felt the need to match their behaviour to their appearance and turned their attention, instead, to observing and mapping their surroundings with greater care, as well as to tending their herds of sheep and goats. Allowing

85

their livestock to graze their way across the western slopes of the Kailas range, they slowly moved south again. As they crossed the Jerko La, Moorcroft was once more seriously affected with altitude sickness: Hearsey notes in his log that, in an unsuccessful attempt to purge himself, the doctor took ten grains of Calomel, three of James's Fever Powder and two of Dr Robinson's Brown Pills.

On 31 July they were back beside the Sutlej but now almost at its source. Camped at the village of Tirthapuri Hearsey learned from its inhabitants that the river came from the nearby lake of Rawan Hrud (Rakas Tal). Yet as they made their way east he could see no connection between any of the streams flowing into the Sutlej and the lake. He therefore assumed – incorrectly – that the outlet from Rakas Tal must be further south and marked it in accordingly on his map.

A week later they were crossing the extensive meadows that sloped down from the foot of Mount Kailas to the shores of the lakes. Below lay the turquoise lake that they had travelled over three hundred miles to see, with the Gurla Mandhata Range beyond, stretching out along the southern horizon. They made their way through herds of grazing yak, goats and sheep, and down past a series of *mani*-walls – 'terraces of stone with the usual inscriptions' – until they came to a lamasery at the lakeside, where they camped. The next morning Moorcroft and Hearsey celebrated their arrival, each in his own style.

Hearsey's log for 6 August 1812 begins, as usual, with a note on the weather: 'Morning early raining & very cloudy Therm 47°.' Then comes a cryptic remark – 'Amamus today at 11 AM' – which suggests that his earlier efforts to engage the interests of the opposite sex may not have been in vain. After breakfast he prepared to have a swim and a shave but then decided that the weather was against him. Instead he got out his fishing tackle and started to walk along the shore of the lake, in the path of Dr Moorcroft, who had set out about half an hour ahead of him: 'I followed his footsteps looking for a place proper to throw in my tag line, but could not find one, the surf being so very high and the shore stony.' After walking some three miles he gave up all thoughts of fishing and observing some 'Poland Wild Geese and their young ones unable to fly', attempted to stalk them: 'I made my servants to lay down and they would have come closer, had we not have started up to catch the young Geese; we had a smart run for it & the youngsters were obliged to exert their legs for it & beat us hollow.' Having had his fun Hearsey settled down to begin his survey of the lake.

William Moorcroft's behaviour was equally in keeping with his character. He knew that the lake was considered by Hindus to be 'the most sacred of all places of worship, founded probably on the difficulty of access to it' but he was consumed less by feelings of awe than by an overwhelming curiosity to know what river – or rivers – flowed out of Manasarovar. He now knew that of the several rivers that were said to derive their sources from it, the Ganga could now definitely be discounted. The 'old *pundit*', Harballabh, had told him that there was a channel running between Manasarovar and Rakas Tal, as well as an exit from Rakas Tal, 'which, escaping from its western extremity near the foot of the great mountain, formed the first branch of the Sutlej.' Moorcroft was now 'determined not to leave this point in doubt.'

At about ten o'clock he began walking south-west along the beach – 'although very weak from the frequent attacks of fever to which I had lately been subject'. Soon he passed a number of simple cave-dwellings set back a little from the water's edge, in one of which lived an elderly Tibetan nun. She did her best to solicit Moorcroft but the doctor was 'so ungallant as to refuse the lady's hospitality' and decided to give her motives the benefit of the doubt: 'A weather-beaten face, half-stripped of its natural covering, blistered lips, a long bushy beard and moustachios, in a country where the former is carefully plucked out, had probably raised emotions of Pity.'

He continued to walk along the beach until he reached a high bank of shingle that seemed to form a 'natural barrier' against any exit of water from the lake. A little further ahead he could see a knoll; he climbed up to it, hoping that this would give him a good view of the shoreline further south and so 'put an end to a task which I now found somewhat too

87

much for the little strength I possessed.' However, when he got to the top 'another mountain intervened to prevent my view. When I reached the summit of this, another equally high presented itself. My servants were much fatigued: for my part I was obliged frequently to lay down.' It was not until four o'clock that the indefatigable doctor finally reached a 'small religious pile' that marked the spot where he could get an uninterrupted view:

> The sky, which had frequently been overcast and disturbed with violent gusts of wind, now became clear, and sunshine illuminated the whole of the circumference of the lake, so as to enable me distinctly to define every portion of its shore close to the edge of the water, and up to the foot of the mountains, by which it is embayed.
>
> There were numerous watercourses leading into it, the most important of which was the Krishna, sweeping down a ravine between two high mountains of the Himalayan range, and expanding like a sheet as it approached the verge of the lake; but *not a break, nor any other appearance indicated the escape of any river or even of any small stream from it*. Although this was clear enough from the naked eye, I employed a telescope; and this showed that the Mansarowar sends out no rivers to the South, North or West. (My italics.)

Having established that there was no exit from the lake, Moorcroft began to retrace his steps back to the camp. Hearsey meanwhile had been observing the varied forms of wildlife to be found on and beside Lake Manasarovar – including, it seems, the lake's own monster:

> On returning before sunset I saw an enormous large Animal or Fish take a porpoise. He kept a considerable time upon the Surface, was of a brown colour and had apparently Hairs; I at first mistook it for a dead Chowhur until I saw it in motion when it disappeared.

At sunset a strong wind blew up and it was not until 11 o'clock that the exhausted Moorcroft finally stumbled into

88

camp, 'almost starved from hunger and cold'. Next day the younger of the two *pundits*, Hurruck Dao, and a companion were sent out to check Moorcroft's observations. They returned just before midnight, having completed an astonishing round rip of some thirty-six miles. They had kept close to the shoreline all the way but, as Hearsey noted in his journal, 'could find no Channel by which this Lake had any connection with Rawan Rudd.'

The second day by the lake was spent taking measurements and bearings. Manasarovar revealed itself to be a large, nearly oval-shaped lake sixteen miles wide from south-east to northwest and about ten miles wide at its narrowest point. On the strip of land running between the two lakes were three 'distinct eminences', which took away all probability of any communication between the two. 'From these Observations,' Hearsey concluded, 'it is fully proved that this extensive Lake to which such sanctity is given in the Hindu Shastras has no communication by exit with any River or even with Rawan Rudd. It is perfectly insulated and girt by mountains.'

So that was that. They had reached the fabulous lake of the *Puranas* and had found – to their own complete satisfaction – that the ancients had got it wrong. When the old *pundit* Harballabh was questioned further he admitted that his information was out of date: the river he had spoken of had issued from lake Manasarovar some sixteen years earlier and since then the bed of the channel from the lake had dried up.

Next morning Hearsey cut their names and the date into a stone and set it up 'in a proper place'. He had a last bathe in the lake and then they were off, though Moorcroft was still suffering from the effects of his over-exertion two days before. They made their way past lake Rakas Tal and followed the course of the Sutlej down to a point some ten miles above Daba, where they met up again with their influential friends from Niti, Deb Singh and Bir Singh Rawat. Together they recrossed the pass and on 3 September they were back in Niti.

For the next month all went well as the travellers shepherded their flocks slowly and sometimes precariously back down the Dauli and Alaknanda gorges. On 8 October they passed through the village of Karnaprayag, where the Pindar river flows in from the east to join the Alaknanda. Here they diverged from the pilgrim trail and began to follow a route up the Pindar valley that would take them more directly to the plains. It was a repetition of the mistake that Hearsey had made four years earlier when he was with Webb and Raper, and it provoked exactly the same disquiet among the Nepalese rulers of Kumaon. They were met and questioned by a Gurkha official, but their answers evidently failed to satisfy him; as each day passed harassment by Gurkha sepoys steadily increased.

By 12 October the situation had become serious enough for Dr Moorcroft to consider abandoning the livestock and making a dash for it to the plains. On that day he was forced to cock and aim his gun at a Gurkha officer who had placed himself 'in a menacing position' on the road ahead of him. The Gurkha retreated, but three days later, as they crossed out of the Ganga's river system and descended towards the Ramganga river, they found more soldiers waiting for them. Moorcroft took up a firing position at the head of the party, while Hyder Jung drew up a rearguard into two ranks at the back. Again it was the Gurkhas who had to give way; after a few tense minutes they pulled back and the travellers were allowed to camp without being molested further.

At dawn on 16 October Moorcroft and Hearsey woke to find Gurkhas swarming through the camp. 'Many *jemadars* and *havildars* [senior non-commissioned officers] came round to Mr H.'s tent and the soldiers closed,' wrote Moorcroft later, 'I had my breakfast placed on a stone and ate it with my gun in my hand.' Yet there was still a reluctance on the part of the Nepalese to initiate hostilities: 'Several of the officers came, offered their necks, and desired me to take off their heads, as, if they did not stop us, that would be their fate.' Witnessing the same bizarre ritual, Hearsey took a more jaundiced view of it: 'The treacherous Scoundrels exposed their bare necks to us saying we might as well cut off their Heads as proceed.'

Finally, it was Dr Moorcroft who precipitated the action. He marched over to a large body of soldiers formed up in a semicircle across the trail and ordered them to stand clear:

The main body opened a little, and I independently

90

advanced with too much impetuosity. My gun had in an instant as many hands upon it as could find room to touch it, but they could not wrest it from me. I had at least seventeen or twenty upon me, but this rather prolonged than shortened the contest, as they pulled in opposite directions. It would have been maintained for even a longer time, had not one man got upon my neck and stuck his knees into my loins, endeavouring to strangle me with my handkerchief, whilst another fastened a rope round my left leg and pulled it backwards from under me. Supported only by one leg and almost fainting from the hand around my neck, I lost my hold on the gun, and was instantly thrown to the ground. Here I was dragged by the legs until my arms were pinioned.

Hearsey, meanwhile, had been cleaning his teeth on the other side of the camp and had not heard his companion's warning shout. Much to his indignation he was jumped upon and seized before he had a chance to put up much of a fight: 'The first object I beheld was a drawn sword and a cluster round – as I supposed – the body of Mr M. whom I concluded they had killed – this idea made me prepare for my own Death and I looked for the means of dying revenged!'

Since the means to avenge his friend's death were beyond reach and his friend turned out to be trussed but still alive, Hearsey had to content himself – some hours later, when he found himself a prisoner in his own tent – with giving vent to his anger on paper. His log for that eventful day opens with a crude sketch of himself and Dr Moorcroft with their arms tied behind their backs and the words: 'Vile Cords our Arms do bind by Villains great and Cowards greater.' Much of the entry that follows is taken up with various arguments as to why it would be madness for the Nepalese to kill them – a very reasonable preoccupation in the circumstances.

In fact, Hearsey's reasoning was sound. For all their truculence, the Nepalese had no wish to provoke the British into open war and they had nothing to gain by killing two *feringhis*. Furthermore, it soon became apparent to them that the *feringhis* had powerful local connections; Deb Singh Rawat, the Bhotia trader from Johar, had come to hear of the arrests and brought his considerable influence to bear on the Gurkha military commander at Almora. Nor did John Company – in the shape of its nearest representative in the plains – turn a deaf ear to the pleas for help that were smuggled out of the hills. There was now a new Agent to the Governor-General at Bareilly and by a great stroke of luck he happened to be a Colebrooke – not Henry Colebrooke but an elder brother, Sir James Edward Colebrooke, Bart. He acted promptly to intercede on Moorcroft's and Hearsey's behalf and after sixteen days of captivity they were set free, along with their sheep and goats.

They can hardly have expected a friendly reception from the powers that be in India. They had left the plains under the most dubious circumstances and had returned after their Government's representatives had been forced to beg a favour of a rival power. But the Honourable Company was a curious institution and one of its most powerful axioms was that commercial ends often justified the means. Those who broke the rules and lost could expect no mercy but those who took the chance and came through nearly always found that the light of John Company's countenance shone brightly upon them.

Moorcroft's and Hearsey's journey provides a fine example of the Company's pragmatism. It had, after all, laid the foundations for a profitable trans-Himalayan trade in shawl wool, uncovered several new and potentially exploitable trade routes and put a useful portion of Western Tibet on the map. And that map, on which he had set to work as soon as he and Dr Moorcroft had reached Bareilly, was unquestionably Hyder Jung Hearsey's; this time, the achievement could not be denied him. It was presented to the Court of Directors and earned Hearsey the very handsome donation of six thousand rupees from the Government. In addition, his *jagir* in the *terai* was restored to him and it was officially noted that the arms and forces that he had earlier been reported to have been gathering for his intended invasion of the Dun were, after all, 'insignificant in number and value'.

For Hearsey this marked the end of his exploring days. He devoted his energies, instead, to the forthcoming conflict with Nepal – and no one can have looked forward to the prospect of British military intervention more eagerly. Towards the end of 1813 he drew up plans for the invasion of Kumaon at the request of Lord Moira, the Governor-General designate, and when the war started in earnest in the following year supplied the army with maps of much of the country in which they were to fight. In due course he and his brother-in-law, William Linnaeus Gardner, were allowed to raise their own levies of irregulars and take them into Kumaon. Their advance went well until March 1815, when a large army of Gurkhas arrived unexpectedly from Nepal and fell upon Hearsey's still raw force of irregulars. His men dropped their arms and fled, leaving Hearsey severely wounded in the thigh. He would have been beheaded on the spot but for the personal intervention of the Gurkha commander, who recognized him as the *feringhi* he had held captive near Almora three years earlier.

Fortunately for Hearsey there were no more Gurkha victories. The treaty of Segauli, by which the Nepalese agreed to stay east of the river Kali and the British to keep out of Nepal proper, was signed soon afterwards and, for the third time, Hearsey was released from Nepalese captivity.

And what of Hyder Jung's fellow-pilgrim and friend, the irrepressible Superintendent of the Company's Stud? No sooner had Moorcroft returned to Pusa than he began making it known that he had set his sights on Bokhara, that legendary and impenetrable city set deep in Western Turkestan. The next seven years were spent badgering the government with schemes and appeals for this latest folly. The original plan was that he and Hearsey would travel back over the Niti pass, make a slight diversion to Lhasa and then join the Silk Road at Yarkand, to follow the golden road that led to Bokhara as well as Samarkand. They would return not only with perfect horseflesh with which to strengthen the chargers of John Company's cavalry but also with new markets for British trade. Hyder Jung was all for going to Bokhara but he lacked the sweep of Moorcroft's imagination; he had his own 'safe, easy and extensive' plan by which they would have travelled by sea to the Persian Gulf and then followed the more orthodox route across Persia. When it came down to going along with Dr Moorcroft's plan or not going at all, he opted out.

By the time approval for his venture had finally been wrung from the government, William Moorcroft was nearly fifty-five, the age at which most Company officials began to draw their pensions. He knew this was to be his last great enterprise. He packed a second family that he had started in India off home to England and in October 1819 brought his expedition together under Hearsey's roof at Bareilly. He had three sahibs with him; an Anglo-Indian surgeon named Guthrie, a geologist whom he soon sacked for maltreating the porters, and Hearsey's replacement as his lieutenant, a young Englishman named Trebeck. As well as two *pundit* surveyors they took with them Hearsey's man, Ghulam Hyder Khan – a professional survivor, if ever there was one, for he was the only one to last the course. After seven years he returned alone to Bareilly to recount his version of the events that had overtaken Dr Moorcroft and his companions.

They had indeed reached Bokhara, that most deadly of cities, but Moorcroft, with his insatiable wanderlust, had wanted to go on further:

> Before I leave Turkestan I mean to penetrate into that tract that contains perhaps the finest horses in the world, but with which all intercourse has been suspended during the last five years. The expedition is full of hazard but 'le jeu vaut bien la chandelle' [the game is well worth the candle].

A few weeks later he and his two English companions were dead. For many years conflicting reports about the manner of their deaths continued to be picked up by travellers in different parts of central Asia. Some said that Moorcroft had been poisoned, others that he had been robbed and shot. There was even a report that he had been seen alive and well in Lhasa. Various papers and diaries of his continued to turn up over the years in all sorts of odd places, helping to sustain the Moorcroft legend. Yet as this legend grew so his reputation as a traveller and explorer diminished, partly because no one knew exactly where he had been but chiefly because

94

he was overshadowed by Alexander Burnes, who followed him to Bokhara seven years later. 'Bokhara' Burnes had style; he matched the romantic image of the traveller to foreign parts and played the part accordingly, whereas Dr Moorcroft was too complex a character to fit any sort of mould. Like many of his kind, he suffered the cruellest fate that posterity can bestow, which is to be forgotten while lesser men are remembered.

Hyder Jung Hearsey went on no more expeditions into the hills but he returned occasionally to arms. In 1826 he was in Rajasthan taking part in the siege and storming of Bharatpore, and his death of apoplexy in August 1840 came as he was on the road to join a military column as its prize agent. As well as his unpublished 'Tour to Eastern Tatary' (which remains in the Hearsey family) he left a daughter and three sons who joined the service of the Nawab of Oude, as he himself had done in his youth. The eldest of his sons, born at about the time of Dr Moorcroft's departure from Bareilly, was named William Moorcroft Hearsey. He spent a number of exciting years in the Oude *terai* putting down *thugee*, the secret religious cult that murdered by strangulation, before being caught up in the famous siege of Lucknow, which he survived. By tradition, a number of his male descendants served in Gardner's Horse; one of their number travelled halfway across India to horsewhip the editor of the *Civil and Military Gazette* in Lahore after that worthy had written an editorial questioning the propriety of 'half-castes' serving in such a distinguished regiment.

The story would not be complete without a postscript on Hearsey's rival from earlier days, William Webb. By the terms of the Anglo-Nepalese treaty of 1815 Garhwal and Kumaon were thrown open to British surveyors. His two junior colleagues, John Hodgson and James Herbert, mapped Garhwal – newly divided into British Garhwal and the native state of Tehri-Garhwal – while Webb spent five lonely years completing a survey of Kumaon, much of his work concentrated on the border areas.

In the summer of 1816 he explored the sources of the river

Kali and met the Tibetan governor of Purang on the Lipu Lekh pass in an attempt to gain permission to visit lake Manasarovar. Permission was refused, but he had the consolation of being allowed to look down into Tibet from the summit of the pass, seeing the upper valley of the Karnali, the Peacock river, stretched out before him with the Gurla Mandhata massif beyond. On this same survey Webb also climbed up to the 18,500-foot Darma La. On the northern slopes of this high pass two streams run down into Tibet. One forms the main branch of the Darma Yankti, the main feeder of the Sutlej or Lanchen Khambab. The other is the main feeder of the Karnali or Mapchu Khambab. We have no evidence to suggest that Webb crossed the pass and saw either of these sources – but it would be nice to think that he did.

At the end of the year the report of his survey work in Kumaon was read before a meeting of the Asiatic Society of Bengal in Calcutta. Webb had computed the heights of nearly all the highest peaks in his area and when these were given there were exclamations of disbelief. He had provided the first scientifically-based evidence to support Henry Colebrooke's claim, made twenty years earlier, that some of the Himalayan peaks could be as high as 26,000 feet above sea level. Among the 130 heights that he gave was one for Peak XIV, now better known as Nanda Devi. Webb reckoned it to be 25,669 feet high, which is just twenty-four feet higher than today's estimate.

Three years later he completed his survey of the Kumaon frontier by making his way past Niti village to the head of the Niti pass – but no further. It must have been a sad moment for him. For most of those five years he had worked without the assistance or companionship of another survey officer. 'I am absolutely in a state of banishment,' he wrote plaintively in one of his letters. 'It is now half a year and upwards since I have seen a European face, and but for correspondence I should run no small risk of forgetting my own language.'

In 1821 the Surveyor-General retired and the selection of his successor began. William Webb believed himself to be a strong contender for the post, but to his great dismay the appointment went to John Hodgson, his junior by several years. For Webb this was 'the total destruction of my hopes'. Declaring that the promotion of Hodgson over his head appeared to 'attach some stigma to my professional character', he sent in his resignation, which was accepted.

In January 1822 William Webb handed over his maps and the field books of the Kumaon survey to the new Surveyor-General and sailed for England and retirement.

Chapter 5

Up the 'Burrumpooter':
the Opening of the
Upper Assam Valley

Throughout the period of British rule, India's North-East Frontier, the province of Assam bordering on Tibet and Burma, was regarded by those who served there as the forgotten frontier. It was known for its tea gardens and for very little else. In 1865 one of India's leading newspapers summed up the conventional view of the province as a wild country inhabited by 'savage tribes, whose bloody raids and thieving forays threatened serious danger to the cause of tea'. For all its exotic hill-tribes, jungles and teeming wildlife, Assam could never hope to match that other – far more glamorous – frontier province on the other side of India, the North-West Frontier. A distinguished Governor-General pronounced it to be a bore.

Until the first Anglo-Burmese war of 1824 this beautiful and fertile corner of the subcontinent had been ignored by the East India Company and allowed to 'lie profitless in impenetrable jungle'. So it might have remained but for the expansionist policies of the Burmese royal house of Ava, which were very similar to those employed by the Nepalese a quarter of a century earlier. Had they contented themselves with invading Assam the Company would not have been greatly alarmed, but by pushing into Cachar and East Bengal the Burmese forced the issue. The conflict that followed has some claims to being the worst managed war in British history.

More than a third of the British troops lost their lives, in most cases dying not from wounds but from dysentery and jungle fever. While the main thrust of the British advance on Burma was from the south, along the coast of Arakan and through the Irrawaddy delta to Rangoon, a smaller force of three thousand men was sent up the Brahmaputra river to Goalpara, which then marked the limits of British territory. From there they began to move into the Assam valley, the alluvial plain laid out by the Brahmaputra river between the Himalayan foothills to the north and a succession of lesser mountain ranges running in an arc to the south: the Patkai, Naga, Jaintia, Khasi and Garo hills (see Map B).

The course of the Brahmaputra had long been a subject of dispute among European geographers. 'This river must needs have a very long course before it enters the Bengal Provinces,' James Rennell had written in 1788, 'since 400 miles from the sea it is twice as big as the Thames.' He was not prepared to go along with the current popular belief, much in favour on the Continent, that the Brahmaputra's headwaters lay south of the Himalayas and that the Tibetan Tsangpo was the same river as the Burmese Irrawaddy. There was, he believed, 'the strongest presumptive proof possible of the Sanpoo and Burrumpooter being one and the same river.' He was equally sure that positive proof could be obtained only by actually tracing the river all the way to its source — 'a circumstance unlikely ever to happen to any Europeans or their dependants'. Two centuries later that circumstance still seems just as unlikely as it did in Rennell's day.

Shortly before the military column began its advance into Assam a remarkable young man in the Bengal Civil Service had been appointed Agent to the Governor-General for the North-East Frontier. His name was David Scott and, at the age of twenty-seven, he had already put in no less than eight years as Collector and Magistrate of several districts in the Bengal Presidency. Like the best of his contemporaries during this period he was an all-rounder, a skilled administrator with an open and inquiring mind and a zest for action. Very characteristically, he took up his appointment by taking a dramatic short-cut from the plains of Bengal to the Assam valley that took him through the Khasi hills. This was a diplomatic as well as a geographical coup, for the Khasi hill tribes were then just as warlike and wary of strangers as any of the other Mongolian tribal groups of Assam.

Scott found the Assam field force to be seriously hampered

99

by a lack of accurate information about the surrounding country. He asked the Surveyor-General to send up a survey party as soon as possible and in the meantime set about recruiting his own team from the officers in the column. Two junior lieutenants of artillery soon came to his notice: Philip Burlton, aged twenty-one, and Richard Bedingfield, aged twenty-two, both former cadets of the Company's military academy at Addiscombe. Burlton, who was from a well-to-do Leicestershire family and had been to Winchester, had been saddled with the reputation of a rebel. While stationed at the artillery depot at Dum Dum (near the site of the present Calcutta Airport) he had invited the editor of a Calcutta newspaper, a notorious critic of government policies, to dine at the mess. For this breach of regimental good taste Burlton had been dispatched upcountry to Assam, where he and another involuntary exile, Lieutenant Bedingfield, found themselves in charge of two howitzers and two 12-pounder carronades as the field force advanced on the old Ahom capital of Rungpore.

In January 1825, with the Burmese invaders in retreat, both volunteered for exploration and survey work. In fact, Richard Bedingfield had already provided Scott with measurements of the discharge of the Brahmaputra that showed it to be a mightier river than the Ganga. However, for the next few months he was forced to stay with the field force as it chased the Burmese across the Assam valley. From information gained from captured prisoners he was able to put together the first cohesive map of Upper Burma.

Bedingfield's fellow gunner was given a more challenging commission, which was to explore the 'perfect blank' that lay upriver from Rungpore. Making his way up the Brahmaputra in a Bengali country boat by a laborious combination of sailing, poling and towing from the bank, Philip Burlton eventually came to an area about ninety miles upriver where the Brahmaputra broke up into a complex of several tributaries (see inset, Map B). On the north bank of what appeared to be the main tributary there was a small settlement called Sadiya, with a population of about three thousand. Today the town no longer exists, having been swept away by the floods that followed the Assam earthquake of 1950, but its

100

position had always been precarious, since it was sited on one of the banks of sand and debris known as *chapris* that came and went as the watercourses swung back and forth across the Assam valley. With every monsoon new barriers of vegetation and silt were piled up and new channels gouged out of the plain. In time these *chapris* became overgrown with tall elephant grass and dotted with *simul* trees, providing a natural home for tiger, water-buffalo, swamp deer, pig, elephant and the stubby Indian rhino. Then came the fishermen, with their coarse-thatch *bashas*, and finally more permanent settlements, sited usually where there was a convenient *ghat*.

Its location made Sadiya the obvious base for the exploration of this furthest corner of Assam – and for its future administration, now that the Company had decided to maintain its hold on this newly-liberated land. Just as Peshawar was the lynchpin of the North-West Frontier in later years so, in its own more modest way, did Sadiya become the focal point of the North-East Frontier. It was where the Hindu culture of the plains gave way to the tribal and largely animist culture of the surrounding hills. In its crowded bazaar Burlton soon found himself face to face with representatives of a dozen or more 'rude hill races', people very different from any that he had hitherto come across in India.

The two largest groups in the area were the Mishmis and the Abors. The first inhabited the mountains and dense rainforests north and east of Sadiya and were, according to Burlton's fellow-explorer in later years, Richard Wilcox, 'wild-looking but inoffensive, rather dirty people' who rarely wore more than a G-string and whose most distinctive ornament was an earring 'nearly an inch in diameter, made of thin silver plate, the lobes of the ears having been gradually stretched and enlarged from the age of childhood to receive this singular ornament.' They were also great smokers from an early age, rarely being seen without a bamboo pipe in their mouths.

West of the Mishmis was the tribe that the Assamese called Abors or 'unknown savages', a dozen or so quarrelsome clans tightly packed along both banks of a river known locally as the Dihong, and said to be 'very averse to receiving strangers'.

The men habitually wore arms or armour; cane helmets and breastplates, short stabbing or throwing spears, long swords known as *daos* and crossbows with arrows dipped in poisonous concoctions of aconite and deadly nightshade. 'A very rude, barbarous people of open manners and warlike habits' was how a Political Officer chose to describe them two decades later:

They appear to be descendants of the Tarter race and are large, uncouth, athletic, fierce-looking, dirty fellows. Like all the hill tribes of Assam, the Abors are void of beards: invariably plucking them, and leaving only scanty moustaches. They wear three kinds of helmets, one of the plain cane, and others trimmed with an edging of bear's skin, or covered with a thick yellow skin of species of deer. A more formidable covering of the head could scarcely be worn. The dress of the Abor chiefs consists of Thibetian woollen cloaks, and a simple piece of cotton cloth, about a foot square, which is passed between the legs and suspended by a string around the waist: but not so effectively as to screen their persons from exposure every time they sit down. Of delicacy, however, the Abors are as void as they are of cleanliness.

Soon after coming to Sadiya, Burlton learned from local Hindus that the true source of the Brahmaputra was said to be close at hand. It was believed to be located at a lake called Brahmakund sited at the head of the River that ran past Sadiya, the Lohit. When Burlton set out to explore this eastern branch of the Brahmaputra, however, his cumbersome country boat could only get a few miles beyond Sadiya; the Lohit was far too shallow for its deep draught. Below and west of Sadiya there were two other rivers that flowed into the Brahmaputra – the Dihong and the Dibang. Despite local Hindu opinion, these appeared to Burlton to look much more promising. When he returned to the Agent's headquarters he was able to report to Scott that one of these rivers, the Dihong, carried much more water than either the Dibang or the Lohit and that: 'most probably this branch is the continuation of the Sanpo.'

102

The British advance into Burma and Assam had greatly stimulated public interest in these two regions and the controversy about the sources of the Brahmaputra and the Irrawaddy was then at its height. Addressing the Royal Asiatic Society in London, the German geographer and orientalist Heinrich Julius von Klaproth had expressed his firm conviction that the 'Sanpoo, or River of Tibet' was connected with the Irrawaddy or 'River of Ava'. John Hodgson, now Surveyor-General, dismissed Klaproth as a 'continental coxcomb' but it was clear that in London and Calcutta as well as on the Continent opinion was swinging in Klaproth's favour.

The evidence that David Scott now held indicated that the Brahmaputra was an extremely large river and that it entered India from the north. But its connection with the Tsangpo had still to be proved beyond doubt, and so when the official survey team arrived in Assam in answer to Scott's request it was directed to regard the source of the Brahmaputra as its chief goal. Its officer-in-charge, Captain James Bedford, was ordered to 'unravel the mystery regarding its fountainhead' and to make his way as far upstream as he could.

When he received his orders to take on the survey of Assam, James Bedford was engaged in revenue surveying in Sahaswan in Upper Bengal. He had made Sahaswan his home and was well established there with a *bibi* and two natural sons who would later follow him into the Survey of India. By all accounts, he was a solid and able worker but temperamentally more of an office-wallah than a frontiersman. Accompanying him as his assistant was a young surveyor named Richard Wilcox. Unlike the majority of his contemporaries in the Company's service, Wilcox was not from the landed gentry; his father was a woollen draper from the Strand. But whatever he lacked in his family connections he made up for in talent. Already at twenty-two he was regarded by his employers as 'one of the cleverest young men we have' and was being marked out as someone who would go far.

These two officers began their work in Assam in the early summer of 1824. At first they accompanied the Assam field force as it harried the retreating Burmese through the jungles, then worked independently, each with his own escort of sepoys. But for Richard Wilcox there was one constant source of grievance: his superior officer made it plain from the start that he alone was to be the first to explore 'the upper parts of the Burrumpooter'. One of the very few compensations of working on this dangerously unhealthy frontier was the greater opportunity for recognition and advancement that the survey offered, and evidently Bedford was not prepared to forgo or share the opportunity with his junior. Yet, while he prevented his assistant from going upriver, Bedford himself made little effort to do any exploring there himself. After more than a year had passed without any signs of action, Wilcox finally went over his head and complained to the Agent to the Governor-General.

David Scott immediately wrote to the Surveyor-General calling for positive action. It was a private letter but unmistakably a threatening one. Scott suggested that the young Wilcox be given his head; he was 'quite zealous in the cause and very desirous of being allowed to explore the country north of the mouth of the Dewung [Dihong]. I fear he will not be permitted to do this, or anything else worth notice, whilst under Captain Bedford, there being some sort of jealousy on the Captain's part.' The Surveyor-General was wise enough to take a hint and Richard Wilcox was immediately placed on special duty to trace the Brahmaputra to its source.

When the news came through to Assam, Bedford was at Rungpore while his assistant was downriver at Goalpara. Still determined not to be outdone, Captain Bedford ordered Wilcox first to explore the Subansiri river, another of the main river's northern tributaries, while he himself set off to explore the Dihong tributary. Bedford moved upriver at such speed that he took with him only two sepoys by way of escort, apparently quite unaware that the Dihong river flowed through the territory of the most aggressive of all the Assamese hill tribes.

When Captain Bedford's boats approached the first outlying Abor settlement on the Dihong river – sited a few miles below the first range of foothills at a crossing-point known as Pasighat – he found his landing opposed by a large group of heavily armed warriors. 'I was received by the villagers in arms,' he reported bluntly in a letter to the Surveyor-General. 'All my endeavours to persuade this mountain tribe to permit my further progress proved unavailing – although the water would have admitted my further progress.' Having failed to make any progress up the Dihong he turned his attentions to the second major tributary, the Dibang. But here too his hopes were foiled by the 'prejudices and fears of the inhabitants'; abandoning the attempt he made his way to Sadiya, where he was joined in due course first by Richard Wilcox and then by Philip Burlton.

For the two younger men this proved to be a most happy and fruitful encounter; the Wykehamist and the draper's son soon found that they had a common interest in the subject of the Brahmaputra's source. They both believed the river to be linked to the Tsangpo by the Dihong so they decided to work together to establish the necessary proof. It was some time, however, before they could put their partnership to the test, principally because Captain Bedford was still treating the Dihong-Dibang area as his own special preserve. In his reports written over the next few months Richard Wilcox twice refers to plans to explore promising overland routes leading towards the upper reaches of these rivers that he and Philip Burlton had been forced to abandon 'in deference to Capt. Bedford's wishes'.

This absurd situation was finally resolved by James Bedford's decision to retire from the field. In 1826 he applied for transfer back to his original revenue survey work and then made one final exploratory boat journey up the Lohit tributary. His intention was to reach the fabled lake associated with the Brahmaputra, the Brahmakund – and, indeed, he did find such a place. It turned out to be no more than an insignificant ox-bow lake beside the Lohit river that attracted a small number of Hindu pilgrims to its banks every year; hardly the prize that he had hoped to secure. In January 1827, after a long recuperation, Bedford was back with his family and his revenue surveys in Sahaswan.

Although the field was now clear for Wilcox and Burlton they knew very well that there would be no progress through tribal territory until the inveterate hostility shown towards outsiders by the Abors and, to a lesser extent, by the Mishmis, had been overcome. While Burlton was away from Sadiya on a short spell of military duty Wilcox set himself to learn as much as he could about the languages and the culture of the Abor and Mishmi tribes in the surrounding hills. He evidently made some progress, since he was able to persuade one of the Abor chiefs to meet and parley with David Scott during the latter's visit to Sadiya in 1826.

Encouraged by his success Richard Wilcox decided to put his new-gained knowledge to the test by making an extended trek deep into Mishmi country. This was, he admitted on his return, an error of judgment on his part and one that he was lucky to survive unscathed. His journey took him more than fifty miles up the Lohit river beyond the point reached by Captain Bedford a year earlier, and he turned back only when it had become obvious that he and his party were in imminent danger of attack. Warned by a friendly Mishmi that an assault on his camp would be made at dawn Wilcox had quietly withdrawn his men during the night. He was told afterwards that 'an hour or two before daylight the assembled warriors had invested our position, and concealing themselves in the jungle, while advancing from all sides, they at last rushed upon our huts, and to their infinite disappointment found them empty.' Wilcox was not exaggerating the dangers of his journey; the next Europeans to penetrate as far into Mishmi territory – two French missionaries in 1854 – were attacked and killed.

Towards the end of the year Wilcox was rejoined in Sadiya by his 'staunch friend' James Burlton, and together they prepared to launch their first major expedition into the Abor hills. They received unexpected encouragement from the Abors themselves in the form of a round stone – 'an emblem of the stability of their friendly inclination' – sent from the village of Membu. Greatly cheered by this gesture Wilcox and Burlton set off for Membu in January 1827, taking with them a generous assortment of gifts as well as a modest escort of fifteen musketeers.

They found Membu to be made up of some one hundred houses perched on a hillside. In the middle of the village was the *morang*, a large long-house perched on stilts which served as 'a hall of audience or debate, as a place of reception for

106

strangers, and as a house for the bachelors of the village generally.' They were expected by their hosts to lodge here but, as Richard Wilcox recorded in his *Memoir*, 'the effect upon our olfactory nerves of certain appendages of convenience was so appalling that we made good a very hasty retreat from it.' Pitching a tent nearby Wilcox and Burlton tried to settle down for the night but found themselves plagued by curious Abors determined to make the most of this brief visitation. 'Our situation was worse than that of unfortunate wild beasts,' Wilcox lamented, 'inasmuch as that we had not the advantage of cages and bars to keep our annoyers at arm's length.'

The next day they returned to the *morang*, to distribute their gifts as best they could and to listen to a great many speeches. However, their patience and generosity went unrewarded: 'It suffices now to say that our visit was not attended with any advantageous result; they would not consent to our proceeding further by land, and they assured us of the utter impossibility of our going on by water.' Greatly disappointed, they led their men back to their boats moored at Pasighat. Here the Abors seemed a little friendlier so they decided to follow the river as far up into the hills as they could go. When armed warriors blocked their further progress along the bank they took to a small dugout canoe that they had brought with them and in this way they were able to negotiate a few more miles of the river. Eventually they were brought to a halt by a rapid 'too formidable to ascend and promising destruction to the boat on return'. Before they turned back Wilcox scrambled over the rocks along the bank and saw above the rapid a long reach of undisturbed water leading away into the hills in a westerly direction.

It was now obvious that no further progress could be made either up the river itself or along its banks. They had learned enough about the Abors to realize that the perpetual state of feuding that went on between one Abor village and its neighbour and between one Abor clan and another made it impossible for any visitor to proceed any distance into the hills. What this meant was that the solution to the Tsangpo-Brahmaputra connection would have to be found elsewhere – perhaps in Burma, for if the Irrawaddy could be tracked to

107

its source and shown to be totally unconnected with the Tsangpo then the case for the Brahmaputra would be that much stronger.

Returning to Sadiya, Wilcox and Burlton at once began making arrangements for a journey that would take them eastwards across the Patkai mountains to northern Burma. The only published account of this brave venture is contained in Richard Wilcox's *Memoir of a Survey of Assam*, which was a summary of his three years' work on the Upper Brahmaputra. Fortunately, a fuller account survives in Philip Burlton's notebook, now in the archives of the Survey of India. If Burlton's story had been published – as he had hoped it would be – then a much more dramatic and horrifying picture of the hazards of exploration in India's North-Eastern Frontier would have emerged.

The expedition set out from Sadiya on 15 April 1827, which was an unfortunate time to choose since the *chota bursat*, the little monsoon that precedes the midsummer rains, was now full upon them. 'Very tedious' is how Wilcox describes their passage up the Noa Dihing river in his *Memoir*. 'More the appearance of drowned rats rather than officers and gentlemen' is how Burlton saw themselves as they poled their boats upriver through torrential downpours.

On 26 April they hauled their boat up out of the water and prepared to strike off into the jungle. This was not the open deciduous forest of the Indian plains but tropical evergreen jungle, the beginning of the dense rain-forest of South-East Asia, enclosed overhead by the branches of the tall *hollong* and *hollock* trees, festooned with creepers and made almost impenetrable at ground level by breaks of thorn-covered cane and bamboo and the coarse-leaved *serat* or giant stinging-nettle that could cripple a man who accidentally brushed against it. The hill tracts that it covered, uninhabited and rarely entered by man, were described by Wilcox as 'a wild region where no paths exist but those made by the constant passage of wild animals. For the last two years none had traversed the wilderness, excepting the two Mishmis who were now our guides, and their only means of finding their

108

way was to hunt for the notches left on the trees by themselves.'

Having been warned by the tribesmen that their Bengali servants would not survive the journey Wilcox and Burlton had come prepared to fend for themselves, their party consisting of a 'heterogeneous retinue' drawn from every hill tribe in the area – 'Sing Phos, Kamptys, Mishmis, Moolooks, Kamjauns, all speaking different languages'. However, this collection proved to be insufficient to carry all the supplies that they had brought with them in the boats, which meant that part of their stores – including 'wine and solah hats' (prototypes, perhaps, of that solid symbol of the Raj, the *sola topee*) – had to be abandoned. They had also arranged for an elephant to accompany them through the jungles, but the unfortunate beast kept losing its footing on steeper ground, and after nearly strangling itself on a slipped load it too had to be abandoned. So were a couple of ponies that they had transported upriver; their usefulness came to an end when they reached the first river, which could only be crossed by means of a simple basket and sling suspended from a strong cane rope:

The passenger sits in this and by means of another cane and by his own exertions he is pulled across in perfect safety. To a man unaccustomed to crossing and subject to be giddy, the sensation may be rather unpleasant should he look down on the water roaring beneath him.

Their guides led them eastwards towards a high mountain range that marked the divide between the river systems of Assam and Burma. As they marched deeper into the jungle they saw more of the wild creatures who were its sole occupants; troops of langur monkeys or long-armed gibbons crashing through the branches overhead, large herds of browsing elephants, the delicate *kakur* or barking deer and the larger *sambur*. Burlton recorded in his journal how they were kept amused for most of one day by an unseen bird – probably a coppersmith – that 'for want of a name may be called the Bell Bird from the striking resemblance it makes to the sound of the bell tolling in the distance.'

On 1 May they camped at the foot of the main mountain range. 'The greater difficulties of our journey now commence,' noted Burlton. 'We have before us the pleasant prospect of 12 days journey without the chance of seeing a village or human being besides ourselves.' As they started the climb they made contact with the insects that were to torment them for the rest of their journey, the aptly-named *dam-dooms* (or *dim-dams*):

It flies on a noiseless wing, and has no hum like the mosquito to announce its treacherous attack; neither is the bite immediately felt, but a little blister is soon after seen, filled with extravasated blood, and the itching becomes so intolerable that it defies the utmost exertion of patience.

Dressed in their European clothes Wilcox and Burlton were better protected from the *dam-dooms* than their native companions in their loincloths: 'Our friends with the "bottomless breeks" were infinitely worse off than we were,' wrote Wilcox, 'and indeed those of the plains were in a few days almost disabled by the inveterate sores caused by these abominable pests.' His colleague noted in his journal that it was just as well that the *dam-dooms* appeared to confine themselves to the Burmese borderland: 'God forbid they should ever emigrate westward, for as they make their attacks by day in thousands, they would prove a greater annoyance than any pest at present known in India.'

A week later they crossed the 10,000-foot mountain barrier that effectively marked the divide between India and Burma. As they reached its summit Wilcox's foot struck what he at first took to be a lump of quartz but which turned out on closer inspection to be a human skull, the remains of some 'unfortunate wretch who must have died a miserable lingering death in the snow'. Almost as if on cue two of Burlton's men lay down on the ground and refused to go any further. With their food supply now almost exhausted Wilcox and Burlton knew they had no alternative but to leave the two men where they had fallen. 'To assist them was impossible,' Burlton wrote. 'Carry them we could not, even had we rice sufficient to enable people to bring them on. However melancholy the circumstances, they *must* be left to their fate.'

110

Burlton's entry in his journal on the following day shows how seriously the health of the expedition was being affected:

9th of May. Heavy rain all the morning. A halt would be most desirable, to allow the two unfortunate men to come up and give rest to the whole party. Almost every man is knocked up; swelled feet and dreadful sores the general complaint, & several men with fevers. Leeches and Dam Dooms scarcely bearable; we once took the trouble to count the collection of about half an hour, and 35 leeches were torn from one leg.

One of those suffering from fever was Philip Burlton himself; he put it down to a combination of the rice diet and 'perhaps to too many raspberries'. Meanwhile his companion had become so lame in one foot from the *dam-doom* bites that he could barely hobble along.

Four days after crossing the mountains they came, at last, to a broad river. They camped beside its waters and as they boiled up what was almost the last of their rice one of the two men who had been left to die staggered into sight. His companion was dead and he himself had eaten nothing for four days. On the following day they waded across the river – 'with great difficulty, for many from weakness were unable to stand against the current' – and were met on the other side by some Burmese. They knew then that their troubles were nearly over. 'The sight of some new faces gave us fresh alacrity,' wrote Wilcox, 'and we hailed our approach to a civilized country with that joy which those only could feel who had suffered from fatigue and privation as we had.'

Soon they found themselves looking out across a cultivated plain – 'to us an Eden' – dotted with small, fortified villages and inhabited by Khamtis, mountain people of Shan extraction, who welcomed them with great friendliness: 'They had never heard, even by report, of Europeans, and the crowd attracted by our white faces and the musical snuff box was immense.' This musical snuff box turned out to be an even greater crowd-puller than the two Britons, and was kept in almost constant use during their short stay in Burma. Nor was it forgotten: though sixty years passed before Europeans

111

visited this remote corner of Burma again, they were at once asked to produce their musical box – which, happily, they were able to do.

After a brief rest at the first Khamti village the party continued its journey eastwards until on 20 May 1827 they climbed a low range of hills and saw 'the object of our deepest interest' in the distance: 'the Irrawaddy winding in a large plain, spotted with light green patches of cultivation and low grass jungle.' Also visible were the roofs and pagodas of Mong Se, the Khamti capital (sited about five miles north of the present town of Putao). As they descended they were met by a reception committee led by the son of the Rajah of Mong Se, who had thoughtfully provided two ponies for Wilcox and Burlton to ride. Flanked by their escort and 'noised by incessant beating on two little gongs' they entered the Khamti capital and were led to the town hall. Here they were provided with a splendid meal sent over from the royal kitchens:

It was served up à la mode Kampty on Burman laquered trays, and numerous small china basins. The repast we found so excellent that we hinted that we should not be sorry to dine from the same source during our stay. From that time forth we 'feasted sumptuously every day'. We were also provided with a supply of distilled liquor, very much like whiskey, but not quite so strong; it was very acceptable, our own small stock being nearly exhausted.

For the next week Wilcox and Burlton remained in Mong Se, savouring the Rajah's hospitality and all the comforts that this friendly Buddhist principality provided. After resting his poisoned foot for the first two days Wilcox felt well enough to start taking short walks around the town, visiting the Rajah in his palace and the chief priest in his temple – though always in the company of a great throng of spectators. Burlton had not yet shaken off his fever, however, and he blamed a new attack on the 'suffocating heat occasioned by the crowds'. He had hoped that once the novelty had worn off they would start to disperse but instead they grew steadily day by day, 'pouring in to see us "once before they die".'

Their goal was now less than half a day's journey away to

the east. The two officers set off on horseback early on the morning of 24 May accompanied only by a local guide. Riding at a gallop for most of the way, they reached the banks of the Irrawaddy in two hours. 'I could not help exulting,' Wilcox recalled in his *Memoir*, 'when standing at the edge of the clear stream, at the successful result of our toils and fatigues.' The river was even smaller than they had expected it to be, no more than eighty yards wide and shallow enough to be forded. Wilcox had been determined to secure 'ocular and incontrovertible' proof that the Irrawaddy was not the lower extension of the Tsangpo – and here it was:

> Before us to the north rose a towering wall, stretching from west to east, offering an awkward impediment to the passage of a river in a cross direction. We agreed on the spot that, if Mr Klaproth proved determined to make his Sampo pass by Ava [Burma], he must find a river to his purpose considerably removed towards or into China.

Fortunately for Wilcox and Burlton they went no further; another two days' march eastwards would have brought them to the banks of a second and larger affluent of the Irrawaddy, and to the start of that extraordinary bottleneck between Burma and China where four great rivers (Irrawaddy, Salween, Mekong, Yangtse) run in parallel lines with less than a hundred miles separating the first from the last. Happily unaware of this complication, the two surveyors were able to return to India convinced that they had destroyed the foundation of Herr Klaproth's theory. This proved to be the case: although Klaproth himself still clung to his belief for some years the connection between the Tsangpo and the Brahmaputra was never again seriously disputed.

The expedition had now to get back to Assam before the main force of the summer monsoon – the *burra bursat* – was thrown against the Patkai hills. The Mong Se Rajah provided the party with rice for the return journey, refusing to accept payment. In the face of such generosity there could be only one response: after first taking it to pieces to show him how it worked Wilcox presented the Rajah with his musical snuff box.

The return journey began on 29 May. 'An unconcerned spectator would have laughed had he witnessed the scene a little before our departure,' Burlton recorded. Since most of their coolies were still too weak to carry much more than their own rations they had been forced to make further drastic reduction of their loads:

We were obliged to give & fling away almost everything we had with us; useless articles had gone many days before. Shot belts, powder, flints, clothes, shoes, shaving & hair brushes etc were to be had for the picking; even soap was too cumbersome to carry.

With the help of more reliable guides loaned by the Rajah they were able to make a more comfortable return journey across the mountains. Two weeks later they were back at the village where they had left their boats and stores. Burlton's relief was undisguised:

Here end all our troubles from marching, wading, climbing, slipping & falling, and all our torments from leeches, Dam Dooms, sand flies, bugs, ticks *et id genus omne*.

Unkempt, unshaven and unwashed, they arrived back in Sadiya to find David Scott waiting to greet and congratulate them. And here on 16 June 1827 Burlton closed his journal with one final, emphatic statement:

In the above journal it may be said that too much egotism has been displayed in mentioning our own personal hardships and troubles. They have been mentioned merely that a true idea of the many difficulties to be encountered should be known, in order to warn any European from ever attempting the same journey. The chances are much against a man's ever returning alive; and, even to us who have had much experience in travelling of the same kind, the effects of the journey are not yet known. Lieut. Wilcox is at present confined to his bed with a dangerous fever, and Lieut. Burlton has scarcely recovered. All who accompanied us have also suffered more or less.

Today, when the mountains and jungles of South-East Asia have been mapped and reduced to order, the voids filled, and a hostile world of dangers known and unknown has been neutralized, Burlton's words cannot help but sound a little theatrical. Yet they would certainly have rung true to the survivors of the retreat from Burma, who were forced to find their way through those same hills and jungles in the early summer of 1942. Nor was Burlton exaggerating the poor state of health to which he and Richard Wilcox had been reduced; the sores from the insect bites soon healed but the dysentery and malaria that they had contracted never left them. Wilcox thought seriously of resigning his post and returning, as Bedford had done, to revenue surveying. 'I cannot help reflecting on how many officers have been cut off in Assam', he wrote in a letter to John Hodgson. But the Surveyor-General had no intention of letting such a valuable officer transfer to revenue work. 'It was affected with great difficulty in Bedford's instance,' he wrote back, 'but you have a much more important part to fulfil and I hope your health will bear you out.' It was agreed that as soon as an opportunity arose Wilcox would make his way downriver to Calcutta and from there embark on a long sea voyage as a means of recovering his health. In the meantime he had to survive the Assam rains, and the only effective answer to that was to escape to the hills.

As it happened, David Scott had just come to an agreement with the Khasi chief of Nongkhlao, a small village perched on the northern escarpment of the Khasi hills, by which the British would be permitted to build a road up from the Assam valley through Nongkhlao and Khasi territory to Bengal. The Khasi hills ranged from three to nearly six thousand feet and offered an ideal refuge from the enervating heat and humidity of the plains. Nongkhlao itself was a perfect place for a sanatorium and the Khasis had no objection to a bungalow being built there for this purpose. One of its first occupants was Richard Wilcox, who was carried up from the valley in a closed palankeen.

Not long afterwards he was joined by Philip Burlton, who had been ordered by Scott to take charge of the surveying and building of the new road through the Khasi hills. Both

115

men had set great store by the publication of Burlton's Journal. It had been sent off to Calcutta within a week of their arrival in Sadiya and Wilcox had made it clear to the Surveyor-General that he hoped to see it published as soon as possible. However, Hodgson had other plans. Despite the fact that a number of senior officials in Calcutta showed great interest, he refused to let it be published. Burlton was not a member of his staff and what Hodgson wanted was an official account from Wilcox himself. The end result was a five-year delay before Wilcox's official *Memoir* appeared in print – and the effective concealment (to this day) of Burlton's Journal among the records of the Survey of India.

Wilcox had been recuperating at Nongkhlao for less than two months when he received a message from the Khamtis in Northern Burma inviting him to return to their country and explore the lands beyond the Irrawaddy. Evidently the temptation was irresistible, for Wilcox at once set off from Nongkhlao and almost immediately collapsed. In January 1828 he wrote to Hodgson asking to be recalled to Calcutta: 'I am still suffering for my temerity in venturing thro' the jungles in May & June. Nor am I alone in this, for here I found Lt Burlton obliged to leave his road making to seek medical aid.' It distressed Wilcox to see his friend denied what he felt was due to him and before he left Nongkhlao he tried to do something about it. 'The annoyances endured, with loss of health,' he argued in a letter written on Burlton's behalf to the Surveyor-General, 'ought to incline the Government to act more generously towards him than at present they seem inclined.' Hodgson's reaction is not recorded.

In February 1828 Wilcox bade farewell to his friend and began a slow journey down the Brahmaputra. Hodgson was anxious that he should use this opportunity to complete the mapping of the river that Burlton had started three years earlier, and as a result nearly a year was to pass before Wilcox was able to begin his sea voyage, on a vessel bound for Dutch Batavia.

Some months after Wilcox's departure Philip Burlton was joined in the Khasi hills by his fellow-artilleryman, Richard Bedingfield, who under Wilcox's direction had been surveying large areas of the north bank of the Brahmaputra west of the Dihong. His health had also broken down and so in March 1829 he, too, took up residence at the Nongkhlao bungalow, together with Burlton and David Scott.

Ever since Scott had first entered their territory four years earlier relations between the Khasis and the British had been extremely cordial, so much so that Scott had asked for and secured their permission to open a second sanatorium in the Khasi hills, to be built on the cliffs of Cherrapunji overlooking the plains of Bengal. Suddenly, and without any apparent warning, the Khasis' attitude changed. It was later put about that one of the Bengalis working on the new road had been mocking the Khasis about the ease with which they gave way to British demands. But whatever the immediate cause, the Khasis at Nongkhlao decided to repudiate their treaty with Scott and to expel the British before they could make further inroads.

On the morning of 4 April the occupants of the Nongkhlao sanatorium woke to find the bungalow surrounded by some five hundred armed Khasi warriors. Fortunately for David Scott he had set off for Cherrapunji only the day before, so it was Richard Bedingfield, the older of the two officers, who went out to talk to the crowd. According to the account published in the *Bengal Observer*, he was given no opportunity to find out what the disturbance was all about:

> They immediately seized him, and after tying his hands behind his back and cutting the tendons of his legs, commenced shooting at him with their arrows. It is said that he told them, if it was his life they wanted, to kill him outright at once, which they accordingly did and, cutting off his head, placed it on a rock.

The killing of Bedingfield was over before Burlton could do anything to prevent it, but he quickly mustered a few sepoys who were quartered in the bungalow and successfully repelled the first Khasi attack. His little party held out 'in gallant style' for the whole of that day and the night. But at dawn on the following day the Khasis managed to set the roof of the bungalow alight with firebrands and the defenders were forced to make a break for it. Burlton and his men

117

charged out in a body and by keeping up a constant fire, were able to hold the Khasis at a distance. They began to make their way along the road towards Cherrapunji, still keeping together and successfully preventing the Khasis from loosing off their arrows at close range. Eventually their luck ran out; a sudden shower of rain came down and wet their powder, making their firearms useless. One of the first to be slaughtered was Philip Burlton:

He was in the act of extracting an arrow from his wrist when he was cut down, being in an exhausted state from the intense exertions he had made, and his previous ill-health.

News of the Nongkhlao massacre soon reached Calcutta and perhaps it was no coincidence that Richard Wilcox finally sailed for Batavia on 30 April, within a fortnight of hearing of Burlton's death. He never went back to Assam but, after returning to Bengal at the end of the year, contented himself with finishing his survey work on the lower Brahmaputra. So, over the years, he came to be closely identified with this river; the Brahmaputra became very much *his* river, just as the Ganga had once been Robert Colebrooke's.

David Scott died suddenly at Cherrapunji sanatorium in August 1831, having regained the trust of the Khasis and won for himself a reputation for fair dealing that would keep his name alive among that warm-hearted people for many years. With the retirement of John Hodgson in 1829, Richard Wilcox found a new patron in his successor, George Everest, who recruited him for his monumental triangulation scheme known as the Great Trigonometrical Survey. Everest regarded Wilcox as the brightest star in his department, and when James Herbert, then the Deputy Surveyor-General, followed his old friend John Hodgson into retirement in December 1831, it was Lieutenant Wilcox whom Everest asked for as his new deputy. 'He is the very person whom I should seek as a really efficient assistant,' he wrote in his proposal.

The Court of Directors refused to accept Everest's nomination. Their reason for rejecting Wilcox was that they considered him, at the age of twenty-nine, to be too young – and besides there was another candidate to whom the post should go by virtue of his long service. After six months of dispute Richard Wilcox was informed that the job had gone to the Superintendent of the Sahaswan Survey, Captain James Bedford.

At this point in his career Richard Wilcox seems to have lost something of the drive and brilliance that had characterized his earlier ventures. He stayed with George Everest's Trigonometrical Survey for another three years and then resigned from the Survey of India to become official astronomer to the Nawab of Oude at Lucknow. He was highly paid and had at his disposal the most advanced and best equipped observatory outside Europe, but it was hardly the distinguished position that his talents and his early years had promised. When he died in Cawnpore in October 1848 the work of the observatory ceased and all Wilcox's records were put away into one of the Nawab's storerooms and forgotten.

Shortly after the recapture of Lucknow that ended the siege of 1857 a visitor from the Survey of India walked through the ruins of the observatory. He found some of Wilcox's instruments together with all his papers and observations piled up in a heap in a corner of a cellar. 'The greater portion of the materials are eaten up by insects,' he reported. 'Whatever remain are quite useless.'

Chapter 6

'The Queerest, Coolest
Fish at Rugby': Edmund
Smyth and the Pundits

The Rawats of Johar valley claim that their ancestors were part of the large-scale Hindu exodus from Rajputana following the invasion of Mohammed Ghori in the twelfth century. In about 1680 a leading member of the clan named Hiru Dham Singh went on a pilgrimage to Kailas-Manasarovar. He took with him a large party of retainers and fellow-pilgrims and while he was in Tibet he joined with local forces to help drive out Chinese marauders. For this service he was rewarded by the Lhasa government with a trade agreement that gave him a virtual monopoly of the cross-border trade with Gartok in Western Tibet – an advantage that was exploited to the full by his descendants right up to the early 1950s, when the Chinese finally closed the borders.

On his way back from that eventful pilgrimage Hiru Dham Singh entered a valley east of Nanda Devi which he later occupied and made the home of his clan. Here in the Johar valley the Rawats traded and prospered, living in the lower villages during the winter months and moving up in early summer to Milam, a small settlement below the 17,500-foot Unta Dhura pass leading indirectly into Tibet (see Map A). They mixed and intermarried with people of Tibetan origin called Bhotias or *Shokpas* already settled in that region but maintained a dominant position as a ruling caste. As effective rulers of the valley and leaders among the trans-Himalayan traders they maintained a position of supremacy during the period when Gurkhas overran Garhwal and Kumaon and when the British succeeded them in 1816.

An Englishman who could claim with good reason to know these Bhotia peoples of Kumaon and Garhwal 'perhaps better

120

than anyone else' was Kumaon's first Education Officer, Edmund Smyth. It was he who first recognized their unusual qualities as the go-betweens of the Central Himalayas:

> The Bhotias have Hindu names and call themselves Hindus but they are not recognized as such by the Orthodox Hindus of the plains. While in Tibet they seem glad enough to shake off their Hinduism and become Buddhists, or anything you like. They pass their lives in trade with Tibet and they are the only people allowed by the Tibetan authorities to enter the country for purposes of trade. From June to November they are constantly going over the passes, bringing the produce of Tibet (borax, salt, wool, gold dust, also ponies) and taking back grain of all kinds, English goods, chiefly woollens and other things. The goods are carried on the backs of sheep, goats, ponies, yaks and *jhoopoos* (a cross between the Tibetan yak and the hill cow). Their villages are situated at an elevation of from 10,000 to 13,000 feet, at the foot of the passes leading into Tibet, though only occupied from June to November in each year. During the remainder of the year they move down to the foot of the hills and sell their produce to the Buniahs or traders.

The first British contact with the Johar Bhotias had been made in 1812 when Moorcroft and Hearsey met the Rawat brothers, Deb Singh and Bir Singh, in Niti; but the first Englishman to penetrate the Johar valley was William Webb, during the five years of his lonely survey of Kumaon. In 1830 the first Commissioner of Kumaon, G. W. Traill, made a spectacular entry into the valley across the south-eastern shoulder of the Nanda Devi massif, over what is still known today as 'Traill's pass'. Traill stayed on as Commissioner for nearly twenty years, earning himself the unofficial title of the 'King of Kumaon' and preserving the friendship of the Bhotia traders by a policy of benevolent non-interference.

After the Anglo-Nepalese war the focus of British attention had shifted away from the Himalayas to the fertile land of the five rivers, the independent state of the Punjab ruled over by the old Sikh warrior Ranjit Singh. With his death in 1839 the

121

usual internecine struggles for power began – exactly the sort of unsettled border situation that the Company deplored. An unwise raid across the Sutlej in December 1845 provided the necessary opportunity for rectifying the position and within a couple of weeks a British victory at Sobraon brought the first Anglo-Sikh war to a close.

During this same period there was an equally ill-judged Sikh military incursion into Western Tibet. In 1841 an army of Sikhs and Dogras from Ladakh and Kashmir advanced across the plateau, scattering an undisciplined Tibetan army and establishing itself at a winter camp on a knoll overlooking Taklakar, the district capital of Purang, two days' march south of lake Manasarovar. Tibetan records state that it was the Tibetan winter rather than their own forces that finally destroyed the invaders. Caught in an unusually heavy fall of snow the half-frozen Sikhs were chased for five days up the Purang valley, losing some three thousand men who were rounded up and beheaded. Among them was the Sikh commander, whose body was chopped up in the traditional Tibetan manner with portions of his flesh being distributed to every house in the area to be kept as talismans. In the circumstances, it was hardly a good moment for any foreigner to think of entering Tibet unbidden.

The first to do so after the Sikh invasion was Henry Strachey, a lieutenant in the 66th Bengal Native Infantry stationed on the coast at Chittagong and a member of one of the most outstanding and influential British families in India. During the hot weather of 1846, ostensibly on sick leave but determined to visit the holy lakes and undeterred by a new government ban on travel across India's northern border, he made his way to Milam, where he met Moorcroft's old friend and protector, Deb Singh Rawat. On his advice Strachey made no attempt to cross the Unta Dhura but made his entry into Tibet by way of a less well-guarded crossing further to the east, the Lampiya Dhura pass. Like Moorcroft and Hearsey before him, Henry Strachey disguised himself as a Hindu pilgrim – and regretted only that he had not dyed his three pairs of pyjamas to a 'dirt colour' to match those worn by his Bhotia companions.

Theirs was a small party and it travelled fast and inconspicuously, keeping off the well-known paths and making elaborate detours to avoid contact with nomads and other travellers. Five days of hard marching brought them to the south-west corner of Rakas Tal, the lesser of the two lakes, and to the point where – according to Hearsey's map – the Sutlej took its source. Here, to Strachey's surprise, he found water flowing *into* the lake instead of out of it. Moving northwards along the western shoreline he went on to discover that there was no real channel of water leading out of Rakas Tal, merely a seepage from its north-western corner across marshy ground – which Hearsey and Moorcroft had failed to see.

Strachey was even more surprised when he began to cross the isthmus between the two lakes and found a large stream a hundred feet wide and three feet deep running from east to west along a well-defined channel between the two lakes. This was undoubtedly the outlet from Manasarovar – and yet Moorcroft, Hearsey and their pundits had all walked along the western rim of Manasarovar without finding any such outlet.

It was one of the Bhotias who provided an answer to this curious discrepancy – and Moorcroft's own description of his walk along the shore that confirmed it. Blocking the Manasarovar entrance to the channel was a raised bar of shingle through which the water from the lake percolated. Moorcroft had noted this raised bank of shingle but because he and his companions had all stuck to the shore they had failed to see what lay on the other side – and so had failed to link the Sutlej to its original source, the Manasarovar lake.

But not all Strachey's attentions were fixed on the two lakes. A few miles to the north was the most beautiful peak he had ever seen, 'a king of mountains, full of majesty', which he estimated to be 21,000 feet high:

the general height of it, I estimate to be 4250 feet above the plain, but from the west end the peak rises some 1500 feet higher, in a cone or dome rather, of paraboloidal shape; the general figure is not unlike that of Nanda Devi, as seen from Almora. The peak and the upper part of the eastern ridge were well covered with snow, which contrasted beautifully with the deep purple colour of the mass of mountain below; the stratification of the rock is strongly marked in successive ledges that catch the snow falling from above, forming irregular bands of alternate white and purple: one of these bands more marked than the rest encircles the base of the peak, and this, according to the Hindu tradition, is the mark of the cable with which the Rakshasa |demons| attempted to drag the throne of Siva from its place.

Instead of retracing his footsteps back along the high ground that formed the watershed between the Sutlej and Karnali river-systems, Strachey then went south into the Purang valley, scene of the Sikh defeat four years earlier. Travelling by night whenever possible he and his party slipped past the fort and the regional capital at Taklakar and made their way unchallenged up the other side of the valley and back across the border.

It was a bold venture that paid off handsomely, winning Strachey the Patron's Medal of the Royal Geographical Society as well as a place on a British mission to Ladakh. Two years later, in 1848, it was the turn of his younger brother, Richard Strachey, to make a name for himself. Of the many Stracheys who served in India over five generations Richard was perhaps the most talented; although trained as an engineer in the Bombay Army he later became an outstanding botanist and geologist. He too came to Kumaon on what was officially designated sick leave and made his own brief excursion to lake Manasarovar, taking as his guide Deb Singh Rawat's son, Mani Singh. His findings confirmed that there was a channel between the lakes, which he drew and measured with characteristic accuracy. He also established the position and height of Mount Kailas; later topographical surveys showed his figure of 22,000 feet to be just 28 feet on the low side.

After the Strachey brothers came the Schlagintweits, three Bavarian geographers sent to India at the request of Baron Humboldt and received with a marked lack of enthusiasm by the Survey of India. In 1855 Adolf and Robert Schlagintweit went up into the Johar valley and found old Deb Singh Rawat not only alive but still in possession of a *chit* of thanks signed by William Moorcroft and inscribed 'Northern foot of the Himachal Mountains near Daba in Chinese Tartary, August 25th 1812'. On his advice they recruited three members of his family for their expedition: Mani Singh Rawat and two younger cousins of his – Dolpa, described as being 'full of courage, energy and devotion', and the 'well disposed and intelligent' Nain Singh Rawat. Nain Singh was then twenty-five years old, a hillman very much in the traditional Bhotia mould, short and stocky in stature, stubborn and reserved in character. All three Bhotias accompanied the Schlagintweits north to the lakes and on to Gartok and a year later went with them to Ladakh.

When Edmund Smyth first came to Johar is something of a mystery. By conventional Anglo-Indian standards his career was undistinguished, and he left little mark either in public or in government records. Yet enough traces of his activies remain to suggest that he was a most remarkable character.

A contemporary of Thomas Hughes at Rugby, Edmund Smyth was immortalized by him as 'Crab Jones' in *Tom Brown's Schooldays* – 'sauntering along with a straw in his mouth, the queerest, coolest fish at Rugby'. From Rugby he came out to India as a military ensign in 1842 and fought with his regiment, the 13th BNI, through the battles of Chenab and Gujerat in the Second Sikh War (1848–9). In the early 1850s his regiment was stationed at Delhi, which was close enough to the hills to allow him to make brief forays into the Himalayas during his hot weather leaves. According to Dr Tom Longstaff, who met Smyth when he was in his eighties, he was on leave in Almora in 1848 when Richard Strachey set out from there for Manasarovar and in July 1851 actually went swimming in the holy lake – 'although his movements were very much hampered by the necessity of avoiding discovery at the hands of the Hunias.'

These excursions had only one motive behind them; Smyth explored and climbed for *shikar*, for the thrill of stalking or tracking down the rarer species of Himalayan wildlife; the long-haired mountains goats – *tahr*, *serow* and *goral* – and the shy musk-deer that lived in the forests and crags below the

125

snowline, as well as the more elusive game of the northern slopes and the Tibetan uplands – the snow leopard, Tibetan wild yak and gazelle, the *burrhel* and its larger cousin the *nyen*, or *Ovis Ammon*, that stood four feet high at the shoulder and whose abnormally acute senses and habit of keeping to open ground made it almost impossible to stalk.

Smyth shared this passion for *shikar* with another Indian Army officer, Lieutenant John Speke, and on at least two occasions in the 1850s they hunted together in Western Tibet. In one of Smyth's few surviving letters, sent to the Royal Geographical Society in 1856, he writes that he and Speke 'travelled for months together in Chinese Tartary to the North of the Himalyah mountains from the Mansarovar Lake to Askardo (Little Tibet).' Apparently preoccupied with bagging trophies, neither Speke nor Smyth thought it worth their while to provide any further details of their travels.

Officers in the Indian Army were at that time entitled to three years' furlough during their first term of twenty years' service. In 1854 Smyth and his fellow-*shikari* decided to take their home leave together, although John Speke got no nearer home than Aden. Here he met another Indian Army officer named Richard Burton and announced that 'being tired of life he had come to be killed in Africa.' So off Speke and Burton went to Somaliland, taking the first steps that would eventually bring them to the source of another river of legend, the Nile.

Edmund Smyth's leave was also well spent. In the summer of 1854 he joined his two brothers – both of them clergymen, as were more than half the founding members of the Alpine Club – in a climbing holiday in the Alps. Mountaineering as a sport was then barely in its infancy but Edmund Smyth was already an experienced climber; the famous alpinist Edward Whymper was later to write of him that 'the natives used to say that he could climb where birds could not fly, which is the oriental equivalent of "Monsieur has the agility of a chamois".' That summer the three brothers put up a number of first ascents, including the first assault on Monte Rosa – which Edmund celebrated by leaving his shirt flying from a pole on the summit of the Ostspitze.

In the following year Edmund Smyth volunteered for the

Crimea, where he was joined by Speke and Burton, both freshly scarred by the spear-wounds that had ended their first attempt to penetrate the African interior. All three officers were attached to a body of Turkish irregular cavalry known as the Bashi Bazouks. It was a period of bitter frustration for all the Indian Army officers present. Despite the fact that they were really the only seasoned group of officers that the British Army could call upon, prejudice against 'Nigger Army' officers, as they were widely known, prevented them from playing any useful part in the war. As the campaign dragged on Smyth and Speke spent much of their time drawing up plans for an ambitious shooting expedition that would take them over the Caucasus and round the Caspian Sea. But at the same time Richard Burton was preparing to make a second attempt on the Nile – and it was Smyth's intended companion that he chose to take with him on that second, fateful journey.

Three years later Smyth again missed his chance when invited by John Speke, the now famous discoverer of the source of the Nile, to join him on his third African expedition – only to be abruptly dropped for an officer from Speke's old regiment, James Grant. Speke evidently had a very high regard for Smyth, whom he describes in a letter to the Royal Geographical Society as 'a chap who won't go to the devil, full of pluck and straight-head foremost . . . a man of precisely my habits, and one entirely after my own heart.' But perhaps he was too much a man after Speke's heart for his ultimate comfort. 'Smyth is feverishly inclined,' was all Speke had to say by way of explanation, 'I won't have him with me . . . I am as hard as bricks.' What Smyth had to say about Speke is not recorded.

Meanwhile in India the sepoy mutiny that had flared up outside Calcutta in May 1857 had spread up the Gangetic plain to other regiments of the Bengal Army. All that summer the fate of the British in India hung in the balance, needing only the smallest shift in numbers from one side to the other to tip the scale. Smyth's regiment, the 13th BNI, was then stationed in Lucknow, where the Nawab of Oude had only recently been deposed by the British for alleged misgovernment. The majority of the sepoys there went over to the rebels

127

but three hundred men of the 13th BNI chose to remain faithful to their salt. They paid a high price for their loyalty, for during the eighty-seven days of the siege a third of their number were killed and a third wounded. But without them the small garrison at Lucknow could not have held out – and if Lucknow had fallen a second army of mutineers would have been freed to march on Delhi and drive the British out of India.

By the time Edmund Smyth got back to India the fighting was all but over. His regiment had been disbanded and the future of the Bengal Army was itself in doubt. During this uncertain and unhappy period Smyth was again able to escape to the mountains of Kumaon and Garhwal, climbing summer after summer in regions hitherto unvisited by Europeans. It is known that he liked to travel fast and light – very much in present-day alpine style – using a small two-man tent that he shared with his servant, but his mountaineering activities are largely unrecorded. Among his few known achievements was the reopening of a long disused pass between Niti and Badrinath, at the head of the famous 'Valley of Flowers' that British mountaineers were to rediscover sixty years later.

Another keen *shikari* who hunted over the same ground at this time was the Hon. Robert Drummond, a younger son of the Eighth Viscount Strathallan and a member of the Indian Civil Service. He, too, did things with a certain style; on his first Tibetan journey Drummond was said to have launched an 'India-rubber' boat on Manasarovar, 'to the great indignation of Hindus and Thibetans alike' – an act of sacrilege that resulted in the local Dzongpon (district governor) losing his head.

Neither Smyth nor Drummond ever publicly acknowledged having made such journeys – and with good reason: both were government servants who entered Tibet in direct defiance of a government ban, and who had nothing to show for it but antlers and skins. The records of the Indian Government for this period show only that one application by Edmund Smyth, to lead an expedition to Lhasa, was considered and rejected. For Robert Drummond the position was complicated

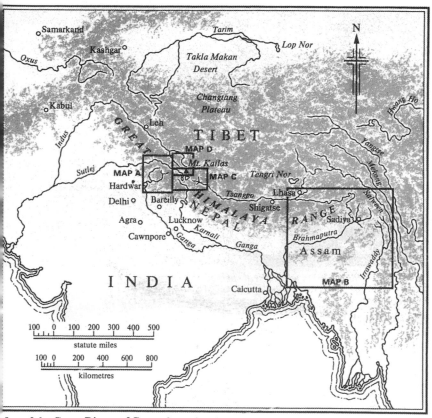

Map of the Great Rivers of Central and South Asia

The Drummond brothers gathered at their ancestral home in Perth. The Hon. Robert Drummond is seated second from the left; his elder brother, Edmund, 9th Viscount Strathallan, stands at his shoulder. (Lord Perth).

The south face of Kailas with its distinctive 'swastika' striations, observed by Dr Tom Longstaff and a companion after their unsuccessful attempt to climb Gurla Mandhata five years after Kawaguchi's visit to the holy mountain. (Royal Geographical Society)

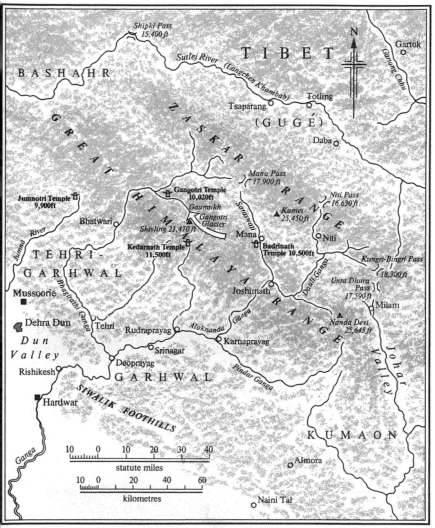

Map A: Uttarakhand and the Sources of the Ganga

The lion-hearted Kinthup, dressed in robes similar to those worn by him in Tibet, photographed in Simla shortly before his death in 1913. (Records of the Survey of India)

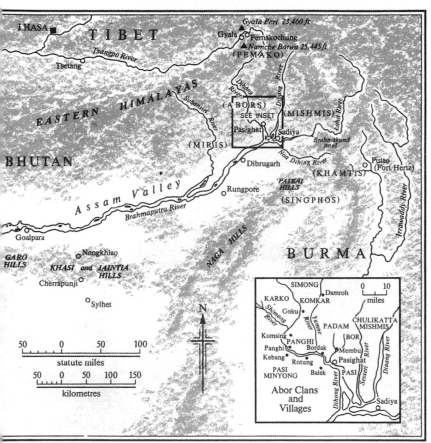

Map B: Assam and the Sources of the Brahmaputra

The English gentleman and the Japanese monk; Henry Savage Landor, in travelling attire, and Ekai Kawakuchi, dressed in the robes of a Tibetan lama.

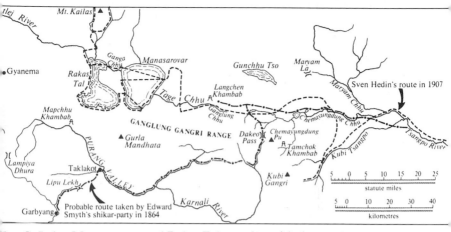

Map C: Lakes Manasarovar and Rakas Tal, together with the
sources of the Tsangpo-Brahmaputra.

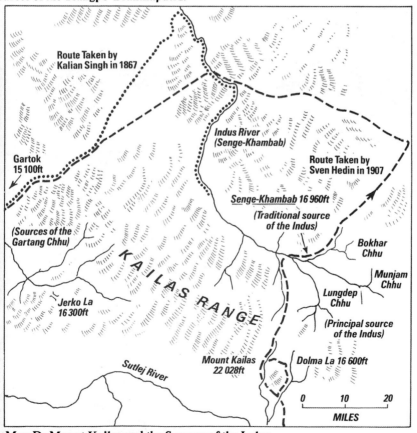

Map D: Mount Kailas and the Sources of the Indus

The sacred mountain: the sheer north face of Kailas, glimpsed by
only a handful of Europeans. Secretly photographed by the Swiss
geologist Augusto Gansser in July 1936.

by the fact that his elder brother happened to be the Lieutenant-Governor of the newly-formed North-Western Provinces.

It was not the first time that Drummond had proved to be a source of embarrassment to his brother. At the time of the outbreak of the Mutiny he had been acting as Magistrate and Collector at Agra, and it was at his insistence that the European population in that station had withdrawn to the fort there, leaving their homes to be looted and fired by the rebels. This firm action undoubtedly saved lives, but the manner in which he had performed his duties was greatly resented and shortly after the relief of Agra Drummond was transferred to Bundelkund, an arid plains district south of Patna that offered few attractions.

In 1861 Edmund Smyth was appointed to the newly-created post of Inspector of the Kumaon Circle Public Instruction Department, with instructions to set up Indian vernacular schools throughout the hills. It was not a demanding job and the prospects for advancement were nil but it offered marvellous opportunities for further mountaineering and *shikar* – as evidenced by the brief but lively guest appearances that Smyth makes in two sporting memoirs of the period. He features prominently as 'that well-known old Indian sportsman' in Major-General Donald McIntyre's *Hindu Koh; Wanderings and Wild Sports on and beyond the Himalayas* (published in 1889) and rather more dramatically in *Forests of Upper India*, the memoirs of a retired forest officer named Thomas Webber.

It was Webber's sporting reminiscences – written in his old age and published nearly forty years after the event took place – that revealed Smyth and Drummond to have been the first Europeans to reach at least one of the major sources of the Brahmaputra. Not altogether surprisingly, when the book was shown to the Swedish explorer Sven Hedin – newly returned from Tibet and claiming the discovery of the source of the Brahmaputra as his own – he dismissed it as worthless. He showed Webber's story to be riddled with inconsistencies, while the map that accompanied it was patently absurd. Yet the fact remains that a journey did take place, one that led four British sportsmen to the headwaters of the Brahmaputra four decades before Sven Hedin got there.

In the summer of 1864, at a prearranged rendezvous with Drummond and two other younger men, Smyth met the future author of *Forests of Upper India*, then a very junior forest officer, and a friend of his named Henry Hodgson. They had made their way into the hills independently – which points to this being a private and unauthorized expedition – and only joined up as a party at a village close to the Lipu Lekh pass. Webber informs us in his narrative that Smyth had come there a year earlier, intending to make for Lhasa, but had been turned back by armed Tibetans from Taklakar. Now the party was able to make quite a show with all its sporting rifles and shotguns as it crossed into Tibet, and when an ill-mounted troop of Tibetan horsemen charged upon them the sahibs, according to Webber, 'simply stood still and roared with laughter'. This reaction so unnerved the Tibetans that they retired in confusion.

As they passed Taklakar they were met by a second group of armed Tibetans, who 'threw themselves in front of us in a compact body, shouting with shrill, strange voices and making signs as if frantic. Some lay on the ground before us, imploring us to stop and drawing their hands rapidly across their necks'. This time it was the British who were put out, for it was plain that the unfortunate Tibetans had been ordered to stop them by non-violent means and risked losing their heads if they failed to do so. A conference was arranged, and over a bottle of Scotch Drummond and the Dzongpon of Taklakar came to an arrangement that allowed both sides to keep face. The Dzongpon would report back to Lhasa that after a great fight the foreign invaders had been diverted towards Nepal and, for their part, the sportsmen agreed to keep well away from the Manasarovar region and return to Taklakar within three weeks.

No doubt the Dzongpon thought he had got the best of the bargain, since the agreement barred the travellers from heading north up the Purang valley and so out onto the Tibetan plateau. He must therefore have watched the foreigners moving downriver and towards Nepalese territory with great satisfaction. What he did not know was that Smyth's Bhotia guides had told him of a high pass to the east of the Gurla Mandhata mountain massif known as the Dakeo or 'wall of death'. It was said to be an extremely difficult route but one that would bring them out onto the Tibetan plateau east of Manasarovar, to a region of 'extensive jungles, frequented by few natives and famous as the haunt of the rarest of all animals, the *bos grunniens* or wild yak'.

Webber records that they went down the Karnali river for some eighteen miles and then marched north-east along one of its feeders, skirting the southern slopes of Gurla Mandhata. A second day's march took them to the entrance of the pass and then on the third day they crossed the Dakeo pass itself – 'a *ghat* or passage between high walls of black basaltic rock, a veritable gate of death' – where by measuring the temperature at which water boiled they determined their altitude to be close on 20,000 feet. 'The scene was most weird,' Webber recalls in his book. 'The view of the peaks and glaciers when the cloud occasionally lifted was stupendous and bewildering. Goggles, of course, had to be worn, but some of the carriers who had neglected to tie on their crepe bandages were howling with pain, half blind.' With their yaks ploughing a path through the snow ahead of them the hunters struggled over the pass and made camp:

> We had now come out on the watershed of the Brahmaputra, having crossed the range which lies to the north of the Himalayas. Descending rapidly to the northward, we found wide valleys and grassy flats opening out, and all the streams trending towards the east.

It was Hedin's contention that Webber's party never crossed this second range and that it would have been impossible for them to have reached the watershed of the Brahmaputra within three days of leaving Taklakar. Sven Hedin devotes six pages of his monumental *Southern Tibet* (published in eight enormous volumes in 1917) to demolishing Webber's story point by point: 'There are no dates, no distances, no directions, no co-ordinates, no camps, so the reader is completely lost.' He concludes: 'If Webber has proved anything it is that he has never been at the source of that river [the Brahmaputra]. The fact is, as I have proved above, that

131

Webber never had the faintest idea where the source or sources was situated.'

Webber's map made him an easy target for Hedin's ridicule. He identifies the sources of the Sutlej as 'Sources of the Indus' and the sources of the Karnali as 'Sources of the Ganges'. How seriously, Hedin asks, can we take a man who can make such grotesque errors? He suggests that we should regard Webber's story as a romance or a 'phantom picture from the time of the Jesuits'. A less committed reader might feel that since Webber's story and sketch map were put together from memory nearly forty years after the event they deserve to be read with caution rather than scepticism. If Webber talks of three days to reach the Dakeo pass when in all likelihood it needed five or six it seems more reasonable to interpret this as a failure of memory rather than an attempt to construct a romance.

Webber tells us that the four sahibs hunted in pairs, the two older men – Smyth and Drummond – moving ahead and further afield while he and Hodgson stayed closer to their camp. However, on one occasion the younger men crossed 'another lofty divide' and found themselves looking down on the holy lake: 'Far beneath us, some miles away, lay the most brilliantly beautiful blue sea, the celebrated Manasarowar Lake, as it proved, which we had promised not to approach.'

From their vantage point Webber and Hodgson sat and munched biscuits, listened to the familiar sounds of skylarks and, 'as a record of our tramp', sketched the view:

The foreground was flat, rolling hills and ridges sloping gradually towards the lake, all bare and tinted in most crude colours – reds and pink and orange – while hundreds of miles to the north and west in the violet distance there stretched range after range of low, jagged hills, all alike and succeeding one another in endless succession. Conspicuous, and towering above them all, was the snowcapped summit of the sacred Kailas.

Hedin was not impressed by this description of the view. 'From the neighbourhood of none of the southern sources |of the Brahmaputra| can the lake be seen,' he declares. 'It is

132

invisible from the whole region of the uppermost Tsangpo.'
But Webber was not then at the southern sources but the
western ones, where the streams were 'trending towards the
east . . . into a great river which ran towards Lhasa'. Satellite
photographs of the Brahmaputra sources show this area as a
clearly defined rectangle of open ground, about twenty miles
by ten and dotted by lakes, lying between two mountain
ranges. The watershed between the Sutlej and Tsangpo-
Brahmaputra lies more or less at the centre of this rectangle,
at a distance of about thirty miles from Manasarovar. There
is no clearly marked ridge here separating the two catchment
areas, as Sven Hedin himself noted when he crossed the
watershed in July 1907, only a series of hills. If the *shikaris*
had indeed crossed the Dakeo pass into the eastern half of
that rectangle then Webber and Hodgson had only to climb
one of those hills – or the range that formed the northern
edge of the rectangle – to be able to see Manasarovar spread
out before them and Kailas in the distance.

On the day after their sighting of lake Manasarovar Webber
and Hodgson 'marched a long way eastward along the
northern slopes of the Gurla range, following the valley of the
Brahmaputra'. On the way they observed 'a very fine peak
called Limi belonging to this range, where some great glaciers
exist at the head of the valleys which debouch into the river
flowing towards the east'. Coming the other way forty-three
years later, Sven Hedin also observed an outstanding peak,
which he named Chemayungdung Pu, whose 'very extensive
glacier' fed the western tributary of the Tsangpo known as
the Chemayungdung Chhu.

Webber and Hodgson continued to a point where their
valley 'opened into wide plains, sloping gradually to the river
Tsampu [Tsangpo]'. From here they could see a great distance
down the main valley of the Tsangpo-Brahmaputra, even
distinguishing in the clear, rarefied air livestock and tents on
the camping-grounds of Tuksum, fifty miles downriver.
Webber noted that here, too, were the 'sources of the great
Brahmaputra, originating from the glaciers of Gurla'.

Hedin finds this sequence of events absurd, chiefly because
he chooses to interpret Webber's references to 'Gurla' and
'Gurla range' not as Webber himself defines it – as 'the range

running eastwards of Gurla Mandhata' – but as the Gurla Mandhata mountain itself. Since its main peak is over forty miles away from the most westerly of the Tsangpo-Brahmaputra feeders he deduces that Webber and Hodgson would have had to march some seventy miles in one day to cover the ground that they said they did. But the truth is that from their eyrie on the watershed Webber and Hodgson would have had to march no more than thirty miles before coming to a point where Tsangpo valley lay spread out before them.

Thanks to satellite photography we can now plot a more realistic course for Webber and his fellow-*shikaris* than that ascribed to them by Sven Hedin. There is in fact a high and difficult pass, the Takhu (Dakeo?) or Tabsi La, that cuts through Webber's Gurla Mandhata 'range' just west of the Chemayungdung massif, and if this is where the hunting party crossed into Tibet then they would have emerged onto one of the glaciers that feed the streams flowing into the Chemayungdung Chhu. Webber and Hodgson could then have had their view of Kailas from a high point on the Tsangpo-Sutlej watershed and afterwards marched down the broad, open Chemayungdung valley, observing that the river had its source in the glaciers at the foot of the 22,230-foot Chemayungdung Pu – which they knew as Limi. They then spent a week in this area 'hunting all the valleys for miles for yak,' while the two older men went after Hodgsonian antelope and Ovis Ammon. All the evidence in Webber's book, supported by a brief outline of the trip from General McIntyre, suggests that Smyth, Drummond, Webber and Hodgson have a good claim to the European title of discoverers not only of the longest, highest and most western source of the Brahmaputra but also its traditional source – for the Tibetans place the head of their Tamchok-Khambab at the glaciers of the Chemayungdung mountain.

Robert Drummond died in 1887 but Edmund Smyth was still alive when Webber's book was published in 1902. He was an active but silent Fellow of the Royal Geographical Society, apparently indifferent to the claims made on his behalf by others. But then he was, as Thomas Hughes had said, the 'queerest, coolest fish'. Indeed, he left only one really solid piece of public evidence about his Tibetan travels, a 'splendid specimen' of a wild yak that is to be found stuffed and mounted at Leeds Museum.

Edmund Smyth seems only once to have ventured into public print. This was in the form of a letter published in the Proceedings of the Geographical Society for the year 1882 and written after Smyth had received a report – false, as it turned out – of the death from cholera of the great Bhotia explorer known simply as 'The Chief Pundit', Nain Singh Rawat. Perhaps it was in this context, as the man who selected the first generation of that remarkable group of Indian explorers known collectively as the Pundits, that Edmund Smyth wished to be remembered.

The story of the Pundits has been told before, most notably and with the greatest artistic licence by Rudyard Kipling. In *Kim* the Pundits are linked inextricably with the political struggle between British India and Tsarist Russia known as the Great Game. In fact, the Pundits were never 'players of the Game' in the political sense, whatever Kipling and British public opinion in India may have wanted to believe. Secrecy, disguise and political subterfuge were certainly vital ingredients in their work, but the intelligence they gathered was essentially topographical and their masters were always the Survey of India.

By the middle of the nineteenth century the lack of accurate geographical information from beyond India's borders had become very apparent. Nowhere was this deficiency more obvious than in the vast unexplored regions of Tibet, where the famous Chinese imperial edict – that no Mogul, Hindustani, Pathan or *feringhi* should be admitted – was now being enforced with ever-increasing strictness. But if Europeans and other foreigners were forbidden to enter Tibet there were certain groups of semi-Tibetans, such as the Bhotias, who could do so.

The Survey of India had made good use of Indian assistants for many years but it had never thought to train them beyond a certain level or use them in anything but a subordinate capacity. It was now proposed that a number of carefully selected men from the border areas be engaged on a modest salary of sixteen rupees rising to twenty a month, to be trained in all the necessary skills, given an appropriate cover and disguise and then sent off on various missions across the border. The first of these men came from Johar.

In 1861 Edmund Smyth had appointed Nain Singh Rawat, the sharpest of the three Bhotia cousins who had worked for the Schlagintweits, as the headmaster of the government vernacular school in his home village:

In 1862–3 I was in correspondence with Colonel (then Captain) Montgomerie of the Survey of India – I think it was about an expedition I was going to make into Tibet – and hearing he wanted some trustworthy men to train as explorers in that region I strongly recommended him to engage some of these Bhotias, both on account of their sound knowledge of the Tibetan language and also because they had the entrée into the country. He asked me to select two and send them to him to be trained. I accordingly chose our friend Nain Singh, who was then employed as a Pundit (or schoolmaster) of the government school of Milum, in Johar, and the second man I chose was his cousin Manee or Maun Singh.

In 1863 Nain Singh and Mani Singh Rawat were sent down to the Great Trigonometrical Survey Offices at Dehra Dun, where they were first given practical instruction in such matters as taking latitude by sextant, direction by compass and height by boiling water. Then they began a more unusual course of instruction under the personal direction of Captain T. G. Montgomerie, a surveyor with a distinguished record of fieldwork in Kashmir. They learned to measure distances not with chains or perambulators but by being drilled by a sergeant-major with his pace-stick to take regular paces – two thousand paces to the mile and 31½ inches to each pace – with every hundredth pace being registered by the dropping of a bead on a rosary: not a standard Hindu or Buddhist rosary, which carries one hundred and eight beads, but a special Survey of India rosary eight beads short. They learned also to code their notes and measurements in the form of written prayers and to conceal them inside specially-adapted Tibetan prayer-wheels, and how to memorize details by constant repetition as they walked along, chanting them aloud in the way that Tibetans chant their prayers. They were taught how to assume all manner of disguises that would allow them to pass as traders or pilgrims or whatever role seemed best suited to the occasion. Finally they acquired their own professional working identities, *noms de guerre* that came usually in the form of a fairly simple sobriquet or by reversing the first and last letters of their names. Thus Nain Singh became known as 'the Chief Pundit' or 'No. 1' and his cousin Mani Singh as 'the Patwar' or 'GM' (from Mani SinG).

In the next few years Smyth sent other recruits from the Rawat clan to join this remarkable brotherhood of explorer-spies. Nain Singh's second cousin, Kalian Singh, became known as the 'Third Pundit' or 'GK', and another rather younger cousin, Kishen Singh, was known as 'Krishna' or 'AK'. It was this last cousin, Kishen Singh, who in time inherited Nain Singh's mantle and rose to become the greatest of the Pundit explorers. Appropriately enough, he was the son of Bir Singh, that other Bhotia brother who had helped Moorcroft and Hearsey so many decades earlier.

Partly because of the clandestine nature of their work, partly because that work has been regarded, since Indian Independence, as being in some way unpatriotic, the achievements of the Pundits have never been widely acknowledged. Yet it was through them that the outside world first gained detailed information about the Tibetan interior. When they entered the country only the Manasarovar area, one tiny corner in Western Tibet, had been mapped with accuracy. The rest of Tibet, all its river systems, its great lakes and vast mountain ranges, was still *terra incognita*, a blank waiting to be filled. At only one crossing point along its entire length had the course of Tibet's main artery, been accurately determined. The Pundits' first order was to put the Tsangpo clearly and accurately on the map.

Their earliest journey began in the summer of 1864; the same summer in which Smyth and his fellow-*shikaris* visited the sources of the Brahmaputra. In fact, as Nain Singh and Mani Singh made their way northwards from Milam they met Smyth coming the other way – a most inopportune meeting as it turned out, since the Tibetan border guards had been fully alerted. After conferring with Smyth the two cousins returned to Dehra Dun and made arrangements to enter Tibet by way of Kathmandu. However, this second attempt was equally unsuccessful; an unusually perceptive Dzongpon on the Tibetan border refused to believe that they were horse-dealers from the Punjab border-state of Bashahr. It was, he pointed out, not only the wrong time of the year for horse-trading but also the wrong place.

It was at this juncture that Nain Singh's strength of character first began to assert itself. Mani Singh admitted defeat and set off across Western Nepal towards his native Kumaon but 'No. 1' hung on in Nepal and eventually talked his way back into Tibet, this time disguised as a Ladakhi trader, complete with pigtail. He and a servant named Chhumbel managed to attach themselves to a caravan bound for Ladakh that was heading north to the Great River, and then westwards along the Tasam, the Lhasa-Leh highway.

They reached the Tsangpo in August 1865, but it was not the happiest of occasions, for while the travellers waited to be ferried across the river in coracles they saw one of these unstable-looking craft overturn, drowning its three passengers. They crossed the river higher up and eventually arrived at the large monastery of Tradom, beside the Lhasa-Leh trade route. Here Nain Singh had to choose between sticking with the Ladakhi caravan as it made its way westward up the Tsangpo valley or making his own way independently down-river towards Lhasa. The temptation to take the easier course must have been great but Nain Singh resisted it; he announced that he was sick and the caravan moved off without him.

It was too risky to think of going on to Lhasa without company so Nain Singh and Chhumbel sat it out at Tradom monastery and waited for another escort to come by. A month later a large body of traders from Ladakh appeared and Nain Singh introduced himself as a pilgrim in need of protection. The giving of such protection, as with alms or shelter, conferred merit on those who gave it so there were no objections to this most devout of pilgrims accompanying the caravan to Lhasa. Seeing him noisily immersed in his prayers by day and silently preoccupied with his curious rituals by

138

night – always performed at some distance from the tents – the Ladakhis left Nain Singh undisturbed. Nor did they find it odd that while they covered some sections of the journey down the Tsangpo valley by boat their pilgrim preferred to pace steadily along the river bank.

After a long halt at Shigatse, Tibet's second city and capital of the Tsang province, the caravan left the river and crossing over the mountains in bitterly cold winter weather arrived in Lhasa in January 1866. Nain Singh hired a couple of rooms on the top floor of the caravanserai where the Ladakhi traders had established themselves and from its windows took observations of the stars with his sextant, putting the Holy City firmly and indisputably on the map.

At first Nain Singh explored Lhasa without any fears for his safety, even securing a brief audience with the *Gyalpo Rinpoche* or Dalai Lama, a 'fair and handsome boy' of thirteen who clearly exercised no real authority at the Lhasa court. But after a month his funds began to run out and to supplement them Nain Singh started to give lessons in book-keeping. This revelation of Western learning aroused the suspicions of two Moslem merchants who questioned him so persistently that he was forced to reveal his true identity. Soon afterwards he saw the Dzongpon of Kyirong riding through the streets of Lhasa – the same man who had penetrated the Pundits' original cover as Bashahri horse-traders. These two events were followed by a third – the public execution of a Chinese monk – which convinced Nain Singh that Lhasa was no longer a safe place for him. To his relief he learned that the Ladakhi traders were almost ready to return to Leh with a consignment of Chinese brick-tea and would be happy to find a place for him in their caravan.

They left Lhasa in mid-April and for the first six weeks Nain Singh retraced his footsteps to Tradom monastery. West of the monastery the Tasam road never veered far from the river; it was a well-worn track marked at intervals by *lapchas* – which made the taking of compass bearings much easier for Nain Singh. A frequent sight that made a great impression on him were the special messengers galloping between staging posts, exhausted men with cracked faces and sunken eyes, often with wounds and sores on their bodies. This relay system was the key to Tibet's security, for these messengers were required to cover the 800 miles between Lhasa and Gartok in twenty days and were forbidden to halt except to eat and change horses. The letters they carried were tucked inside their long-sleeved, all-enveloping *chogas* and closed at the breast with a special seal that only the official to whom the letter was addressed was allowed to break.

Early in June the caravan crossed the grazing meadows of Tuksum – seen in the far distance by Webber only two years earlier – where sheep, goats, horses and yak were gathered in vast numbers. From here they began a slow climb which took them to the head of the valley and the crest of the Maryum La. According to Captain Montgomerie's account of the Pundit's journey, based on Nain Singh's notes and a verbal report, the road led 'to the north of the main source of the Brahmaputra, and within sight of the gigantic glaciers which give rise to the great river'. Unable to leave the caravan route Nain Singh could only observe this source, which he fixed at 'about north latitude 30½° and east longitude 82°'.

From the Maryum La the highway went down past the ten-mile-long Gunchhu lake and on to Manasarovar, where Nain Singh and Chhumbel left the caravan and crossed over the border to Milam. In due course Nain Singh reported to Montgomerie at Mussoorie, where the Survey had established a station on the Landour ridge. 'The Pundit' had been out of British territory for eighteen months.

From the Survey of India's point of view Nain Singh's journey was a triumphant vindication of Western scientific method and training, even though it owed far more to resourcefulness and courage than to anything else. But it was a method that worked – and was too good not to be tried again. Montgomerie saw an obvious and tempting gap of unexplored country between the territory that he himself had surveyed in Ladakh and that covered by Nain Singh and others since Moorcroft's time in the Manasarovar region:

It appeared to me very desirable that this gap should be filled up, the more especially as it embraced a portion of what was said to be the course of the great river Indus, a

140

portion, moreover, that had never been traversed by any European.

Montgomerie was aware that a number of Europeans – the Schlagintweits as well as Moorcroft and Hearsey – had travelled down part of what they had believed to be the main branch of the Indus, but he took a different view: 'The information I have received led me to think that there was a large eastern branch of that river.' The search for this eastern branch, as well as the exploration of the fabled goldfields that were said to lie beyond became the Pundits' next objective.

By now Nain Singh and Mani Singh had been joined by the 'Third Pundit', a strapping young man named Kalian Singh Rawat. The three cousins chose to make their approach by way of Badrinath and the Mana pass and in the familiar guise of Bashahri horse-traders. After collecting a good stock of merchandise and asses to carry them, they crossed into Tibet in midsummer 1867 and in less than a fortnight had reached the Gartok branch of the upper Indus, known to the Tibetans as the Gartang Chhu. Skirting the tents of Gartok they climbed the mountains to the north-east and found themselves on a vast and desolate plateau known as the antelope plain. A grim six-day ride across this waterless table-land brought them to the banks of a large river flowing towards the north. Nomads camped nearby confirmed that they had reached the Senge-Chhu or Lion River – the name by which the Indus is known in Tibet.

Their satisfaction at having reached what was clearly the larger tributary of the Indus was cut short, however, by the hostility of the nomads when they announced that they were horse-traders from Bashahr. The nomad chief flatly refused to accept their story, for if they had been Bashahris, he said, they would never have dared to admit it. Some Bashahri traders had brought smallpox into Tibet the year before and as a result all travellers from Bashahr were forbidden entry to Tibet. The leader went on to assert, with devastating accuracy, that in his opinion they were Bhotias from Milam and very probably working with the British.

Concealing their shock as best they could the three Pundits tried to persuade the chief that, whoever they might be, they

141

intended no harm. Eventually it was decided that Mani Singh would stay behind in the nomad encampment, together with the asses and their loads, while the other two explored further afield. At Nain Singh's direction, Kalian Singh set off with one porter, with orders to follow the Indus south to its source – while the Chief Pundit himself crossed the river and set out northwards for the goldfields.

A hard four-day climb over a high snow-range brought Nain Singh out on a new plateau, a windy plain dotted with small piles of earth like ant hills – the excavations of the fabled goldfield of Thok Jalung. There is a curious story told by Herodotus of a great desert north of India inhabited by giant ants, who threw up nuggets of gold as they burrowed in the ground. Nain Singh's visit provided some support for this story, for while there were no giant ants he did find large numbers of miners living with their families more or less permanently underground. Even as he approached the first diggings he could hear, but not see, the diggers singing in chorus as they worked. It was then high summer, but Nain Singh thought it the coldest place he had ever visited, with a chilling wind blowing ceaselessly across the 17,000-foot plateau. It was to avoid this wind that the goldminers stayed below ground, pitching tents inside their digs and sleeping in a most extraordinary position: 'They invariably draw their knees close up to their heads and rest on their knees and elbows, huddling every scrap of clothing they can muster on to their backs.' Despite their privations, Nain Singh found the miners and their families to be remarkably cheerful and always ready to break into song – and if their methods seemed a little crude that did not prevent them from digging up plenty of gold; even as he watched Nain Singh saw unearthed a nugget weighing more than two pounds.

While the Chief Pundit was visiting the goldfields of Thok Jalung, the Third Pundit made his way up the valley of the Senge-Chhu. The river's course took him south-east for some distance and then swung round to the south, leading him directly towards Mount Kailas – but also into a region notorious as prime bandit country. Its reputation appeared fully justified when Kalian Singh's porter was ambushed by three nomads. The attackers had been waiting for a moment when the two travellers became separated and when this happened they jumped on the porter and began to wrest his pack from him. Fortunately, Kalian Singh saw what was happening and came to the rescue; he swung one assailant round by his pigtail and threw him to the ground, whereupon the other two ran off.

After another day's march they reached the last inhabited site on the river and Kalian Singh was warned that it would be madness to think of going further along the valley. He turned back, with great reluctance and knowing that only 'three or four marches more' would have brought him to his goal. From his local informants he learned that the Indus took its rise at the base of a snowpeak, where it was called the Senge-Khambab. The surrounding mountains had remained shrouded in mist and cloud throughout this period, making it impossible to get any bearings, but what was now certain was that the sources of the Indus would be found where legend had long placed them – close to the northern slopes of the holy mountain.

All this valuable new information reached Captain Montgomerie shortly before he sailed for England on furlough, with the result that in March 1868 he was able to present to a meeting of the Royal Geographical Society the first public account of the work of the Pundits. He took some trouble to conceal their identities and origins, and it would be many years before the remarkable accuracy of Nain Singh's work could be verified and recognized as such, but even so his achievements were widely applauded by European geographers. In the circumstances, the award of a gold watch by the RGS seems rather less then generous, but it was, after all, only a beginning.

There was still plenty of exploration to be done, as Montgomerie was at pains to point out at the end of his address. The Ganga, Sutlej and Indus had been traced almost throughout the whole of their respective courses but one mystery remained to be resolved:

This last exploration [by Nain Singh] tends to show that Wilcox was right in concluding that the great river which flows through the Lhasa territory is the upper course of the

143

Brahmaputra, the largest river in India. Positive proof as to whether this river is or is not the upper course of the Brahmaputra can only be afforded by tracing the river from Lhasa downwards. Every endeavour will be made to supply this missing link.

Chapter 7

The 'Missing Link':
the Exploration of the
Tsangpo Gorge

In unadministered frontier areas and Indian native states the authority of the British Raj was usually vested in the political agent or the political officer. His powers were limited, so his effectiveness as an administrator was largely dependent on the degree to which he could impose his will on peoples who were often actively engaged in resisting government attempts to curtail their independence. In consequence politicals tended to be strong-minded individuals who, because they often served for long periods in isolated corners, tended to become a little idiosyncratic – if not downright eccentric – in their ways.

One such political who left his mark on the North-East Frontier was John Butler, who had special charge of the hill tribes from 1844 until his retirement in 1865. His son, also called John, followed him into political service on the Assam frontier and was later killed in an ambush in the Naga hills. The older Butler had a great reputation as an up-country character or what his fellow Anglo-Indians would call an 'old *Koi Hai*', being chiefly remembered for his habit of touring with two glass windows, which were inserted into the bamboo walls of the *bashas* and huts in which he put up for the night. It was largely on Butler's advice that the government followed a policy of non-interference with the awkward and intractable peoples scattered along the edges of the Assam valley. This was perfectly satisfactory so long as the tribals kept to themselves, less so when they came down to raid the plains.

The greatest mischief-makers were the Abors, those same aggressive defenders of their privacy who in the 1820s had

145

stopped Bedford, Wilcox and Burlton from exploring the Dihong river. In 1858 they attacked a village within cannon-shot of the military headquarters at Dibrugarh, killing a number of villagers. A punitive force was at once sent after the raiders, only to be drawn deep into the Abor hills and ambushed. Retiring in disorder, the government forces were harried and repeatedly ambushed all the way back to Dibrugarh, with considerable loss of life. So cockahoop were the Abors after this episode that they sent a challenge down to the plains, calling upon the British to give them a return match.

It was now decided to restore the prestige of the Raj by 'inflicting such chastisement as will teach these savages to respect its power'. This second military expedition, complete with elephant-drawn howitzers, was as much of a fiasco as the first and ended with the loss of three of its officers. A third expedition in 1862 ended in a political victory for the Abors when it was agreed that they would keep to their tribal lands in return for government *posa*, the annual payment in cash or kind of a sum amounting to 3400 rupees. This Danegeld did little to stem the raiding and the depredations continued, presenting a contant threat to the new tea gardens that were fast taking over from the jungle scrub in the alluvial plain. A further element in this policy of appeasement was the prohibition of any kind of mapping or exploration into sensitive tribal areas, which meant that any attempt to close Montgomerie's 'missing link' would have to be made from the Tibetan rather than the Indian side of the Himalayas.

After his two Tibetan missions Nain Singh Rawat had taken over the role of instructor at Captain Montgomerie's academy for aspiring Pundits, where his first and most brilliant pupil was his younger cousin, Kishen Singh Rawat. By then Mani Singh had been pensioned off but Nain Singh's other cousin, the stalwart Kalian Singh who had so nearly reached the source of the Indus, was still active in the field. In 1868 he travelled through Western Tibet from Ladakh to Shigatse, crossing the ice-covered Brahmaputra in mid-December and making his way back through Nepal. Three years later it was twenty-one-year-old Kishen Singh's turn. In July 1871 he led a party to Lhasa by way of the holy lake and was able to map 300 miles of unexplored country north of the capital before being set upon by bandits and robbed of everything but his surveying instruments. After a nightmare journey back to Lhasa, Kishen Singh successfully brought his party back to India.

In the meantime Nain Singh Rawat had been attached to a British mission in Chinese Turkestan. When it pulled back to Ladakh in 1873 General Walker, the new Surveyor-General, suggested that here was an opportune moment to send 'No. 1' on a final mission. 'He does not at all fancy having much more exploration,' wrote the General, but he thought that Nain Singh could be prevailed upon to 'make one grand push' if he knew it was going to be his last.

So, with a little arm-twisting and the offer of a generous pension that would be waiting for him when he came home, Nain Singh Rawat was induced to make his grand push, with orders to make for Lhasa along a more northerly route than had so far been attempted, and from there either to attach himself to a China-bound caravan or follow the course of the Tsangpo down to India. He set off from Leh in July 1874, taking with him three companions, one of whom was his personal servant, Chhumbel. This time they travelled as Ladakhi monks, with their belongings stowed in packs on the backs of a herd of sheep, moving at a grazing pace eastward for a thousand miles until they came to the lakeland region where Nain Singh's younger cousin had been robbed in 1871. In view of the argument that was to rage thirty-five years later it is worth noting that it was on this second great traverse, not on his first, that Nain Singh saw and noted the existence of 'a vast snowy range lying parallel to and north of the Brahmaputra river'.

Skirting the lake of Tengri Nor the Pundit led his caravan to Lhasa, where to his consternation he almost immediately picked up a rumour of his impending arrival. He became even more alarmed when he ran into a Ladakhi trader of doubtful character who knew him to be in the employ of the Government of India. Fearing that he was about to be betrayed Nain Singh lost no time in getting out of the city. To throw any pursuers off his scent he marched eastwards along the Peking highway for two days and then abrubtly left the road and took his party up into the mountains into the south. A few days later he and his companions found themselves looking down into the Tsangpo valley.

They followed the river downstream for about thirty miles to the town of Tsetang. Here they left the Tsangpo and made their way south over the Himalayan range. Once they had reached Assam Nain Singh enlisted the help of the local Assistant Commissioner and brought his party down to Calcutta in a river steamer. It was undoubtedly his own poor health that accounted for the Chief Pundit's abrupt termination of the march down the Tsangpo: prolonged exposure to the harsh Tibetan climate had seriously damaged his eyesight, making it almost impossible for him to continue his surveying.

Now 'No. 1' was at last allowed to retire, with a pension and a plains village granted to him as his *jagir*. In 1877, the year in which Queen Victoria was proclaimed Empress of India, he was made a Companion of the new Order of the Indian Empire (CIE) and awarded the Patron's Gold Medal of the Royal Geographical Society, the highest honour that the geographical world could bestow.

Rai Bahadur Nain Singh Rawat Milamwal lived on in comfortable retirement in the Johar valley for many years, finally dying of a heart attack while on a visit to his *jagir* in 1895. Besides his fellow-Pundits there were others in the Rawat clan who maintained the tradition of service either in the Survey of India or in the armed forces, right up to the present day. One of those who reached the summit of Everest during the successful Indian expedition of 1965 was Harish Chandra Rawat, a grandson of Kishen Singh Rawat.

It was Kishen Singh, long regarded as Nain Singh's natural successor as the leading Pundit, who took on the work that his elder cousin had been forced to abandon. In 1878 he was ordered rather bluntly by General Walker to proceed to Lhasa and to keep going until he reached Mongolia. Four and a half years passed before 'A-K' and his one surviving companion – the faithful Chhumbel, whom he had inherited from Nain Singh – reappeared in India. Penniless and dressed in rags, they amused themselves by wandering through Kishen

148

Singh's native village of Milam begging for alms. His friends and relatives there had long since given him up for dead, and when he eventually revealed his identity they refused to believe him. Even his wife failed to recognize him, and it was not until Kishen Singh had given the right answers to a series of questions that she agreed to let him enter his own house.

Most of Kishen Singh's efforts had been concentrated on the exploration of Northern Tibet, but he too had attempted to return to India by way of the Brahmaputra. He had taken an extraordinarily difficult route from China which cut across the headwaters of the Mekong, Salween and Irrawaddy and brought him to a point only just short of the Lohit branch of the Brahmaputra. After hearing fearful stories of the savagery of the Mishmis, whose lands he would have had to cross if he went any further, he decided to turn back. He had then made his way to Lhasa along the watershed between the Tsangpo and Irrawaddy river systems – and in so doing had established once and for all that the two rivers were well and truly separated.

There now remained no more than 300 miles of unexplored country between the point where Nain Singh had left the Great River at Tsetang and the gap in the Abor hills out of which the Dihong emerged onto the Assam plains. It was known that Tsetang stood at nearly 10,000 feet above sea level and Pasighat a mere 500 feet – but how and where did the water from the one point reach the other? Did it squeeze through the Himalayan chain in a series of tight bends or drop in a succession of cataracts? Were there mighty gorges, or even one great waterfall to rival the Victoria Falls, still waiting to be discovered? The possibilities – and the speculation – were endless.

In 1878 the challenge was taken up by Lieutenant Henry Harman of the Survey of India, who had already spent some time in Sadiya measuring the flow of the various Brahmaputra feeders before being transferred to survey work in the hills and mountains round Darjeeling. Described in Survey reports as 'fertile in ideas' and 'enthusiastic to rashness', Harman immediately set to work to learn Tibetan, employing as his *munshi* Sikkimese *sirdar*, a foreman of coolies from a road-building gang, named Nem Singh. This was not so that

Harman could himself go to Tibet; the system of using surrogate explorers like the Pundits had now become too entrenched for this to be possible and, under General Walker, an element of exploitation had undoubtedly begun to show itself.

Sirdar Nem Singh had none of the qualities that distinguished the Bhotia Pundits, and he lacked their familiarity with conditions inside Tibet; nevertheless, when he showed an interest in Harman's work he was at once dispatched to the home of the retired Chief Pundit in Kumaon for a crash course on clandestine surveying. On his return to Darjeeling in October 1878 Nem Singh, now code-named 'G-M-N' (from NeM SinGh), was immediately put across the Tibetan border with orders to follow the Tsangpo downstream from Tsetang as far as he could go. Accompanying him as his servant and companion was one of the Sirdar's coolies, an illiterate, brawny young man named Kinthup, the 'Almighty One'.

The two men followed the Tsangpo due east from Tsetang for about 120 miles (see map B). Then as it approached the final 'upward' curve of the eastern end of the Himalayan chain the river made a 45° shift in course and turned towards the north-east, continuing in this direction for another hundred miles, still flowing placidly through a wide valley. Gradually birch and oak forests took over from the familiar Tibetan scrub, villages and other signs of human occupation became fewer and the walls of the valley started to close in. Ahead of them there rose what seemed to be an unbroken wall of rock and snow, pushing out across the path of the river. Two magnificent peaks stood out above the rest; the breasts of the goddess Dorje Phangmo, Demchog's consort, now known as Namche Barwa and Gyala Peri. At the foot of the first of these peaks the river turned northwards, dropping into a deep gorge and changing within the space of a few miles from a wide, smooth-flowing river into a roaring torrent of white water, with less than a hundred yards between its banks.

Climbing up onto the terraces above the gorge the two men could see and hear how the river first doubled back on its tracks and swung westwards for a short distance before finding a passage that brought it back round to the east again,

150

until finally it was seen to disappear not round but *between* the two mountain peaks – which formed, in fact, the portals of a gigantic cleft in the Himalayan wall.

This was as far as Nem Singh and Kinthup went, to a small village named Gyala, which they estimated to be 8000 feet above sea level. But they made inquiries and learned that below Gyala the river entered a mighty gorge that led down to the country of Pemako, whose inhabitants spoke their own language and followed customs that were very different from those of the Tibetans. From Pemako the Tsangpo passed through another, wilder country before finally reaching the Indian plains.

The two Sikkimese might have been pardoned for thinking that 'G-M-N''s report on their journey would be enthusiastically received in Darjeeling – but it was not. Henry Harman had expected too much from his amateur Pundit; when he found that Nem Singh had more or less made up his figures as he went along his reaction was to sack him and appoint a new Pundit to take his place. As it turned out, this, too, was a disastrous error of judgment.

'G-M-N''s replacement was a Mongolian lama, a temporary visitor to Darjeeling with no strong ties to guarantee his return. His lack of scientific training presented no particular handicap, however, since all Harman wanted him to do was to perform a comparatively simple task – but one that would provide incontrovertible proof that the Tsangpo and Brahmaputra were one. With Kinthup acting as his guide, the lama was to proceed to the point on the river at which the two Sikkimese had turned back. Here – while Harman and his men kept watch at the Assam end of the river – he was to cut five hundred logs to a prescribed length, drill a hole in each, insert a short metal tube and then throw the logs into the Tsangpo at the rate of fifty a day over a prearranged period.

The scheme was an ingenious one, and would probably have worked but for the fact that the Mongolian lama was a complete rogue. Before they had even crossed into Tibet he had drunk and gambled away most of the Survey's money, and Kinthup had been forced to use his own funds to buy the lama out of an entanglement with another man's wife. After

151

seven months of dawdling they finally reached Gyala in March 1881, and even penetrated some distance into the great gorge, ending up at a small monastery called Pemakochung perched above the river. From here, according to the official version of his report, Kinthup saw the Tsangpo plunge over a 150-foot waterfall into a large pool.

Why at this point the Mongolian lama and Kinthup did not sit down and prepare their logs remains a mystery. Perhaps it was because they had missed the agreed date for their launching and had assumed that Harman would have given up waiting. Whatever the reason, the Mongolian lama now decided it was time for him to return to his native land. His final gesture was to sell the luckless Kinthup into slavery.

After seven months of servitude Kinthup managed to escape, but instead of heading back to Darjeeling as might have been expected, he elected, heroically, to complete the lama's task. Finding it impossible to get any further into the Tsangpo gorge from the north he made a detour over the surrounding mountains until he came to what was clearly the southern end of the gorge. Here there was another monastery, which Kinthup had just entered when servants dispatched by his former slavemaster caught up with him. After a tussle the head abbot intervened and bought Kinthup for fifty rupees.

Although still a slave Kinthup now found himself in happier circumstances, and after four months at the monastery he was given leave to make a short pilgrimage downriver. This gave him the opportunity to cut and prepare his 500 logs and hide them in a cave beside the river. Before they could be launched, however, he had first to inform the Survey of India of his plans, so after a two-month interval he asked for permission to go on a second pilgrimage, to Lhasa. Here he found a fellow-countryman from Sikkim to whom he dictated a letter to be delivered to Sirdar Nem Singh in Darjeeling. The letter – which Nem Singh was expected to translate into Enlish and pass on to Lieutenant Harman – was a masterpiece of restraint:

Sir, the Chinese lama who was sent with me sold me to a Jongpon as a slave and himself fled away with government instruments that were in his charge. On account of this, the journey proved a bad one. However, I, Kinthup, have prepared 500 logs according to the order of Captain Harman and am prepared to throw 50 logs per day into the Tsangpo river from Bipung in Pemako, from the 5th to the 15th of the tenth Tibetan month of the year called Chhuluk of the Tibetan calculation.

After seeing his fellow-Sikkimese safely out of Lhasa Kinthup returned to his monastery, passing up a third chance of escape to serve his head lama for another nine months. When it was time for the logs to be launched he again asked for leave to go on pilgrimage – and was told by the head lama that his devotion to his faith had won him his freedom. He made his way back to his cave and in mid-November 1883, over a period of ten days, finally launched his logs. Having completed his self-appointed task Kinthup then set out to close the 'missing link'. He very nearly succeeded. He walked south alongside the river for several days until he came to the land of the Simong Abors, where the men wore little else beside breech-cloths and always carried swords and bows. Here he found himself being increasingly harassed and threatened as he passed through their villages and finally, at the Padam Abor village of Damroh, he turned back. By his own calculations he was only thirty-five miles from British territory.

After an absence of four years, of which two had been spent in servitude, Kinthup returned to Darjeeling – where he learned that his message had never reached its intended destination: his logs must have floated unnoticed through Assam to the sea. Nem Sing had died some two years earlier of malaria and had never read Kinthup's letter. Captain Harman was also dead. He had kept watch on the Dihong river for many months, still hoping to catch sight of the logs, but in the end had abandoned the project and returned to his surveying in the mountains. In the summer of 1882 he had suffered severe exposure while mapping the 18,000-foot Donkya pass leading from Sikkim into Tibet and had been brought back to Darjeeling with frost-bitten feet and lungs.

He was invalided out of the service and died in Florence in the following spring.

With neither his former employer nor his friend alive to support him Kinthup found that his story carried little weight. However, this scarcely explains his appalling treatment at the hands of Harman's successors. His 'dogged obstinacy' was noted with approval but the contents of his report, which was taken down and translated into English, were almost entirely disregarded – apart from the reference to the 150-foot waterfall, which matched public expectations. There was no expression of thanks for Kinthup's exceptional devotion to what he saw as his duty and no offer of support or compensation for what he had endured.

According to popular legend, Kinthup disappeared into the backstreets of Darjeeling, where he scraped together a living working as a tailor – a skill that he had acquired as a slave in Tibet. However, the records of the Survey show that Kinthup continued to work for them on a casual basis; a year after his return from Tibet he accompanied another of the Survey's Pundits on a circuit of Bhutan – although still working as a servant. Six years later, in 1892, he was being employed as an expedition *sirdar* by Dr Waddell on his reconnaissance of Mount Kangchenjunga. Waddell's vivid portrait of the Sikkimese suggests that Kinthup bore his disappointments lightly and was more than capable of looking after himself, He describes him as:

> a thick-set, active man with a look of dogged determination on his rugged, weather-beaten features. His deep-chested voice I have often heard calling clearly from a hill-top some miles away, like a ship's captain in a storm. He has all the alertness of a mountaineer and with the strength of a lion he is a host in himself.

If there was anyone in India of Kinthup's generation who could match him for 'dogged obstinacy' it was a contemporary of his named Jack Needham. For a period both men were actually working towards the same goal at the same time, Kinthup from the north and Needham from the south –

154

although it is unlikely that either knew of the other's existence.

Jack Needham was possibly the most remarkable and least rewarded of the many British officers who worked on the North-East Frontier during the British period. His record of twenty-three years' unbroken service at Sadiya suggests either that he refused to accept any alternative posting or that there was a strong reluctance on the part of the Assam Government to promote him. Indeed, what evidence there is suggests that he was just the sort of unorthodox figure who most upset those in authority. He was difficult to handle, he quarrelled with his colleagues and would not put up with what he regarded as interference, but at the same time he clearly had a genius for establishing a rapport with tribal peoples – so much so that it was noted, against him, that he allowed himself to be 'cheeked by the men and pulled about by the young women'. Above all it was said of him that 'he had a dash', an enthusiasm and an energy that he concentrated on one particular subject: 'Needham's eyes were constantly turned towards the north and he lost no chance of gleaning information on the unknown tract.'

Needham came from one of the established Protestant families of Northern Ireland, where the export of younger sons of the gentry had long been a vital ingredient in the shaping of British India. He was a grandson of the 1st Earl of Kilmorey and the eldest of a family of fifteen, several of whom followed him to India. He began his career in the Bengal Police and his appointment as Assistant Political Officer at Sadiya started a tradition of police service in political posts that was unique to Assam.

In 1884 Needham became the first British officer to enter Abor territory for thirty years. He was received by the villagers of Membu in a relaxed, if not entirely friendly, manner. Having learned to speak the Abor tongue fluently he was able to communicate on a very informal level with his hosts. 'They could not understand why I had come up empty-handed,' he wrote in a characteriscally unguarded report. 'No amount of even legitimate excuses seemed to satisfy them, for they grumbled out, "Oh you are a pretty Saheb to come here in this manner".' Like Wilcox and Burlton sixty years earlier, Needham and a 'private gentleman' who had come with him were then forced to submit to a very public examination of their persons:

> Each and everything we wore was felt, and then we were asked to take off our things. We took off our coats and explained that we had got nothing on under our *banians* [loose cotton shirts], but until we had opened these also the gaping crowd were incredulous, and they appeared to disbelieve their eyesight, as they put their hands on our skins and felt our chests. Then we had to take off our boots and socks, as they declared we had not feet, and when we had done so, the girls got hold of our feet and petted them as an old maid would a friend's pet lap dog. The women, I may here remark, are excessively rollicky and jolly, and the unmarried girls have apparently any amount of latitude given to them. They are utterly shameless.

The report must have caused a few eyebrows to be raised in government circles since Needham had no qualms about writing in explicit terms about Abor sexual practices. He displayed the same frankness in his private life, living quite openly with a tribal girl from the attractive Miri river people in his bungalow in Sadiya. Half a century earlier this would have caused no comment but now, in the era of high Raj, any form of sexual alliance between the rulers and their subjects was frowned upon. Such liaisons, it was officially argued, could only demean the former in the eyes of the latter and so undermine the prestige of the master race. Needham thought otherwise; when asked by a local missionary to get rid of his *bibi*, as it was causing a scandal, he replied that he was damned if he would – and married her instead.

Needham found much to admire in the Abors' social code: 'Wives are treated by their husbands with a consideration as marked as it is singular in so rude a race.' Cases of adultery were rare, but where they did occur the punishments were discriminatory to say the least. Male adulterers had to pay a fine that varied from four to eight *mithun* or domesticated Indian bison 'according to the nature of the case', with the aggrieved party opening proceedings by 'going to the adul-

156

terer and giving him a severe crack on the head with the back of his *dao*.' But if the woman was held to be partly to blame she suffered a penalty that was very clearly intended to fit the crime: 'Viz. stripped and tied up and, a chillie having been inserted into her vagina, she is kept tied up until she is almost hoarse from roaring on account of the pain it causes, and this is done in front of the whole village.'

After a tribal dance in their honour in the evening Needham and his companion retired to their tent, both sleeping with revolvers under their pillows. The next morning they were summoned to a conference in the *morang* or tribal long-house, which Needham measured by pacing it out and found to be eighty yards long and ten wide, with twenty-four fireplaces laid out along the floor. Its side walls were crammed with hunting trophies and all down the centre were bamboo trays containing arms and cane armour of every description. When Needham protested about the heat and smoke from the fires and asked if they could gather under the shade of a tree instead he was met with a howl of protest and told that he would have to put up with it whether he liked it or not. So he sat it out and talked for the best part of a day, determined that nothing would prevent him from building up friendly relations with the Abors.

Eventually a dialogue of sorts was re-established between the Abors and the Government, but it was not an easy one to maintain. The Abors had asked for wire to strengthen their cane bridges, but when Needham returned to Membu with the wire and an engineer to help install it the villagers refused to accept it. Subsequent visits only confirmed Needham's fear that the tribe was 'so excessively suspicious' that the chances of a non-military expedition being allowed to explore up the Dihong were minimal.

Needham's hopes of leading a peaceful expedition through Abor country had come no nearer to fruition when, in December 1893, Padam Abors from Bomjur village raided a Miri settlement and made off with a number of captives. While negotiations were in progress for their release three sepoys from the military police were killed in an ambush. On Needham's advice a punitive force of five hundred infantry-men and police was assembled, under the military command of a Captain Maxwell but with Needham as its political officer. It advanced on Bomjur village but, finding it to be deserted, moved against a neighbouring village, Dambuk, which was stormed and taken after fierce hand-to-hand fighting. Several other settlements in the vicinity were razed before Needham settled down to peace negotiations with local headmen.

These talks convinced Needham that the real source of all the trouble among the Padam Abors was to be found some distance to the north at Damroh, the village where Kithup had been forced to turn back on his one-man expedition down the Tsangpo. If Damroh could be subdued then Needham believed that effective resistance among the Abors on the left bank of the Dihong would be ended for good. He telegraphed the Chief Commissioner of Assam for authority to proceed to Damroh, adding that if he would also give him permission to go on northwards from Damroh it would allow the question of the Tsangpo-Brahmaputra connection to be solved once and for all. The Chief Commissioner's reply was brief and to the point: 'Advance on Damroh but no further.'

Because of a shortage of porters Needham and Maxwell decided to leave the bulk of their food and supplies behind, taking with them only enough food to last them eight days. These supplies, together with a small force of some sixty sepoys and camp followers, were left at the small Padam Abor village of Bordak, on the river bank not far above Pasighat.

The column spent a week hacking its way through the jungle before it became obvious to his joint commanders that they were still nowhere near their goal. Then as the column was preparing to retire, runners arrived with the news that the supply depot at Bordak had been destroyed. Returning by forced marches with an advance party Needham found the camp completely gutted. There were twenty-seven dead bodies lying scattered over the site and a further nine were later recovered from the jungle. From a wounded *dhobi* who had managed to jump into the river Needham learned that a group of Abors had entered the camp pretending to be porters and at a given signal had drawn their *daos* and rushed the guard.

The massacre at Bordak not only destroyed Jack Needham's career but also his chances of further exploring Abor territory, for he was never again allowed to exercise any local initiative in his dealings with them. While he and Maxwell blamed each other, both were publicly censured by the Government of India, the one for failing to take elementary military precautions and the other for his 'want of judgement and political foresight.'

Apart from the ending of the annual tribute of *posa*, no action was taken against the perpetrators of the Bordak massacre; once again the Abors had got away with it. Jack Needham's disappointment and bitterness are shown in a private letter sent to a cousin in England in 1895, a year after the massacre: 'I told you in my last |letter| about Maxwell having received a brevet! Does not this show how poor wretched uncovenanted devils, like myself, are treated! Had I been a covenanted man I should have been made a csi for the frontier work I have done since I came here long ago!'

Despite the setback of the Bordak massacre, Needham still had hopes of leading an official expedition up the Dihong to Tibet. Throughout his second decade of frontier service he went on drawing up plans and lobbying for support and official sanction, but even the Royal Geographical Society was powerless in the face of the disapproval of the Government of India. Only the intervention of the Viceroy himself could change the situation.

George Nathaniel Curzon was not yet forty when he was installed as India's youngest and most dazzling Viceroy. Not for him the 'sordid policy of self-effacement'; despite the handicap of spinal curvature, he had already built up an unrivalled knowledge of the countries bordering on British India, infuriating fellow mps whenever the fate of some exotic country was debated in the House of Commons by announcing that he had 'been there'. During five extended journeys through various parts of Asia – which included the tracking of the Oxus river to its source in the Pamirs – Curzon had acquired not only a passionate belief in Britain's 'sacred' mission in the east but also a deep-rooted fear of the 'Russian peril'. It was said of Curzon's six years as Viceroy (1899–1905) that his 'special obsession as to the advance of Russia in Central Asia marred his judgement.' Nowhere was this

159

obsession more obvious than in his aggressive dealings with Tibet, where the Viceroy's unfounded fears of Russian involvement finally led to the dispatch of the Younghusband Mission to Tibet in 1903.

The mission amounted to an armed invasion and as it fought its way through to Lhasa it brought fierce protests from many quarters. One of Curzon's strongest critics was also one of his most ardent admirers, the Swedish explorer, Sven Hedin, who compared his action to the 'victories' of Cortez and Pizarro. Hedin was better placed than any to champion the Tibetan cause and he had no illusions as to what his stand might cost him: 'I am quite prepared to lose 50 per cent of my English friends but I cannot help it,' he wrote to the Viceroy. 'I should regard myself as an ass and a poltroon if I remained silent when I can and must talk. War against Tibet? Why? The Tibetans have never asked for anything better than to be left alone.' It was the first in a series of defiant gestures that would eventually turn nearly all Hedin's friends in England against him.

By occupying Lhasa the Younghusband Mission did indeed – as a member of the expedition put it – destroy the isolation of the one mystery that the nineteenth century had left to the twentieth to explore. But before the mystery could be explored any further Frank Younghusband had drawn up the Anglo-Tibetan Convention of 1904, which effectively put Tibet out of bounds to all the great powers except China. Its purpose was to ensure that Russia kept her nose out of Tibetan affairs, but its effect was once more to place Tibet off limits to explorers. However, Colonel Younghusband had with him a number of young army officers who were determined to make something of their privileged position in the heart of Tibet and he himself was anxious to give them as much leeway for exploration as he could. As the British forces prepared to pull back to the Indian frontier he gave the go-ahead for three light expeditions, each of which would strike from Lhasa in different directions.

The most important of these three expeditions was to head down the Tsangpo to Assam, and it was to be led by the most experienced of the three British officers involved, Captain C. H. D. Ryder, who five years earlier had already made an unsuccessful effort to approach the Tsangpo from China. In the event, his second attempt was also doomed to failure. Just as the three expeditions were preparing to set off, news was received in Lhasa of an attack on a mail party on the road back to Darjeeling. As a consequence Younghusband decided that it would be safer to combine the three lightly armed parties into one stronger expedition, which would follow the safest and best known of the three projected routes, the Tasam highway up the Tsangpo valley.

His decision was a bitter blow both to Captain Ryder and to Lieutenant F. M. ('Eric') Bailey, who had hoped to travel from Lhasa to Peking. What made it all the harder to bear was Bailey's discovery that it was not Tibetans but Indians who had ambushed the mail caravan. Visiting the scene of the attack he found the frozen corpses of the mules and their Tibetan drivers still lying where they had fallen. He examined the bodies and found that they had been killed not with Tibetan weapons but with modern rifles; the murders had been committed by frustrated soldiers from an Indian Army unit which had arrived too late to participate in the general looting. With this ugly little episode in an even uglier war the best chance of exploring the Tsangpo gorges from the Tibetan side was lost.

Together with Captain Cecil Rawlings, Ryder and Bailey made their 'race against winter' up the Tsangpo in the last months of 1904, with Captain Ryder and his surveyors using a plane-table to confirm the astonishing accuracy of much of Pundit Nain Singh's work over the same ground. However, their fears of being cut off in Tibet by winter snow on the Himalayan passes led them to confine their plane-tabling to the highway, and as a result the mapping of the ultimate source of the Brahmaputra was left uncompleted.

At Manasarovar they found and examined the channel between the two lakes, the wide steam-bed first discovered and explored by the Stracheys more than half a century earlier. It was dry, but they were assured by local Tibetans that it filled up when the snows melted in the summer months. Two days later the officers rode along the western shore of Rakas Tal and finding no outlet other than an old stream bed, also quite dry, concluded that the Sutlej now took its source from one of the tributaries flowing down from the Himalayas and not from the lakes. As soon as they were back in India both Ryder and Bailey began lobbying their respective contacts in Simla. However futile it may have seemed in the wake of the Anglo-Tibetan Convention, both men hoped to win permission to enter the Tsangpo gap.

It was a long-established feature of Anglo-Indian society that no significant advancement could be secured without the help of powerful allies, and here Ryder had the edge on his rival since he had a friend at court in the person of Sir Louis Dane, the Viceroy's Foreign Secretary. Yet even the Viceroy had ultimately to defer to the Secretary of State for India in London – who was adamantly opposed to any further interference in Tibet. While Ryder waited and hoped for a change of heart, Bailey was offered the job of Trade Agent in Gyantse, midway between Darjeeling and Lhasa. Here he spent the next four years, learning the language and familiarizing himself with Tibetan ways. In 1908 he went on leave and began to lay plans to approach his objective from China.

What both Bailey and Ryder, as well as a number of other well qualified contenders, were waiting for was the renewal of the Anglo-Tibetan Convention in August 1910, with the possibility that the ban on exploration would then be lifted. However, it was not to be. Chinese attempts to win control of the Lhasa government provoked widespread disturbances in Tibet and made an easing of restrictions out of the question. These same disturbances also prevented Eric Bailey from reaching his goal. Having crossed the Yangtse, Mekong and Salween rivers, he got within fifty miles of the Tsangpo gorges before being deflected from his course. He was on his way down the Lohit river towards Sadiya and the Assam valley when a runner arrived bearing a message from the British Consul-General in Szechwan. It was a cable from his father in Scotland and it read simply: 'Warn Bailey Massacre Sadiya.'

In fact, the massacre had taken place not in Sadiya but again in Abor country, and its chief victim was Jack Needham's successor, Noel Williamson. Needham had finally retired in 1907 and had gone to live with his wife and family in Shillong, Assam's hill station in the Khasi hills. His successor evidently shared Needham's ambitions; he too expressed a desire to be the first *sahib* to travel up the Dihong into Tibet and in 1909 he actually managed to take a dugout some twenty miles up the river. Instead of an armed escort he took with him a gramophone and a magic lantern, and was received by the villagers of Kebang, in Minyong Abor territory, in a very friendly manner (see inset Map B). Two years later, in March 1911, he set out with the intention of again visiting the Minyong Abors on the right bank of the Dihong. Again he travelled without a military escort but with forty-seven porters bearing gifts and medicines, and a tea garden doctor named Gregorson.

The massacre was triggered off by the most trivial incident. Some rations and a bottle of whisky were stolen at the village of Rotung, ten miles east of Kebang, and Williamson told the villagers that he would require satisfaction on his return. He and his party then crossed the Dihong into the territory of the Panghi Abors. Here there was some sickness among the coolies and Williamson decided to split up the party. He sent the three worst cases back down the trail with a mail-runner, left Dr Gregorson with other sick porters at Panghi village and set off with the rest of the party for Komsing.

The Rotung Abors had just been debating how best to respond to Williamson's demands when his mail-runner arrived. He was carrying three letters from Williamson for posting in Sadiya, which he proceeded to flourish in front of the villagers. These letters were to all intents his death-warrant; they were in white envelopes edged in black as a mark of mourning for the recent death of King Edward VII, and were sealed with red wax. Having no written language the Abors set great store by signs and symbols and they chose to interpret these envelopes in their own terms: the white envelope they saw as representing the white man, the black border was his soldiers and the red seal government anger. In consequence, the mail-runner and the three sick coolies with him got no further than the outskirts of Rotung, where they were surrounded and dispatched. A war party about a hundred strong then descended on Dr Gregorson and his invalids at Panghi and killed them all on the spot.

The next day warriors from Rotung and Kebang caught up

163

with Noel Williamson just as he and his party entered Komsing. Williamson was hacked to death with *daos* on the edge of the village while the coolies, gathered in the village long-house, were speared as they tried to escape.

At first it seemed to the Abors as if they had got away with it yet again; weeks and then months went by without any sign that the British Raj would seek reparation. Then in late September, six months after the massacre, came word that an avenging army was on its way.

The news caused great excitement in the Abor hills and for the first time all the main villages got together to plan a united defence. The women and children were sent up into the mountains and the warriors gathered and prepared to meet the enemy on their own terms. Cane bridges were cut down and fords demolished; trees were felled and piled into stockades across the valleys; rock-chutes were built overlooking trails, and the trails themselves were further booby-trapped with concealed pits lined with poisoned stakes and ingenious spring-traps that sprayed the track with poisoned arrows. The Abors had shown themselves to be supreme masters of jungle warfare, and they had no reason to suppose that their supremacy was about to be challenged.

The expeditionary force that landed on the banks of the Dihong in October 1911 was certainly no military sledge-hammer. But the bulk of its 725 fighting men were Gurkhas – some from the military police battalions in Assam, others from regular Indian army units, but all hillmen who knew the style of the country and what they were up against. And they were backed by what must surely have been the most warlike bunch of coolies ever assembled – 3500 spear-carrying Naga tribesmen. It was the ideal army for jungle combat.

In charge of the Abor Field Force was Major-General Hamilton Bower, known as 'Buddha' Bower because of his unusually solemn and self-contained manner – and thought by many of his young officers to have been the wrong choice. He was a man who won not by flair or dash but by dogged persistence, and had become famous throughout India for having pursued a murderer the length and breadth of Central Asia. The murder in question took place in 1888 in the High Karakoram when a traveller named Andrew Dalgliesh was

164

killed by a Pathan. Hamilton Bower, then a subaltern in the Bengal Cavalry, was sent after him and after months of inquiry and several false trails he and his agents tracked him down to Samarkand, where the fugitive eventually hanged himself in a Russian jail. This exploit had been followed by a succession of journeys through Chinese Turkestan and Northern Tibet. Cautious Bower may have been, but no one could accuse him of lacking either courage or application.

Commanding a detachment of the 2nd Goorkhas was a young major called Alec Lindsay, whose letters to his grandmother – herself the widow of an Indian Army general – give a far more honest and livelier account of the Abor campaign than any published version. His early letters overflow with good-humoured optimism:

Don't be worried if you read in the papers that the Abors used poisoned arrows. The poison (aconite) is not usually strong and rarely has ill effects if the wound is treated properly at once. We all carry squirts and an antidote. So there is nothing to worry about – especially with the Vicarage prayers – so don't worry at the exaggerated stories you see in the Daily Mail.

You would love to see our daily quinine parade. As the NCO comes along with the quinine tablet each man opens his mouth and the NCO throws it in! We all take 5 grains a day to enable us to defeat the fever in the Abor jungles.

An object of particular delight to the British officers was the presence of the head-hunting Naga warriors in camp. 'Our lot are stark,' wrote Lindsay:

The others are practically so, having only a 2" excuse for a rag in front of them. All carry long spears. They are quite warlike and are out for heads. In fact there seems some fear that when we are attacked in the jungle they will drop their loads, shout their war-cries, and dash into the jungle after the Abors whom they hate.

Lindsay appreciated the irony of putting the Nagas up
165

against the Abors: 'It is amusing having to fight savages with savages. That is the way we make an Empire!'

The Nagas very definitely had style. When they were on the march, in columns six abreast, they employed a peculiar two-note chant – He-hah! He-hoh! – that could be heard at a great distance through the jungle and was rightly calculated to put the fear of God into all who heard it. They had come in high hopes of taking a few heads from the Abors and there was a marked drop in morale when General Bower announced that head-hunting would not be countenanced and that the fighting was to be left to the militia. Acting as official interpreter to the Nagas was a young Anglo-Miri policeman named Jack Needham, son of the former Assistant Political Officer. He was briefly accompanied by his sixty-nine-year-old father, who had come up with him to Pasighat in the hopes of being allowed to join the Abor column but was ordered to leave. He returned to Shillong where he died in 1925, disappointed and embittered.

Another frustrated visitor to headquarters was Eric Bailey; he too was out of luck. His first action on returning to Indian soil had been to race across to Simla, where he now had a powerful patron in the person of the new Foreign Secretary, Sir Henry McMahon. Bailey's journey from China to Assam was held to be a success and the Viceroy was persuaded to overlook any breaches of regulations that might have occurred. A position on the Abor Field Force was fixed for him and Bailey was back in Sadiya in time for the start of the push into Abor country. But here he was not made welcome; the local commander did not look kindly on those who were known to have pulled strings to get on the column. Bailey was 'that damn fellow from Simla', and for some weeks was forced to kick his heels in camp.

Bower's conduct of the campaign very soon began to exasperate both the Abors and his own officers. He moved forward with snail-like caution, clearing the surrounding jungle and road-building before every advance, and after a month in the field he had progressed only twenty-three miles. Lindsay's Gurkhas had been allowed to scout ahead on the left flank of the main force but they too had been kept severely in check. 'War by this method I don't understand,' he wrote in early November. 'The General's slowness is painful and we fret at his inaction. Given a free hand I would have cleared the country and taken Kebang 10 days ago.' Soon the unhealthy climate began to take its toll of the troops:

The rain has continued incessantly since 9th – ie. for 14 days – and this is their dry month here! It is too awful for words. Every-one is going down with fever and five out of our 11 officers with this column are in bed taking 40 to 60 quinine grains a day. It is inconceivable that any general should let his troops rot in these malarial jungles and not push forward.

However, once the position of the troops had been well and truly consolidated Bower finally allowed Lindsay to give his men a taste of Abor warfare:

After marching for 6 hours we found the path blocked with fallen trees and poisoned bamboo stakes. Soon afterwards the enemy, who were in a stockade above us, fired off two stone chutes towards us. I glued myself to the *khud* |steep hillside| hoping the horrid rocks would miss me and was lucky to escape with only a bruise above the knee from a smaller stone which knocked me down, while the Adjutant and men near me were swept off the path. Capt. Nicholson and I and the five leading scouts then ran forward and scrambled up the stockade walls helping each other up and shooting down on the men inside who were firing arrows at us. Fortunately for us they ran away.

By this time Bower's slow, inexorable advance had begun to wear down the resistance of the Abors. The combination of the hard wedge at the centre and the fast moving column on its left allowed them little opportunity to follow their traditional tactics of withdrawal and ambush. One carefully prepared defensive position after another was abandoned, often without a fight, until eventually the united Abor front collapsed. One after another of the headmen from the Abor villages on the left bank of the Dihong began to come in with offers of assistance, until only those villages who had been

167

directly involved in the Williamson massacre were left to fight on.

The Abor war came to a spectacular conclusion on a cliff above Rotung village, where some six hundred warriors were holding out in what appeared to be an impregnable position, a natural fortress of rock crowned with a stockade and ringed by some fifty rock-chutes. Here the two columns came together for the final attack: under covering fire from their five Maxims, assault parties worked their way up on both flanks and stormed the position. A few days later the two columns advanced on Kebang, the Minyong Abor stronghold, which was deserted and in flames. All the surrounding villages were razed and all the stockades and defences dismantled, and one by one the hostile chiefs came in waving newspapers as flags of truce. By Christmas the little war was over.

Now that the Abors had been subjugated it was at last possible for the long and eagerly awaited exploration of their country to begin. Several survey columns were sent out, one of which explored to the head of the Shimang river, running north-west off the Dihong into the Himalayan ranges. Here, from an 11,000-foot survey point, its officers caught a first glimpse of one of the twin guardians of the Tsangpo gorge, the 25,500-foot snowpeak of Namche Barwa. Among them was the younger Jack Needham; it was the closest that a Needham ever came to the missing link.

Alec Lindsay led a survey party up the Yamne river, on the left bank of the Dihong. After marching north for several days his party crossed an intervening ridge and arrived back at the main river at the village of Geku. Without venturing further they returned to their base at Rotung, since the job of exploring the Dihong itself had been set aside for the main survey column.

The prospect of solving the mysteries of the Tsangpo river had now at last become a reality, but it called for a leader with the single-mindedness of a Needham or a Wilcox – and no such man was present or available. Eric Bailey had been sent off to Mishmi country as the political officer of a military column, and the other main contender, the unlucky Major Ryder, was surveying on the North-West Frontier and was about to be sent off to Persia to join the boundary commission. Lacking the right sort of charged and committed leader the Dihong survey party advanced no more than thirty miles beyond Geku. It stopped at the last of the Abor villages and went no further upriver. The country of Pemako, which Kinthup had crossed nearly three decades earlier, lay close at hand. There was nothing to prevent the survey column from going on, but its political officer preferred to concentrate on forcing the local Abors to eat Government salt, as a gesture of allegiance, while its military officers evidently felt that exploration was not soldiers' work.

Major Lindsay had also decided that he was not 'cut out' to be an explorer:

I loathe walking day after day for miles . . . and climbing up and down hills over impossible paths. One is bored with sleeping on the ground and getting wet for the sake of geographical additions to a map.

Early in March 1912 he was playing rounders with his Gurkhas at headquarters when a telegram came through ordering him to proceed to Simla. 'It was a sorrowful parting in many ways,' he wrote. 'I shall probably not return to the Regiment. I shall be a Lieut. Colonel before my billet expires. However – that is a long way off. The German war and conflagration in Europe comes first.' But Lindsay died before the outbreak of war; the strains of the Abor Campaign had fatally weakened his heart.

It was left to Eric Bailey to close what was left of Montgomerie's 'missing link'. In October 1912 he secured a place for himself on a second mission that was being sent into Mishmi country, with specific instructions from on high that he was to be allowed as much scope for the exercising of his initiative as he required. After spending the winter months surveying in the Chulikutta Mishmi territory east of the Dibang, he and Captain Henry Morshead of the Survey of India set off northwards into Tibet. When they re-emerged six months later onto the Assam plains south of Bhutan they looked more like tramps than British officers, and it was only with the greatest difficulty that they were able to borrow

169

money to travel second class by rail and steamer down to Calcutta. There they once more resumed the conventional garb of sahibs and proceeded to Simla, believing that 'it was a 50-50 chance whether we would be congratulated or hauled over the coals.' Needless to say, the old criterion still applied, and Sir Henry McMahon offered only his warmest congratulations.

It was generally accepted that with their journey Bailey and Morshead brought the mystery of the Tsangpo-Brahmaputra connection to an end. They had established that between the peaks of Namche Barwa and Gyala Peri the river Tsangpo cut through the main Himalayan range in one of the deepest, longest and most spectacular gorges on earth, and that it then turned back on itself in what Bailey called a great 'knee-bend' to run parallel – but in an opposite direction – with its upper course for sixty miles before again turning south and into Abor country. They had found no great waterfalls but were able to confirm many of the details left by an earlier traveller, the Sikkimese Kinthup.

One of Bailey's first actions on arrival at Simla was to ask the Survey of India for news of this by now almost legendary figure. The Survey had nothing to offer: they assumed that Kinthup was long dead. Bailey then wrote to a friend of his in Darjeeling, who discovered Kinthup working as a tailor in the bazaar. After further pressure from Bailey Kinthup was summoned to Simla, where at last his worth as an explorer was publicly recognized. He and the young man who had not even been born at the time of his great adventure met and talked – and as they compared notes it emerged that Kinthup himself had never claimed to have found any great falls at the Tsangpo gorge. In his verbal report he had described a 150-foot waterfall from a sidestream as well as a lesser 30-foot fall in the main river, which in the written report had been merged into one.

Bailey had hoped that the Government of India would now make amends by awarding Kinthup with a pension. It was opposed on the grounds that Kinthup might live to be ninety, and an *ex gratia* payment of a thousand rupees was made instead. Kinthup returned to Darjeeling with his award, and a few months later Bailey received word that he was dead.

After the disruptions of the Great War both Bailey and Morshead returned to the Himalayas. Bailey continued his career in the Political Service with long spells as a Political Agent in Sikkim and elsewhere. He retired in 1958 and died at home in Scotland in 1967. By then his fellow explorer had already been dead for many years. In 1921 Henry Morshead had again gone to Tibet, this time as a member of the first Everest expedition. In the following year he and George Leigh Mallory became the first men to set foot on the upper slopes of Everest, an exploit that cost Morshead several frostbitten fingers and toes. A few years later, while out on a morning ride in Burma, he was attacked and murdered by unknown assailants.

Although Bailey and Morshead's journey of 1913 effectively settled the last doubts about the exact course of the Tsangpo, one short gap remained unexplored. It was a forty-mile stretch of river into which neither they nor Kinthup had been able to penetrate – the mighty Tsangpo gorge itself. In 1924 the botanist Captain F. Kingdon Ward and a companion, Lord Cawdor, managed to close that gap still further by climbing down into the gorge at several points. Their explorations convinced Kingdon Ward that although the river dropped fast and dramatically through many thousands of feet in a more or less unbroken series of rapids and cataracts there was no longer any possibility that the unexplored sections might conceal a waterfall of any size.

Since Kingdon Ward's day there have been no significant advances. The Tsangpo gorge still guards its secrets, and will continue to do so until the last great Asian adventure – a journey all the way up the Tsangpo-Brahmaputra from the Assam valley to the Tibetan plateau – is undertaken.

Chapter 8

The Monk and the
Gentleman-Traveller:
Ekai Kawaguchi and
Henry Savage Landor

In the Spring of 1897 two travellers were preparing to depart for Tibet. In London a thirty-year-old gentleman of private means, Henry Savage Landor, was collecting letters of introduction from the Prime Minister and a handsome commission from Alfred Harmsworth, propietor of the newly-launched *Daily Mail*, to write a series of articles on his adventures. In Tokyo a Buddhist monk in his mid-thirties, Ekai Kawaguchi, was calling on all his friends and relations and extracting from each a pledge of abstinence from some particular vice that offended him. One was asked to give up drinking, another smoking, a third fishing and a fourth running a restaurant that specialized in chicken dinners. The Japanese was off to Tibet to study Buddhist texts in their original Sanskrit rather than in the Chinese translations on which Japanese Buddhists were forced to rely. Savage Landor's stated reasons changed according to circumstances, but perhaps the dominant motive was Tibet's legendary isolation. It presented a challenge that no Englishman of highly developed sporting instincts could ignore.

It would be hard to imagine two more sharply contrasted personalities than Savage Landor and Kawaguchi. The first was the Victorian traveller in full fig, characterized by overwhelming self-assurance and conceit, a man who required thirty porters for his camping gear and provisions prepared by the Bovril Company 'after instructions furnished by me'; the other was the solitary pilgrim personified, a traveller impelled by something beyond himself, something of a prig but a true innocent.

172

Henry Savage Landor was the grandson of the poet Walter Savage Landor, and had the same vile temper that distinguished his grandfather. Both tended to resort to violence at the least provocation; the poet is remembered for having thrown a servant out of an upstairs window for breaking a soup tureen, and his grandson was to employ much the same technique, with even less provocation, when it came to dealing with Tibetans. Sven Hedin was to describe him as the Baron Münchhausen of Tibetan exploration but Landor's account of his Tibetan adventure, written at speed while he was still recovering from its effects, suggests that he had more in common with the Marquis de Sade and Count von Sacher-Masoch. Published in 1898, *In the Forbidden Land* was, quite literally, a *tour de force*, a lurid catalogue of assaults that matched the late-Victorian appetite for bloody tales of derring-do from the far-flung corners of the Empire. His story made a great impression both in Europe and America and evoked a good deal of public sympathy. Modern readers might be inclined to feel that Henry Savage Landor got what he deserved.

Savage Landor set out for Tibet shortly before Kawaguchi. his original scheme had been to ride through Russia and across Central Asia, but at the last moment he decided to catch a P & O steamer instead, landing in Bombay in March 1897. From there he made his way to the railhead below the foothills of Kumaon and caught a tonga for Naini Tal, the lakeside hill-station that had become the summer residence of the United Provinces (UP) government. He waved his letters of introduction in front of a startled Deputy Commissioner and informed him that he was off to Tibet. The DC would not take him seriously, so Savage Landor rode on to the regimental depot of the 3rd Gurkhas at Almora, where he asked the colonel of the regiment for the loan of some thirty of his men to act as porters. When the colonel sent him packing Savage Landor recruited some coolies from the baazar, including an ex-policeman called Chanden Singh, whom he engaged as his personal servant.

Chanden Singh proved to be a man of exceptional devotion and stupidity. He enraged his new master almost at once by cleaning his shoes with a hairbrush and discharging a soda-water bottle into his face. Savage Landor responded by throwing him out bodily into the street, the first act of gratuitous violence recorded in his book, together with the comment that: 'firm if not too severe a punishment administered in time is absolutely necessary with native servants and generally saves much trouble and unpleasantness in the end.'

The route Savage Landor took was the same as that followed by Henry Strachey six decades earlier. He had hoped to cross over the Lipu Lekh to Purang, but his attempt was frustrated by the Tibetans. So highly developed was Savage Landor's aptitude for picking up native languages as he went along that when he met his first Tibetan official, at Garbyang, he knew at once that he was telling the assembled Bhotias that the English were cowards and afraid of the Tibetans. This provoked Landor into taking immediate action:

> Throwing myself upon him, I grabbed him by his pigtail and landed his face a number of blows straight from the shoulder. When I let him go, he threw himself down crying and imploring my pardon. To disillusion the Tibetan on one or two points, I made him lick my shoes clean with his tongue, in the presence of the assembled Shokas [Bhotias]. He tried to scamper away but I caught him once more by his pigtail and kicked him down the front steps.

Not surprisingly, when Savage Landor set out from Garbyang he found that Tibetan soldiers had turned out in force to block the Lipu Lekh. They had also dismantled a bridge, providing him with the opportunity to make a spectacular detour which later became the subject of one of his highly imaginative watercolours. Prevented from crossing the Lipu Lekh, Savage Landor made for the passes at the head of the Kuti valley. The most frequently used of these was Strachey's Lampiya La, but there was another, rarely used, pass to the east, the Manshang La, which he decided to cross instead.

After setting up camp below this pass Savage Landor took out a small party on a reconnaissance. Undeterred by the fact that it was already half-past four in the afternoon he set off with three Bhotias and a Methodist missionary named Harkua Wilson, an Anglo-Indian doctor whom he had persuaded to come with him part of the way. Landor alone reached the head of the pass – shorty before midnight. It was a bright, moonlit night and he could see the 'immense, dreary Tibetan plateau' stretched out before him. Indeed, so very bright was it that he could see from his aneroid barometer that he stood at 22,000 feet above sea level; which was not at all bad considering that the pass was only 19,000 feet and that he was dressed in Norfolk jacket and breeches, together with a stout pair of walking shoes. Only the straw hat that usually completed his travelling outfit was missing; a few days earlier one of his coolies had been carrying some swan's eggs in it and had stumbled and fallen, squashing both eggs and hat.

Savage Landor was evidently a great believer in sworn depositions; forty-six pages of his book are given over to them. One is from Dr Wilson certifying that Savage Landor reached 22,000 feet on the Manshang pass. He knew this to be a fact because Savage Landor told him so: 'Owing to the rarefied air, I and the other men accompanying Mr Landor were unable to go as far as he did. Mr Landor was at the time carrying on him a weight of 30 seers (60 lbs) consisting of silver rupees, two aneroids, cartridges, revolver, etc.'

The next day Savage Landor and his party crossed the main pass, the Lampiya La, and after various excitements came to the edge of the great camping grounds west of lakes Rakas Tal and Manasarovar, now rich with spring grass and covered with large herds of *kiang*, the Tibetan wild ass. The gentleman-traveller considered these beasts to be extremely dangerous: 'their apparent tameness is often deceptive, enabling them to draw quite close to the unwary traveller, and then with a sudden dash seize him by the stomach.' Beyond the wild asses Savage Landor could see through his telescope the tents of Tibetan nomads and Bhotia traders, surrounded by thousands of sheep and goats.

As they approached this encampment, Gyanema, a gong was sounded and the Tibetans began to run for cover inside a small fortification in the centre of the camp. After a while the more courageous ones re-emerged, carpets were laid out

175

and Savage Landor sat down to parley with the local officials. They urged him to go no further; if he did either his head or theirs would be forfeit. Savage Landor's reaction was predictable:

'Cut off my head?' cried I, jumping to my feet and shoving a cartridge into my rifle. 'Cut off my head?' repeated my bearer, pointing with his Martini-Henry at the official.

The Tibetans withdrew and soon afterwards messengers could be seen galloping off in different directions. The coolies now began to show signs of unrest, which Savage Landor quickly resolved by threatening to shoot the first man that deserted him. The next morning a posse of horsemen arrived, escorting the senior official of the district, the Tarjum of Barka. Savage Landor took an instant dislike to him – 'he never looked us straight in the face and he spoke in a despicably affected manner' – and when their negotiations began to falter he pointed his rifle at the Tarjum's head: 'He tried to dodge the aim right or left by moving his head but I made the weapon follow all his movements. With every meekness he expressed himself ready to please us in every way.'

Having thoroughly frightened and humiliated the Tarjum of Barka, Savage Landor suddenly announced that he had had enough. He unloaded his Mannlicher, ordered his tent to be struck and led his coolies back towards the Indian border. He had decided that his goal was nothing less than Lhasa itself – and that his only chance of success lay in getting there undetected. But to do this he had first to convince the Tibetan authorities, as well as the troop of armed horsemen set on to his tail, that he had left their country.

His chance came during a blizzard. During the night he and nine men – including the bearer, Chanden Singh – slipped out of the camp, leaving Dr Wilson and the remaining porters to continue the journey back to India in the morning. The ruse appeared to succeed and the next few days and nights were spent dodging nomads and groups of armed Tibetans in the hills south of Rakas Tal. Then it became apparent that the Tibetans still believed them to be in the area. Four of his Bhotias sent down to Taklakar to buy salt and flour brought back news that a thousand soldiers were out looking for him and that a price of five hundred rupees had been set on his head. That night, so Landor informs us, he feigned sleep and saw his remaining porters draw lots to decide who should kill him. He was, of course, too quick for the would-be assassin:

> I lost no time in placing the muzzle of my Mannlicher close to his face, and the perplexed *Shoka*, dropping his *kukri*, went down on his knees to implore my pardon. After giving him a good pounding with the butt of my rifle, I sent him about his business.

After adventures and escapes 'too numerous to mention' Savage Landor brought his little band to the southern end of the strip of land between the two lakes. 'Here,' he records, 'it was my good fortune to make quite sure from many points that the ridge between the Rakas and Mansarowar lakes is continuous and no communication between the two lakes exists.' Of the many implausibilities and downright whoppers in Henry Savage Landor's narrative this was one that could be – and was – easily disproved. In nearly every other respect, the gentleman-traveller would beat his critics hands down; for he had actually been to Tibet and they had not, and who was to say which mysteries were genuine and which were exaggerated or fraudulent?

By now Savage Landor's credit was all but exhausted. At a monastery on the southern shores of the holy lake he detected further signs of treachery among his porters and sacked five of them. The remaining pair defected two nights later, leaving him with two yaks and two men, the faithful Chanden Singh and Mansing, a leper of uncertain origins who had attached himself to the expedition and had become Chanden Singh's dogsbody.

From Manasarovar, Savage Landor led his forlorn hope up past the Tage Chhu towards the Maryum La; but now they no longer made any attempt to conceal their movements: there was a large body of armed horsemen following

177

them at a safe distance and another group of horsemen riding ahead. When Savage Landor pitched his tent beside the Gunchhu lake, the Tibetans set up their own camps nearby. Some of the soldiers even helped to gather dried yak dung for his camp fire and brewed Tibetan tea for him. 'They seemed decent fellows,' Savage Landor acknowledged, 'though sly, if you like.'

The Maryum La marked the division between the western province of Nari Khorsum and the Tsang province, and it was as far as the two squadrons of cavalry could go. To Landor's great satisfaction they allowed him to proceed over the pass without hindrance, a fact which he put down to their fear of him but which was more likely a simple matter of passing the buck:

> We descended quickly on the eastern side of the pass, while the soldiers, aghast, remained watching us from above, themselves a most picturesque sight as they stood among the *obos* [cairns] against the sky-line, with the sunlight shining on their jewelled swords and the gay red flags of their matchlocks, while over their heads strings of prayer flags waved in the wind.

Soon after beginning the descent Savage Landor came to a small rivulet which he decided was the source of the Tsangpo-Brahmaputra and accordingly named the 'Landor source'. He evidently knew nothing of Desideri and Freyre's crossing of the Maryum La in 1715 or of Smyth and Drummond's visit to the area in 1864, and the Chief Pundit obviously did not count:

> I must confess that I felt somewhat proud to be the first European who had ever reached these sources, and there was a certain childish delight in standing over this sacred stream which, of such immense width lower down, could here be spanned by a man standing with legs slightly apart.

Some years later, when the whole business of Sven Hedin's claims had come out into the open, Savage Landor was also to assert that it was he and not a certain 'Swedish traveller' who was the true discoverer of the great range of mountains north of the Tsangpo to which Sven Hedin gave the name Trans-Himalaya. This assertion found no supporters because by then Savage Landor's claims were not to be trusted. His map, for instance, was said to have been drawn 'entirely from my surveys of an area of twelve thousand five hundred square miles of Tibet proper' – although all that Savage Landor had had with him when he emerged from Tibet was a rough sketch on a scrap of paper drawn in blood. Yet, to be fair to our gentleman-traveller, he was certainly the first European to set down an accurate appreciation of the mountain range north of the Tsangpo:

From the Maium Pass a continuation of the Gangri chain of mountains runs first in a south-easterly direction, then due east, taking a line almost parallel to the higher southern range of the Himahlyas, and forming a vast plain intersected by the Brahmaputra. This northern range keeps an almost parallel line to the greater range southward; and, though no peaks of very considerable elevation are to be found along it, yet it is of geographical importance, as its southern slopes form the northern watershed of the holy river as far as Lhasa.

The journey down the Tsangpo valley lasted for five days. There were more narrow escapes, more close encounters with armed horsemen and, inevitably, more one-sided fisticuffs. But now even Savage Landor had to admit that his luck had run out:

We were in the centre of Tibet, with no food, no clothes, no extra shoes, and no way of really defending ourselves if it actually came to a fight. We were surrounded by enemies. Still we went on, here and there picking up what we could, but the days were long and dreary and the daily adventures – each of which would provide a lifelong subject of conversation for most Europeans – almost passed unnoticed.

179

Nemesis finally came in an unguarded moment when Savage Landor briefly laid down his rifle. He was immediately rushed by several men and after an epic brawl that lasted twenty minutes and involved thirty men he and his two servants were overcome and tied up.

Henry Savage Landor remained bound and a prisoner of the Tibetans for the next twenty-five days, during which time he and Chanden Singh were starved, beaten, tortured, shot at and then finally put through a mock execution. He put his eventual release down to the fact that the provincial governor who was presiding over these various activities – all graphically illustrated in Savage Landor's book – noticed that his fingers were partially webbed, which was said to be a most auspicious sign. A more likely explanation is that having given Mr Savage Landor a severe going-over the authorities decided to leave it at that. He and his two men were put on yaks, still with their hands bound, and taken under escort to the fortress at Taklakar. It was during this uncomfortable return journey that Savage Landor drew his sketch map in blood, which in one feature at least – the detail in his drawing of the several lakes at the head of the Chemayungdung Chhu – confirms that he certainly visited the Tsangpo's most westerly tributary.

At Taklakar the prisoners were met by Dr Harkua Wilson, together with a leading Bhotia trader from Garbyang, who had heard rumours that Savage Landor had been executed and had hurried over the border to find out what had happened. At first the missionary was unable to recognize the gentleman-traveller, unshaven, unkempt, his clothes in tatters and covered in wounds. 'He was in a very low condition,' wrote the doctor in his deposition:

I examined his injuries and found that his forehead had the skin off and was covered in scabs. His cheeks and nose were in the same state. His hands, fingers and wrists were swollen and wounded. On his spine at the waist he had an open sore and his seat was covered with marks of wounds caused by spikes. His feet were swollen and so were his ankles. The flesh about the latter was much hurt and contused, showing marks of cords having been tightly bound round them.

Despite his wounds Savage Landor insisted on Dr Wilson tying him up exactly as the Tibetans had done and photographing the result for posterity. He topped this some days later by having himself photographed half-naked at 16,300 feet with Chanden Singh emptying a pitcher of water over his shoulders: 'I reproduce it to show that even in my reduced condition I was able to stand an unusual degree of cold.' The incident carries the hallmark of vintage Münchhausen: 'The water immediately froze on my shoulders, with the result that in a second I had icicles hanging on each side of my neck and a shawl of ice over my shoulders.' The uncharitable might add that the photograph reveals that Savage was rather less 'reduced' than he had claimed.

Savage Landor's adventures created a minor sensation in England – though not in India, where he found British officials entirely lacking in sympathy – and did wonders for the circulation of Alfred Harmsworth's newspaper. Landor sailed for Europe with Chanden Singh, stopped off in Italy to be received by the King and Queen and then proceeded to London. Here Chanden Singh became a great favourite with the British press and was briefly arrested after catching a pickpocket on Victoria station and kicking him into a coma. However, London life did not entirely agree with him. He grew morose, got drunk, attacked Savage Landor's cook and finally went for his master with a knife and had to be soundly thrashed. Eventually, Savage Landor sent him home, together with a pension and a double-barrelled shotgun.

Savage Landor's stirring account of his Tibetan adventures, *In The Forbidden Land*, was rushed through the printers and became an immediate bestseller, doing much to reinforce Western preconceptions of the Tibetans as a benighted and savage people. For the next two years its author toured Europe and America, thrilling capacity audiences with detailed and well-illustrated recitals of his tortures. Then – to the horror of the UP government – he suddenly turned up

181

once more in Kumaon, with the declared intention of re-entering Tibet.

This time officials from both sides of the border worked together to ensure that Henry Savage Landor stayed out of the country. He had to make do, instead, with some suitably dramatic exploits in neighbouring Nepal, of which the high point was a daring night climb with straw boater, walking shoes and malacca cane that took him to the summit of a mountain 23,000 feet high – an altitude hitherto unapproached by any mountaineer. A magnificent feat, indeed, but too esoteric ever to find its way into the pages of the *Alpine Journal*. It was of particular interest to a young mountaineer named Tom Longstaff, who in 1907 reached the 23,350-foot summit of Trisul, then – and for the next twenty-three years – the highest mountain ever climbed. Six years after Savage Landor's Tibetan adventure Tom Longstaff was on his way to attempt an assault on Gurla Mandhata when he decided to make a short detour through Western Nepal. Taking with him three of the Bhotias from Garbyang who had accompanied the gentleman-traveller on his epic ascent, Longstaff followed Savage Landor's route into Nepal. His guides led him to a pile of stones on a mountain ridge, which Longstaff reckoned to be at an altitude of about 16,500 feet. This was Savage Landor's 23,000-foot summit, they assured him; the *sahib* with the straw hat had gone no higher.

His Nepalese adventure by no means marked the end of Henry Savage Landor's travels. From the Himalayas he rushed off to China, where he was just in time to take part in the general looting of Peking that followed the collapse of the Boxer rebellion. Later he was to embark on an ambitious ride from Russia to Baluchistan, sail round the Western Pacific islands, and make safaris through darkest Africa and the Amazon jungles. After the First World War he became a vociferous supporter of Signor Mussolini and his *fascisti* in Italy. Appropriately enough, he called his memoirs *Everywhere*; he was the epitome of John Earle's Jacobean character, the 'affectate traveller, who hath seen all and perceived nothing'.

While Henry Savage Landor had been beating his curious path across Western Tibet the Japanese monk, Ekai Kawaguchi, had been travelling by steamer to Calcutta and thence by various ways and means to Darjeeling. Here he spent a year and a half studying Tibetan under a remarkable teacher named Sarat Chandra Das, the last of the great explorer Pundits. It was on this Bengali Tibetologist that Rudyard Kipling based the character of his *babu*-spy in *Kim*, Hurree Chunder Mookerjee, MA, alias R.17. It is nice to think that while Kawaguchi sat at the feet of Sarat Chandra Das as his *chela* (disciple) in Darjeeling, halfway across the world, on the Sussex coast at Rottingdean, Kipling was shaping the character of another *chela*, the young Kimball O'Hara. He too would soon be travelling 'far and far into the North', to play the Great Game for Colonel Creighton-*Sahib* and the British Raj, and to help his old Tibetan lama in his search for his mystic River, hidden somewhere in the hills. Perhaps one of the happier by-products of Savage Landor's adventure was that it stimulated public interest in Tibet. The publication of his book in 1898 was followed within a year or two by a flurry of publications with Tibetan or Himalayan themes – one of which was Rudyard Kipling's *Kim*, published in 1900.

Kawaguchi's search began in January 1899 at Buddh-Gaya, on the plains of Bihar. Here he spent a night in meditation beside the 'undying' banyan tree under whose branches Gautama Buddha first attained enlightenment twenty-five centuries ago. Then he went north by train to the Nepalese border, where by strange coincidence he met the one man in Nepal to whom he carried a letter of introduction, the Tibetan abbot of the monastery of Bodnath, the Chini Lama. Passing himself off as a Chinese monk on pilgrimage from Lhasa, Kawaguchi accompanied the Chini Lama to Kathmandu valley and spent a month as his guest, living under the shadow of the great stupa of Bodnath, where the all-seeing eyes of the Compassionate One look out across the valley to the four points of the compass.

Although Kawaguchi's final objective was the Sera monastery outside Lhasa he had long hoped to make a pilgrimage to the holy mountain and lake that he had read of in Chinese religious texts. With help from the Chini Lama in the form

183

of a pony and a guide as far as the Nepalese border, he travelled up the gloomy Gandaki gorge to Lo Manthang, the kingdom of Mustang, that juts into Tibet like an isolated tooth. Here he said goodbye to his escort and his pony and went on alone, carrying all that he owned in a large bundle strapped to his back. He made his way to the capital of the kingdom, Tsarang, where he was welcomed as a learned lama and immediately installed in the palace chapel.

For reasons that he never made clear, Kawaguchi lingered here in Mustang for a full year, studying Buddhist texts and occasionally being drawn into furious arguments with his host, a Mongolian priest whose tantric lamaism Kawaguchi regarded as 'Lewd and detestable'. He found his surroundings in Tsarang enchanting, even though his Japanese sense of cleanliness and propriety was often deeply offended. The days he spent in Tsarang, Kawaguchi wrote later, were the days of his tutelage in the art of living amidst filth and filthy habits:

> In Tibet people wash themselves occasionally but in Tsarang they almost never do. I only twice saw a person wash himself, the washing even then being confined to the face and neck. I have no courage to dwell here on their many other doings, which are altogether beyond imagination for those who have not seen them done. The natives hereabouts are merely creatures of animal instincts. True, they engage in agricultural work to some extent during the summer months, but at the other seasons they think of nothing but eating, drinking and sleeping, their minds being otherwise filled with thoughts pertaining to sensual love.

This uncomplicated though by no means easy life gradually began to wear down the monk's defences, and it was not until the start of the new year that Kawaguchi forced himself to take stock of his situation:

> I gradually perceived that traps were being set for me, so that I might be tied down to Tsarang for life. The arch-spirit in this conspiracy was my instructor, who brought

all his ingenuity to bear upon assisting the youngest of my host's daughters to make a captive of my heart and person. Fortunately, my faith proved stronger than temptations. Had I yielded then, Tsarang would have had today one more dirt-covered and grease-shining priest among its apathetic inhabitants.

In March 1900 Kawaguchi finally dragged himself away from this perilous Shangri-La and crossed into Tibet. He avoided the popular trade-route that led directly to the border and instead chose a less frequented passage further to the west that took him high over the barren, rolling hills north of the Dhaulagiri range. In this open country he observed a profusion of wildlife, from Tibetan antelope and wild yak to snow leopards and wolves – as well as large numbers of bones lying scattered about. Some of these were undoubtedly human, but were never complete: 'The curious thing was that the skull and the leg-bones were missing from every one of the skeletons that I came across.' Only later did Kawaguchi learn to his disgust that these missing bones would have been put to good use either as ritual vessels or as drums and trumpets in tantric lamaist ceremonies.

Walking alone across the Pindu La, forty miles due west of the Kore La that leads from Mustang to Tibet, Kawaguchi entered his Promised Land. It was an emotional moment, which he acknowledged in Japanese style by composing a short poem.

His progress westwards up the Tsangpo valley was in marked contrast to Landor's journey eastwards three years earlier. Of course, the Japanese had considerable advantages; his appearance and physique allowed him to blend more naturally into his surroundings and his priestly calling made him practically inviolate. He also presented no threat to anybody and in consequence even the poorest nomads treated him with the greatest kindness, while the richer ones went out of their way to offer him the hospitality of their tents or their firesides or the use of a pack animal. One wealthy herdowner went so far as to present Kawaguchi with a pair of sheep to carry his belongings, which were later to save his life by keeping him warm during an all-night blizzard.

Kawaguchi's one great drawback was his hopeless sense of direction. Most of this first period of his travels he spent alone, walking from one campsite to another, and he frequently strayed off course. After being guided over what he calls 'the upper course of the Brahmaputra' and pointed in the direction of the path that led over the western watershed, he lost his way completely and wandered in and out of the mountains for several days until he found himself near the head of a stream that flowed towards the west. Here Kawaguchi met some nomads who told him that this was the river Ganga and that it flowed into lake Manasarovar. The stream came from a range of high snow peaks to the south-east and following it back in that direction for about four miles Kawaguchi arrived at a clear, bubbling pool of water called *Chumik Ganga*, the Spring of the Ganga.

'We drank deep of the sacred water,' he relates, 'then we continued our climb and arrived at another spring, which was welling up in a most picturesque way from under an immense slab of white marble.' This second spring was apparently called the *Chumik Thonga Ranchung*, the Spring of Joy, and it too was said to be a prime source of the Ganga. Undeterred by any need for geographical accuracy, the Japanese monk was quite happy to regard it as such.

Soon afterwards Ekai Kawaguchi caught his first sight of the holy mountain:

> It inspired me with the profoundest feelings of pure reverence, and I looked up to it as a natural mandala, the mansion of a Buddha and Bodhisattvas. Filled with soul-stirring thoughts and fancies I addressed myself to this sacred pillar of nature, confessed my sins, and performed to it the obeisance of one hundred and eight bows.

Only two days later his joy was complete was he finally came in sight of the clear, placid waters of Manasarovar – 'a huge octagon in shape, with marvellously symmetrical indentations'. It, too, appeared to him as a natural mandala, the ideal image upon which to concentrate his meditations:

The hunger and thirst, the perils of dashing stream and freezing blizzard, the pain of writhing under heavy burdens, the anxiety of wandering over trackless wilds, the exhaustion and the lacerations, all the troubles and sufferings I had just come through, seemed like dust, which was washed away and purified by the spiritual waters of the lake; and thus I attained to the spiritual plane of Non-Ego, together with this scenery showing Its-Own-Reality.

As a good pilgrim should, Ekai Kawaguchi went on to make complete circuits of both lake and mountain. His *parikarama* of Manasarovar took him over the isthmus between the two lakes, where he noticed a ravine with what appeared to be a communicating channel from the one to the other. It was quite dry, however, and when he made inquiries he learned that it now filled only after exceptionally heavy rains:

> Hence arises the Tibetan legend that every fifteen years or so Lakgal [Rakas Tal], the bridegroom, goes to visit Manasarovara, the bride. This will account for the statements of the guidebooks to Kang Tisé and Mount Kailasa that the relations between the two lakes are those of husband and wife.

Joining a party of Tibetan pilgrims, the Japanese monk walked over the pastures above the lakes until he came to the first of the Kailas temples, Nyandi Gompa, where to his intense disgust he found the images of Buddha and Naro-Bonchung, the unsuccessful defender of the Bon religion against Milarepa, sharing the same altar:

> I already knew the strange history of the founder of this Tibetan sect, and so, when I noticed the two images worshipped side by side, a sensation of nausea came over me. It was really a blasphemy against Buddha, for Lobon [Naro-Bonchung] was in practice a devil in the disguise of a priest, and behaved as if he had been born for the very purpose of corrupting and preventing the spread of the holy doctrines of Buddha.

From the abbot of Nyandi Gompa, Kawaguchi learned that there were three paths of pilgrimage round the holy mountain. All pilgrims started on the lowest and widest of the three circuits and only after they had completed twenty-one *parikaramas* were they judged to have attained sufficient merit to attempt the middle circuit, which ran high across the four faces of the mountain itself. Few survived this middle path, let alone the higher one, which was attainable only by those who had achieved an advanced state of Buddhahood – or its Hindu equivalent.

Although well aware that it reduced the merit of the act, Kawaguchi made his circuit on a borrowed yak, lent to him by the abbot of one of the four surrounding monasteries. But even mounted he found the Kailas *parikarama* a far from easy act of penance. The crossing of the 18,600-foot Dolma La, in particular, which brought the traveller back over the Kailas range and was the highest point on the lower circuit, gave Kawaguchi a severe bout of altitude sickness.

It was now September and Kawaguchi was anxious to get to Lhasa before the winter set in, so without further delay he began to retrace his footsteps towards the east. But he was never a fast mover and it took another six months before he reached the Tibetan capital, two years and three months after setting out from Darjeeling.

Kawaguchi had hardly settled down to his study of the ancient Sanskrit texts in Sera monastery – as he had so long before vowed to do – before his false identity as a Chinese monk was challenged. Helped by a sympathetic lama from the monastery – who afterwards paid for his act of kindness with his life – Kawaguchi was able to make a hurried exit from Lhasa and in June 1901 turned up once more on the verandah of Sarat Chandra Das's bungalow in Darjeeling.

As the Japanese monk leaves the Tibetan plateau so Savage Landor's 'Swedish traveller' takes his place; it is now Sven Hedin's turn to set out in disguise for Lhasa. Two years earlier, in March 1899 – as Ekai Kawaguchi was beginning his journey on a borrowed pony westwards from Kathmandu – Sven Hedin had written from Stockholm to John Scott Keltie, Secretary of the Royal Geographical Society:

188

As to my future plans and projects of travel I can't give you the details now but I will wright [sic] you from the way. I will keep it secret for many causes, specially for the Russians. I think the[y] are afraid I have become to[o] much of an Englishman.

But I can tell you that if my scheme will be carried out it will be one of the most extraordinary journeys ever made on the globe. I hav[e] the plan ready when in the heart of Asia, and I will have to carry it out – or never return.

PS What about Landor?

Chapter 9

Sven Hedin:
Hero and Martyr

Happy is the boy who discovers the bent of his lifework during childhood. At the age of twelve my goal was fairly clear. My closest friends were Fenimore Cooper and Jules Verne, Livingstone and Stanley, Franklin, Payer and Nordenskiöld, particularly the long line of heroes and martyrs of Arctic exploration.

Sven Hedin, My Life as An Explorer

Swedish by birth, part-German by extraction, Sven Anders Hedin was born in Stockholm in 1865, the eldest son of the city architect, Ludwig von Hedin. From his behaviour in later years one might be forgiven for assuming that Hedin was born and raised in conditions of extreme social or emotional deprivation, but nothing could be further from the truth. Hedin grew up in the security and comfort of a large bourgeois household dominated first by his mother and in later years by his elder sister. These were the two women in his life and between them they provided Hedin with all that he required to sustain him between his extended bouts of exploration. Hedin himself declared that he proposed marriage twice during his lifetime – in his youth and in middle age – and was twice rejected, but without a doubt it was to the women of his own family that he turned in moments of despair and crisis. These moments came often in Hedin's life, brought on by two irreconcilable elements in his character: his single-minded ruthlessness in the pursuit of his goals and his craving for recognition and approbation, a wish to be seen as one of the 'heroes and martyrs' whose exploits had filled his boyhood dreams.

This fatal contradiction in his character – a tragic flaw in the classical mould that sets him apart from all his rivals in the field of Asian exploration – was already evident when at the age of fifteen Sven Hedin witnessed the return to Stockholm of one of his heroes, the Swedish explorer Baron Nordenskiöld. 'All my life I shall remember that day,' Hedin records, 'it decided my career. From the quays, streets, windows, and roofs, enthusiastic cheers roared like thunder. And I thought, "I, too, would like to return home that way".'

From that moment on Hedin began systematically to prepare himself to become a professional explorer. He trained his body to withstand the lower extremes of temperature with a regime of cold baths, open windows and naked plunges into snowdrifts; he taught himself to draw and to map; he studied a variety of potentially useful languages that included Russian, Tartar and Persian; finally, he went to Berlin to become a student of the German geographer and South-East Asian explorer Baron von Richthofen. This German phase of his apprenticeship, when he lived with a German family and enjoyed the carefree life of a student, made a lasting impression on him.

Hedin's first opportunity to put his training to the test came when he was twenty-one and working as a tutor to the son of an engineer employed by the Nobel family on the Russian oilfields at Baku. When his term of service was over he took a steamer across to the southern shores of the Caspian Sea and from there rode south for a thousand miles across Persia to the Gulf. He then travelled by steamer up the Tigris to Baghdad and made a second journey across Persia that eventually brought him back to Baku.

His tour took him less than three months but it established Hedin's reputation in Sweden and Germany as a bold and enterprising traveller. More importantly, it showed Sven Hedin that his future as an explorer lay not in the polar regions but in the desert wastes of Asia. Within a few years he was back in Persia as the official interpreter for a Swedish delegation, a visit highlighted by a grisly act of daring that shocked his colleagues but was perfectly in character. A Swedish craniologist had asked him to be on the lookout for some Parsee skulls that he could add to his collection – and Hedin obliged by robbing a Parsee 'tower of silence', one of the amphitheatre-like towers with high walls in which orthodox Parsees leave their dead to be picked over by

191

vultures and carrion-crows. Mounting his raid on a midsummer afternoon when the heat had driven most people off the streets, Hedin climbed over the wall of the tower with the help of a long ladder, and with a saddlebag full of watermelons over his shoulder. He selected three adult male specimens from the many corpses laid out in various stages of putrefaction, wrenched off their heads, shook out the brains and put the empty skulls in his bag under the watermelons. Afterwards he buried his trophies in the earth for a month and then boiled them in milk until they were 'white as ivory'. It was perhaps as much an act of bravado as anything else but it could well have led to Hedin's own head being removed from his shoulders. It showed for the first time his capacity for ruthless action, in which neither his own nor anybody else's feelings could be allowed to stand in the way.

Once the Swedish mission's visit was over Hedin was free to travel again. This time he went eastward, following the ancient Silk Route, James Elroy Flecker's *Golden Road* that led through Meshed, Bokhara and Samarkand into the heart of Central Asia, to Kashgar in Chinese Turkestan (Sinkiang). Here, camped in an orchard outside the city walls, he met another young traveller who had plans to go far, Captain Francis Younghusband. Hedin seemed to Younghusband to be 'of the true stamp for exploration – physically robust, genial, even-tempered, cool and persevering.'

It was now midwinter, a season which most travellers in Central Asia preferred to sit out in some safe refuge. But for Hedin the horrors of a journey over the Tien Shan mountains and across the Russian steppes in winter conditions presented a challenge, another chance to put the self-mortification of his adolescent years to the test. 'A jolly journey,' was how he described it. 'A wild and whizzing expedition on horseback, by sleigh and carriage through all of Western Asia.'

With this second Asian journey behind him Sven Hedin considered himself fully qualified, in his own words, to 'conquer all Asia, from west to east.' The years of preparation were over and from now on he would be content only 'to tread paths where no European had set foot.' The next journey would last for three years and seven months, during which

Hedin would ride or walk the equivalent of more than half the world's circumference.

It began in Tashkent in January 1894 and it led Hedin back to Chinese Turkestan. The first task he set himself was to explore and map part of the Kun Lun mountains, the barrier lying between Chinese Turkestan and Tibet. A year later he turned his attentions to the Takla Makan, the great sand desert that extended for a thousand miles east of Kashgar. The same perversity that had driven him to explore mountain ranges in winter now drove him to make a desert crossing in early summer, regardless of the dangers. 'I did not hesitate for a moment,' he wrote later. 'I would not retrace a single step of my trail. I was swept away by the irresistible *desiderium incogniti*, which breaks down all obstacles and refuses to recognize the impossible.'

Hedin never allowed himself to regret his decision to go forward into the Takla Makan, just as he never abandoned his Nietzschean view of exploration as the affirmation of Superman in the form of a 'struggle against the impossible', but the horrors of that journey across the dunes stayed with him for many years. Even by the standards of Superman it had come as close to being impossible as any journey could be.

He had set out with eight Bactrian camels and four camel-drivers from Kashgar, knowing only that at some unknown distance ahead a river bed lay across their intended route – which *might* contain a few pools of water left over from the winter. But as the days passed the dunes only grew higher and the progress of their camels slower. Their water ran out and one after another the camels faltered and died. Two of the camel-drivers drank camel's urine and became delirious. Hedin abandoned them, together with all the baggage, continuing with the two stronger Kashgaris and the five remaining camels. When these were either dead or dying he and the one Kashgari still able to walk went on by themselves, with Hedin dressed in his best suit, 'for if I was to die and be buried by the sandstorms of the eternal desert, I would at least be robed in a clean, new shroud.'

For two days and nights Hedin and the Kashgari walked on over the dunes, trying to escape the burning afternoon sun by resting through the heat of the day, buried up to their noses in the sand. On the afternoon of the second day they saw their first tamarisk bush, the first hint that the desert sea had a farther shore. Then they came to some isolated poplars but were too weak to dig for water at their roots. At dawn on the third day they saw a dark green line on the horizon that marked the riverbed, but before they reached it the last Kashgari collapsed. Hedin went on alone and as night approached he reached the riverbed – and found it dry. He continued walking across:

The bed still remained as dry as before. It was not far to the shore where I must lie down and die. My life hung on a hair. Suddenly, I started and stopped short. A water-bird, a wild duck or goose, rose on whirring wings, and I heard a splash. The next moment I stood on the edge of a pool, seventy feet long and fifteen feet wide! In the silent night I thanked God for my miraculous deliverance.

It was a measure of the man that when he was eventually rescued Sven Hedin began immediately to lay plans for a second – and wholly successful – crossing of the Takla Makan. But he took the lessons of the disaster to heart and never again courted danger without first establishing the odds. On one point only would he never compromise; once begun the journey had always to be accomplished, by one means or another and regardless of the cost in terms of men or pack animals. Success and the endeavour always came first, and nothing could be allowed to stand in its way.

This ruthlessness was tempered, to some extent, by Hedin's sentimentality. He refused to shoot any animal himself, preferring to employ a professional *shikari* instead, and it always upset him when a favourite riding pony or camel died under him, as many did. His attitude towards his men was really no different. While he regretted their deaths or their sufferings and felt them deeply he never considered himself to be in any way responsible. This seeming callousness disgusted his critics but for Hedin there was no contradiction in his behaviour. The men with him were almost always natives of Chinese Turkestan and

Ladakh, professional travellers and caravan-men who accepted that the world was a hostile place and life a struggle against the odds. Fatalism was a necessary part of their philosophy and they could follow Hedin's orders to march into the unknown without needing to fathom the strange faith that required his restless, apparently pointless travelling from one empty quarter to another. And Hedin himself commanded their faith like a good general, sharing everything with them, good or bad, so that they in turn supported him with dog-like loyalty and devotion – in several instances, even unto death.

After another year spent exploring the Tarim basin along the northern boundary of the Takla Makan – and in the process discovering two ancient cities that had lain abandoned in the desert for nearly two millennia – Hedin made his way eastwards into China. In May 1897 he returned to Stockholm by way of Mongolia and the Trans-Siberian railway. To his chagrin there was no hero's welcome awaiting him – 'no trace of the triumphal procession that I had dreamed of as a boy.' The triumph had gone instead to Nansen, who had returned to Stockholm only a fortnight earlier after crossing the Arctic Sea in his ship the *Fram*. There was only Hedin's family waiting for him at the quayside.

But if the Swedish people were slow to recognize Sven Hedin's achievements the geographical world was not. Awards, medals and honorary memberships were lavished upon him from all over Europe. Most gratifying of all was the award of the Royal Geographical Society's Founder's Medal, and honorary fellowship of the most prestigious and exclusive geographical body in the world. There were dinners in London with the Prince of Wales and Henry Stanley, the African explorer. In Stockholm he was toasted by his patron, King Oscar. Without a doubt, Sven Hedin had arrived.

A year later Hedin, funded jointly by the King and Emanuel Nobel, was on his way back to Central Asia, with a plan that he had been nursing for three years. It had been with him ever since the aftermath of his death-march across the Takla Makan, when he had dreamed night after night of crossing Tibet. He told Keltie at the RGS that his reason for keeping his plans secret was to forestall any Russian rivals, but what Hedin most feared was that the Tibetans might somehow get to hear that the foreigner who had for so long prowled about their northern walls was now about to force an entry. In the previous half-century more than a dozen Westerners had tried to enter Tibet from the north, but always news of their approach had run ahead of them and all had been apprehended or deflected well short of their goal. Russians (Ruborobovsky, Prjevalsky and Kosloff), Frenchmen (de Rhins, Bonvalet and Grenard), Americans (Crosby, Rockhill and Littledale) and Englishmen (Deasy, Carey, Wellby and Bower) – all had dreamed of reaching Lhasa, and all had been frustrated. But Hedin believed that he had the edge over them: by a triumph of will a Swede would succeed where others had failed.

The dash to Lhasa was to be the culmination of many months of painstaking work – sketching, notetaking, measuring, sounding, mapping by theodolite and compass. First, there was a slow journey by boat down the Tarim, the sluggish river that drains eastwards into the saltmarshes of Lop Nor. After that, more than a year was spent in a series of extended loops and countermarches across thousands of square miles of no-man's-land between the Gobi desert and the Tibetan plateau. And then, at last, the attempt on Lhasa – begun in late July 1901, just a month after Ekai Kawaguchi had returned to Darjeeling.

Hedin's plan was based on the false assumption that by going flat-out on horseback he could move faster than news could spread. What he had not reckoned with was the quite amazing efficiency of the Tibetan relay system. He and two Mongol companions slipped away from their main encampment on the edge of the Tibetan table-land and rode hard towards the south. Hedin was dressed as a Buryat lama from Siberia, his skin darkened by a mixture of fat, soot and brown pigment and with his moustache and hair shaved off. He could not, however, alter his stature. Not a tall man by European standards, he nevertheless sat head and shoulders above his fellow-riders and as they passed their first Tibetan encampment at a fast and bone-rattling trot Sven Hedin heard a bystander call out that he was a *peling* (European).

Five days of hard riding brought them to within a few days' march of Lhasa, but as they drew on towards Tengri Nor, the lake first put on the map by Pundit Kishen Singh Rawat in 1871, a troop of Tibetan militia rode up and began to skirmish in front of them. Hedin and his companions had no choice but to make camp, and as night fell they saw one campfire after another light up the darkness around them. Hedin knew then that his plan had failed – and the defeat was made more galling by the realization that he was in exactly the same predicament as that in which Henry Savage Landor had found himself three years earlier.

Hedin accepted his failure with rather better grace than did the gentleman-traveller. He remained in camp until the local Dzongpon appeared, and discussed the situation with him amicably over several cups of tea. Then he allowed himself and his two companions to be escorted without fuss back to the border. A few weeks later he tried again, making a second dash south by another route, but was again trapped by the Tibetan intelligence system. This time the two governors of the northern province came to meet him and after some hard bargaining they agreed to a valuable concession: instead of being sent north once more to the northern border, Sven Hedin was allowed to take a short cut that led him through Western Tibet to Ladakh. Four months later he was dining in Government House, Calcutta, with Lord Curzon, and by June 1902 he was back in Stockholm, proclaiming new discoveries but inwardly sick with shame and disappointment.

Again the Swedish nation let him down and, as he felt himself becoming increasingly isolated in his own country, so Hedin began to look elsewhere for the moral support that he so badly needed – to people who would recognize his worth. He found the support he was looking for in England and the Royal Geographical Society. This was partly Lord Curzon's doing. Hedin's travels were drawing him increasingly into what the Viceroy regarded as a British sphere of interest, and despite Hedin's protestations that he travelled 'only in the service of geography', there were many besides

Curzon who felt that the Swede's links with Tsarist Russia were too strong for India's comfort. A determined effort to woo him over to the British camp was mounted; at Curzon's prompting, the RGS presented him with a second gold medal, the Victoria Medal. Hedin was highly gratified, and responded with a wholehearted acceptance of British good faith. He had never read or heard a word of jealousy from England, he declared, in direct contrast to the criticism he had been forced to suffer in Sweden: 'The higher one reaches the less friends remain at home; not in the RGS, where I have more *real friends* than anywhere else.'

Chief among these friends was John Scott Keltie – 'my dear oncle Keltie' – who for nearly twenty-five years as the Society's Secretary and Editor of its *Geographical Journal* acted as confidant and father-confessor not only to Hedin but to scores of lonely explorers and geographers scattered round the globe. When ultimately Keltie had to make it clear to Hedin that his loyalties lay elsewhere the Swedish explorer felt deeply wounded and betrayed.

But all that lay in the future. In the spring of 1903 Hedin still basked in the full approbation of the British geographical establishment. He considered Lord Curzon to be 'one of the two greatest scholars living on Asiatic questions' (who was the other, one wonders?) and described his time spent in the Viceroy's company as 'the most charming and glorious days of my life. It was grand, it was splendid in every way.' With characteristic vigour he set about mastering the English language – and British imperial literature. His future, he confessed to Keltie, was now 'as bright as the sun'. Although he had had enough of Asia for the time being he knew that in a year or two the urge to return would be too strong to resist: 'It will begin again and I will long for the music of the camel bells. "If you've 'eard the East a-calling You won't never 'eard no't else".'

This new-found anglophilia was soon put to the test by Curzon's military assault on Lhasa in the shape of the Younghusband Mission. That it survived at all was largely due to the skill with which the Viceroy, by a mixture of candour and flattery, deflected Hedin's anger. He hinted in his letters that as yet undisclosed actions by the Russians had forced his hand and that as the 'Guardian of India' he could not afford to see Russian influence become paramount in Lhasa: 'Had you asked me 2½ years ago whether I meant to send Younghusband in as I have I would have laughed out loud.' This was nonsense, as Hedin knew very well, but he allowed himself to be at least partially won over to Curzon's view; the fact was that Hedin was now himself beginning to be infected by doubts over Russia's ultimate ambitions in Central Asia – doubts that would eventually develop into the violent anti-Russian sentiments that so warped his judgment in later years. Curzon urged him to be above petty politics, and to stick to exploring:

You are a scientist before anything else – the man who more than any other has shown with what resources a great explorer ought to be equipped. I hope therefore in the interests of the world that you will perform one more big journey before you settle down. From this point of view I am almost ashamed of having destroyed the virginity of the bride to whom you aspired, viz. Lhasa.

With the rape of the holy city by Younghusband and 'thousands of Tommy Atkinses' in August 1904, Sven Hedin appeared to lose all interest in reaching Lhasa: 'The longing that had possessed me to penetrate the Holy City in disguise was completely gone.' It was as if a great weight had been lifted from Hedin's mind, and he began to draw up plans for what he was already describing as his final journey, one that would take him through all the great white patches on the map of Tibet marked 'Unexplored' and end with the triumphant exploration of the Tsangpo-Brahmaputra gap. This time he could begin and end his travels in India, secure in the patronage of a powerful Viceroy who had declared himself proud to render Hedin every assistance.

But India's great pro-consul had overreached himself, both in his intervention in Tibet and in his attempts to contain his ambitious Commander-in-Chief, Lord Kitchener. In August 1905, as Hedin once more prepared to make his departure from Stockholm, he learned that his 'strongest and best protection' was lost to him: Curzon had tendered

199

his resignation as Viceroy. It was, Hedin acknowledged, a heavy blow to his plans. Nevertheless, there was no going back.

The last great journey was preceded by a six-month warm-up on camel-back through Asia Minor, Persia and Baluchistan. Hedin then made his way by train to Simla, where he was met at the station by his old rival, Frank Younghusband. He was taken to see the new Viceroy, Lord Minto, and learned from him that permission to enter Tibet from India had been refused. All the surveyors, assistants, armed escorts and passports so carefully arranged for him by Lord Curzon had been withdrawn: 'I had survived revolutions, deserts and plague, but at the very threshold I met an obstruction more difficult to surmount than the Himalayas.'

In fact, there was considerable sympathy for the Swedish explorer at Viceregal Lodge and a great deal of lobbying was done on his behalf, but to no avail. The home Government, in the person of the Secretary of State for India, Lord Morley, was resolved to keep Tibet isolated. Hedin took this second disappointment badly and blamed the British authorities indiscriminately; they were 'worse than the Tibetans', he declared. Later he was to taunt Keltie about the way in which this closing of the door on Tibet had ultimately worked to his advantage: 'Your liberal government has been a great help to me. They could not do me harm once I *was* in Tibet, but they have been kind enough to hinder everybody else to enter, so I was left alone with my discoveries.'

Now that direct entry to Tibet was out of the question Hedin put the word about that Tibet was no longer on his agenda. He announced, instead, that he would be returning to Chinese Turkestan and, with many expressions of regret, left Simla for Ladakh. This false trail fooled nobody who knew anything of Hedin's record, least of all the authorities in Simla, who correctly deduced that as soon as Hedin had assembled his caravan in Leh he would head straight for Tibet. To forestall this move a message was sent to the British representative in Leh ordering him to stop Hedin from entering Tibet, by force if necessary. But, curiously, this message only got to Leh a week after Hedin's departure; owing to the 'negligence' of a senior official in Kashmir it had been delayed. Hedin went to some lengths to conceal the identity of this anonymous friend but it was almost certainly the gallant Younghusband, already in disgrace for having exceeded his political brief in the Lhasa mission.

Sven Hedin crossed into Tibet on 25 August 1906. He was elated at having successfully outwitted the British authorities and in the highest spirits. He *knew* that this was to be his greatest, most triumphant journey, and the conviction stayed with him for the next fifteen months. 'During the whole journey I have had a feeling of being passive,' he wrote in a letter to Keltie, 'of being simply the means in a stronger and mightier hand. I go on quietly surrounded by all sorts of dangers about which I know little or nothing and the invisible hand bears me and carries me through everything.'

As always Hedin had chosen to travel without the company of a fellow-European but he had with him a 'first-class caravan with first-class men', led by a *bashi*, or caravan leader, of outstanding quality, recommended to him by Younghusband. Mohamed Isa, 'tall and strong as a bear', was of mixed Ladakhi-Yarkandi parentage and had probably seen more of Central Asia than any man alive. Isa had been with Younghusband when he and Hedin had first met in Kashgar in 1890 and had accompanied Younghusband to Lhasa as his caravan leader in 1903. A year later he had been with Ryder, Rawling and Bailey on their ride up the Tsangpo valley. But long before joining Younghusband Mohamed Isa had travelled with other *sahibs* in the Pamirs and Turkestan. Most notably, he had served Dalgliesh as caravan leader on his journeys through Central Asia before his murder on the Karakoram Pass in 1888 and had been with the French explorer Dutreuil de Rhins when he was murdered in Eastern Tibet in 1895. Equally at home among Buddhists or Moslems, he ran his caravan with an authority that tolerated no argument. In fact, from Hedin's point of view, he was the ideal expedition *sirdar*. Hedin gives a vivid portrait of Mohamed Isa's working style in his description of the crossing of the 19,000-foot pass that led out of British territory into Tibet:

From time to time Mohamed Isa's voice growls forth like thunder, shouting out 'Khavass!' and 'Khabardar!' |Take care| We see him standing up above at the last turn of the pass, and hear him distributing his orders from the centre of the circle now formed by the caravan. His sharp, practised eye takes in every horse; if a load threatens to slip down he calls up the nearest man; if there is any crowding, or a gap in the ranks he notices it immediately. With his hands in his pockets and his pipe in his mouth he goes up quietly on foot over the Marsimik La.

For the next six months Hedin's whereabouts remained a mystery. Then in February 1907 he wrote jubilantly to Keltie; he was in Shigatse, midway down the Tsangpo valley and less than 150 miles from Lhasa, after a 'very beautiful and happy journey' that had taken him across the larger of the two great white patches on the map supplied by the Royal Geographical Society. Even by Hedin's standards it had been a tough trip: during one eighty-day period they had seen no other human beings and elsewhere had met only a few bands of nomads, barely enough to allow them to replace their pack animals. Out of nearly a hundred mules and ponies only six had survived, yet Hedin could still regard this as cause for self-congratulation: 'I have lost the whole precious caravan it is true but not a single man.' And by crossing the Chang Tang at its wildest sector and in winter he had managed to evade the Tibetan warning system until he was deep inside the country.

He was stopped by the same man who five years earlier had blocked his first attempt to reach Lhasa, the Dzongpon of Naktsang province. However, fortunately for Hedin the Dzongpon now spoke with less authority. The Dalai Lama, whom he recognized as the supreme power in the land, had fled to Mongolia at the time of the British invasion and much of his authority in the western part of Tibet had passed to a rival pontiff, the Tashi or Panchen Lama, whom Hedin knew to be on rather better terms with the British. The Swedish explorer therefore countered by asking to be allowed to send a message to the Tashi Lama at his monastery of Tashi Lunpo at Shigatse. To his great surprise the

202

Dzongpon gave way and suggested that Hedin might as well go to Shigatse himself and talk to the Tashi Lama in person.

Anxious to make what he could of this valuable concession, Hedin pushed on ahead of the main caravan and slipped through the gates of Tibet's second city late at night without being challenged. The next morning there was an uproar throughout the city as the townspeople woke to find a foreigner camped in their midst. It was widely believed that he had fallen out of the sky during the night. Before very long a messenger arrived from the Tashi Lama with a token of welcome in the form of a *kadakh*, a ceremonial scarf of fine gauze, and an invitation to attend him at the start of the New Year festivities that were about to be celebrated at Tashi Lunpo monastery.

Hedin remained in Shigatse for as long as he could. With the Tashi Lama's support he was allowed to wander into every part of the monastery, one of the largest and most impressive in the whole of Tibet, housing some four thousand monks. He sketched, painted and photographed at will, and frequently joined the monks at their prayers and ceremonies. Their chanting made a deep impression on him. He found them 'full of faith and longing, of mysticism and harmony ... they lead the listener away to the land of dreams and hope.'

Hedin's seven weeks in Shigatse were a blissful interlude, made all the sweeter by the knowledge that his presence there was becoming a grave source of embarrassment and that a furious exchange of notes was taking place between Shigatse, Lhasa, Calcutta, Peking and London. Hedin bided his time: 'I was hard pressed; the quarry of four governments. Yet I won out in the end.' He knew that so long as he remained close to the Tashi Lama he could not be touched – but that as soon as he left the safety of Shigatse he would be bundled across the nearest pass into India. By staying put Hedin hoped that he could eventually force the distracted representatives from Lhasa who came to negotiate with him to give in and let him proceed on down the Tsangpo and its still unexplored link with the Brahmaputra. This was asking too much, and Hedin had finally to be content with a lesser concession: permission to return to Ladakh by way of the Tasam trade-route.

Naturally, Sven Hedin had no intention of sticking to the highway as Ryder, Rawling and Bailey had done three years earlier, and as the Tibetans expected. Instead, he zigzagged his way westwards, criss-crossing the jumble of mountains that formed the northern wall of the Tsangpo valley, until in midsummer 1907 his caravan returned once more to the Tasam highway and began the slow ascent to the headwaters of the great river. Here beside the Tsangpo Mohamed Isa suffered a stroke and died within hours. His fellow-Moslems kept vigil in his tent through the night and next morning, wrapped in a white shroud, he was laid in a grave dug beside the river, his face turned towards Mecca. After the grave had been filled in, Hedin gave a short oration in Turki praising his 'excellent, faithful' *bashi*. He and his men returned to their tents and feasted on a newly-slaughtered sheep in honour of the dead Mohamed Isa. 'Then came the realization of our loss,' wrote Hedin. 'We missed him bitterly.' He appointed a new *bashi* and the expedition moved on.

Four months after Mohamed Isa's death Hedin wrote his second letter from Tibet to Keltie. Sent from Gartok and marked 'Private and Confidential', it gave the first news of what Hedin described as 'some of the most important and splendid discoveries that were left to be conquered on the earth'. Indeed, so important were these discoveries and so hard would it be to 'beat this journey' that Hedin wanted an entire issue of the *Geographical Journal* to be devoted to them. In brief, this issue would contain:

a description of very great discoveries of the new enormous range, which I call Nin-tchen-tang-La, of the source of the Brahmaputra, of the genetic source of the Sutlej, and finally of the source of the Indus, which I discovered a couple of weeks ago. Then some descriptions of Manasarovar and Rakas-Tal and my navigation of those lakes, my pilgrimage round Mount Kaylas and journey N.E. from there.

204

The enormous range that Hedin was claiming as his discovery stretched in an arc along the northern watershed of the Indus, through the Kailas range and on to the mountains north of Lhasa. From west to east it was spread over a distance of nearly a thousand miles and Hedin considered it quite as dominant a feature of Central Asia as the Himalayas to the south and the Kuen-Lun range to the north. What had hitherto been regarded as a comparatively flat table-land stretched out between these two mountain barriers had now to be seen as having its own central range.

The source of the Brahmaputra had been visited on 13 July 1907. Hedin had always known that Nain Singh in 1865 and Captain Ryder's expedition in 1904 had followed the tributary that led up close to the Maryum La and he chose to believe that they regarded this to be the main source, although Nain Singh, Ryder and Rawling had all acknowledged that it lay not at the Maryum tributary – the 'Landor source', as Henry Savage Landor would have had it – but rather (in Nain Singh's words) in the 'snowy ranges to the south-west'.

There were three main affluents involved; one flowing from the north, one from the west and one from the south. Coming down from the north there was the Maryum Chhu, which joined the larger Chemayungdung Chhu from the west. Some six or seven miles downstream their combined waters were joined from the south by the third tributary, the Kubi-Tsangpo. Launching his collapsible-frame boat below the lower confluence Hedin worked out that the combined discharge of all three affluents came to 1554 cubic feet of water per second. He then had the boat pulled up past the mouth of the Kubi-Tsangpo and measured the combined discharge of the Chemayungdung and Maryum streams. This turned out to be no more than 353 cubic feet, which showed conclusively that the Kubi-Tsangpo was by far and away the most significant tributary – and the one most worth exploring.

Hedin got hold of three Tibetan nomads who knew the Kubi-Tsangpo valley well and set off on a four-day reconnaissance, into 'a world of gigantic peaks, black but covered with perpetual snow, pointed like wolves' teeth, mighty glacier-tongues lying between them'. Under the highest of the surrounding peaks, the Kubi-Gangri, was the main glacier – and at its snout the largest of several glacial streams. After fixing the altitude at 15,958 feet, Hedin climbed onto a moraine to sketch and photograph the scene. 'It was,' he wrote later, 'a proud feeling to stand at the three-headed source of the magnificent river that goes out in the ocean near Calcutta, Brahma's son, famous in the ancient history of India.'

Yet this was not to be the high point of his travels, for he was soon able to add a postscript: 'perhaps it was still more wonderful to camp over a night at the little rock from which the Indus comes out at a little spring.' This second source was reached two months later when on 10 September 1907 Hedin 'had the joy,' as he described it, 'of being the first white man to penetrate to the sources of the Brahmaputra *and* the Indus, the two rivers famous from time immemorial, which, like a crab's claws, encircle the Himalayas.'

His journey from the one source to the other took Hedin across the valley of the Chemayungdung Chhu, country that he believed had never yet been visited by Europeans before. In fact it was the same broad valley up which Henry Savage Landor had been led on horseback a decade earlier and through which Edmund Smyth's *shikar* party had hunted in 1864. Apparently satisfied with his discovery of the Brahmaputra's main source, Hedin paid scant attention to this most western tributary. Instead of following it up with a local guide to its farthest point, as he had done with the Kubi-Tsangpo, Hedin simply forded the river and then made his way along the hills north of the Chemayungdung valley. In doing so he missed the traditional source of the Brahmaputra and its accompanying lakes – those same lakes seen and drawn on his rough map by Henry Savage Landor. The largest of these, which is about two miles in diameter, is regarded by the Bhotias as the source of the Brahmaputra and is venerated accordingly as the Brahmakund, while the Tamchok-Khambab, the Horse-Mouth River itself, runs into the lake from the south. Its actual source is still a dozen miles away, sited under the Chemayungdung glaciers and marked by a small stone-walled hut surrounded by cairns.

The area is renowned for its wild yak and has yet to be visited – at least officially – by Europeans.

Ironically, one of the few details that Hedin did observe as he bypassed this area was a 'deep-cut passage' in the snow-range that fed the Chemayungdung Chhu. Only three or four days earlier his Tibetan guides had spoken of such a passage called the Tabsi La, 'with a difficult and hardly ever used road leading across the high mountains to the valley of Map-Chhu |Karnali|.' It is difficult to believe that Hedin could have failed to make the connection between his 'deep-cut passage', the Tabsi La and (when he eventually came to learn of it) Webber's 'wall of death'.

From the Chemayungdung Chhu, Hedin crossed the watershed into the Manasarovar basin. Directly to the south was a stream emerging from an ice-fall that he named the Ganglung glacier; it was the main feeder of the Tage Chhu, the largest of the rivulets that entered the holy lake and therefore what Hedin called the 'genetic source' of the Sutlej. 'I loved this stream,' Hedin acknowledged later, 'for no white man had ever seen its source before me.' As he and his men rode on down alongside the stream towards Manasarovar they passed the first of the two springs that Kawaguchi had been shown during his peregrinations seven years earlier. It came bubbling out from under a rock and was marked by a pole bedecked 'like a scarecrow' with prayer-flags and streamers. Kawaguchi had known it as the Spring of Joy and had believed it to be a prime source of the Ganga. Hedin learned its correct identification; it was the Lanchen-Khambab, the spring of the Elephant-Mouth, which – together with its companion spring lower down the hillside – made up the traditional source of the Sutlej.

On the following day Sven Hedin at last caught sight of the blue waters of the lake itself. It was a moment as much charged with emotion for him as it had been for the Japanese monk seven years earlier, and he responded by bursting into tears. During the next few weeks he often found himself in a similar emotional state, and not without reason. His presence by the lake was the consummation of years of single-minded devotion to his cause, a devotion that was really no different in its self-discipline and self-denial from that of the most dedicated Buddhist monk or Hindu *sanyasi*. No European had ever approached Kailas-Manasarovar with a better understanding of its religious significance and no human being had ever gained such knowledge about its geography as he now possessed. It was indeed a time of triumph; the apotheosis of Superman, victorious against all the odds.

When he reached the lake Hedin reassembled his cockleshell and went for a row in the moonlight. Unaware of Robert Drummond's voyage in his 'India-rubber' boat half a century earlier, he revelled in the belief that his was the first vessel ever to float on these waters. The next day – 'distinguished by three stars in the record of my life' – he again launched his boat and was nearly drowned by a fierce squall that drove him across the lake. He beached the boat near Gossul Gompa, the monastery past which Moorcroft had tramped almost a century earlier, and spent the night with the monks. Early next morning Hedin walked out onto the terraced roof of the monastery, where a profound ecstasy came over him:

The Holy Lake, which yesterday had done everything to drown us, was now smooth as a mirror. The air was slightly hazy. One could not see whether the eastern shore was mountains or sky, the lake and sky had the same values. Objects swam before my eyes. The whole temple swayed under me and I felt as if hurled into infinite space. But beneath lay the Holy Lake, along the shores of which innumerable pilgrims had walked themselves weary to secure peace for their souls. The Manasarovar – the hub of the wheel which is a symbol of life! I could have stayed there for years.

In the event, Hedin spent a month beside the lake, taking several more trips on its waters to sound its depths and coming to the conclusion that there *was* an outflow from Manasarovar into Rakas Tal, even if it now only took place at rare and increasingly infrequent intervals.

The channel between the two lakes, the Ganga Chhu, shows up well on Landsat satellite photographs although this is partly due to salt deposits laid down along its bed. The connection between Rakas Tal and the Sutlej, which Hedin visited next, is not so easily discernible. Hedin's inspection confirmed what Henry Strachey had found in 1846 and Ryder's expedition in 1904 — that there was no longer any visible outflow from the lake, only the old channel that had once linked it to the Sutlej. Ryder's party had ridden several miles down this old bed without finding any signs of water seeping down it. Hedin covered almost the same ground but came to a different conclusion: 'When one comes to parts of the bed which are lower than the lake's present surface one finds several springs breaking through it, which grow in volume as one goes down the course, and could not come from any other source than the Rakas-Tal.' This, together with the evidence that the water of Rakas Tal was still 'as sweet as those of any spring', was enough to convince Hedin that he was justified in placing the genetic source of the Sutlej at the foot of the Ganglung glacier — which he regarded as his personal discovery.

Next there was the holy mountain, which Hedin rather unromantically likened to a tetrahedron set on a prism. With four Buddhists from his retinue Hedin set out to make his *parikarama*. It was somewhat devalued because, like Kawaguchi, he rode most of the way but nevertheless he professed to be deeply moved by the experience and the new insight it gave him into the religious life of the Tibetans and the faith that brought them so far:

From the highlands of Kham in the remotest east, from Naktsang and Amdo, from the unknown Bongba, which we have heard of only in vague reports, from the black tents which stand like the spots of a leopard scattered among the dreary valleys of Tibet, from Ladakh in the mountains of the far west, and from the Himalayan lands in the south, thousands of pilgrims come here annually, to pace slowly and in deep meditation the 28 miles round the navel of the earth, the mountain of salvation. I saw the silent procession, the faithful bands, youths and maidens, strong men with wife and child, grey old men, ragged fellows who lived like parasites on the charity of other pilgrims, scoundrels who had to do penance for a crime, robbers who had plundered peaceful travellers, chiefs, officials, herdsmen and nomads; a varied train of shady humanity on the thorny road, which after interminable ages ends in the deep peace of Nirvana. August and serene Siva looks down from his paradise, and Hlabsen from his jewelled palace, on the innumerable human beings below who circle, like asteroids in the sun, round the foot of the mountain.

At the halfway point of the circuit Hedin was delighted to learn from the monks of Diripu Gompa that the source of the Indus lay a mere three days' journey away to the north. Hurriedly completing his *parikarama*, he divided his caravan into two and sent the main party westwards down the Tasam highroad to Gartok, together with its Tibetan escort. With five men and six horses he then made his way back along the first stages of the Kailas circuit and two nights later they were camped beside the 'insignificant stream' of the Indus, about twenty miles above the farthest point reached by the 'Third Pundit', Kalian Singh Rawat, in 1867. Here Hedin made friends with a group of shepherds and persuaded one of them to guide him to the place they knew as the Senge-Khambab.

Hedin's guide, a young man called Pema Tense, led them eastwards along a broad and generally flat valley. As in the case of the Brahmaputra – though on a smaller scale – the headwaters of the Indus were drawn from three main sources. Hedin and his guide waded across the first of these on the morning of 10 September. This was the Lungdep Chhu, flowing down from the mountains of the Kailas range. Hedin calculated its volume of flow to be no more than three cubic metres a second, but this was still two thirds of the total volume of the Indus as measured at that point. This made the Lungdep Chhu by far the largest of the three affluents, so that if Sven Hedin had applied the same criterion as that by which he had determined the Kubi-Tsangpo as the pre-eminent source of the Brahmaputra then he ought to have settled on this branch as the main source of the Indus. Instead, he chose to accept the view of his nomad guide that the real source lay a few miles further to the east.

They continued in this direction for another four miles, when they came to the second affluent, the Munjam Chhu, flowing down from the east. Beyond it there was only a 'very insignificant brook' named the Bokar Chhu, with a flow of no more than a third of a cubic metre. This was the last of the three affluents, and following it towards the north-east for about a mile they came at last to the Senge-Khambab itself, made up of several small springs running out from under a terrace of white, porous limestone. Set out on the terrace were three small cairns and a little niche containing votive offerings of clay, and piled around the niche were hundreds of *mani*-stones incised with prayers and sacred symbols. On one such stone was an image of the Buddha, which Hedin pocketed as a souvenir.

Hedin himself had no doubts about his discovery – and, indeed, so far as the siting of the source of the Indus is concerned, Hedin's choice has never seriously been questioned. No other Westerner ever came near this particular cul-de-sac before Hedin's time and none has ever been there since. Yet the inconsistency remains: in the case of the Brahmaputra Hedin selected the Kubi-Tsangpo on the basis of its greater volume and ignored the traditional source; in the case of the Indus he did the opposite, rejecting the largest feeder in favour of the traditional source. From the point of view of legend and Indo-Tibetan cosmography both Hedin's choices were the wrong ones; had he reversed the order the head of the Brahmaputra, the Tamchok-Khambab, would have been brought that much closer to lake Manasa-rovar on our maps and the source of the Indus, the Senge-Khambab, would be sited within ten miles of the northern face of Kailas.

Hedin's claims were first set out in a long article that followed his private letter to Keltie. It was, Keltie acknowledged, 'a most gorgeous production' and he was anxious to publish it. The problem was that along with the article came a letter from Hedin's sister in Stockholm asking for a large fee for its publication. It was not the Society's custom to pay its contributors any sort of fee and when Keltie wrote to

Miss Hedin along these lines he received a reply that was, in his opinion, 'simply abusive'. To make matters worse, Keltie soon began receiving reports that the 'cream' of the geographical intelligence that Hedin had given him in confidence and which he had not therefore included in the most recent number of the *Geographical Journal* was being published in newspapers in India and Germany.

In February 1908 John Scott Keltie wrote Hedin a testy letter of complaint (which the latter did not receive until seven months later, when he arrived in Simla). He stated that the RGS could not afford Hedin's asking price, and that the article might, he now thought, be more suitable for a popular magazine or a newspaper. But Keltie's letter also touched on something that was quite as much a source of irritation as Hedin's clumsy attempts to make what he could from his story: 'We are very much annoyed at the attitude of our government towards Tibet . . . agreeing to keep everybody out of the country. As you say, it has been a fortunate thing for you, that you have had Tibet all to yourself.' It was the first indication that Hedin's activities – and his evident success – had aroused deep resentment in England.

Chapter 10

Sven Hedin:
Conqueror and Nazi

The greatest mistake that Sven Hedin ever made was his decision in November 1907 to make yet another great sweep through Tibet. The delay of more than a year between sending news of his discoveries to Keltie from Tibet and arriving in London to substantiate them was to prove fatal to his reputation. There was much wisdom in Keltie's remark: 'It might have been wiser for you to have kept nearly everything to yourself until you actually arrived here, and burst upon England all at once in the Queen's Hall.'

Hedin never gave any plausible explanation as to why, after crossing from Gartok into Ladakh and paying off all the members of his caravan crew, he suddenly headed back into Tibet. Yet back he went, driven by some compulsion to submit himself to further hardship, to complete a final circuit of the unknown tracts of Western Tibet. 'I simply *had* to go there,' he wrote. 'It was unthinkable that I should return home without carrying out my plans or reaching my goal.' He was convinced, too, that if he did not go back, 'one fine day another explorer would come and rob me of this triumph. And this thought I could not endure.' What this goal and the expected triumph were – other than the mapping of more of those blanks on the map that he so often referred to in his correspondence – Hedin never revealed. It seems more than likely that the Swedish explorer's real goal (never publicly expressed because never achieved) again lay east of Shigatse, if not among the golden portals of Lhasa itself then on down the great river whose upper reaches he had now charted but whose lower course would not be determined by Bailey and Morshead for another six years.

Hedin also knew that his time was running out. He had been plagued with eye trouble for over a decade and was already all but blind in one eye. Soon it would be impossible for him to continue his mapping unaided and he would be forced to retire from the field. Another punishing two thousand miles through the wastelands could only produce further revelations, reinforce those already made and ensure that Hedin's worst fear – that he might be judged unworthy by the geographical world – was unfounded. And, indeed, Hedin was to claim that his final journey was 'still richer in discoveries' when in August 1908 he finally crossed the Shipki La into British territory and, looking back across the canyons of the Sutlej valley towards the great Tibetan plateau, took his leave of 'the best years of my life and the finest chapter'. Here he was met and photographed by a Moravian missionary, surrounded by his Tibetan and Ladakhi retainers and his dogs, and striking a curiously defiant pose for the camera.

This last journey was very much in the Hedin tradition. After bidding farewell to his first caravan team in Ladakh he immediately hired a fresh crew and told them that they were bound for Kashgar and Chinese Turkestan. They set off with only one month's supply of grain and fodder for their pack animals, enough only to last them to Kashgar, but were then led eastwards off the road on another of Hedin's terrible winter journeys through the blizzards of the Chang Tang. Once more there was the calculated gamble that they would be able to replace the losses among their animals – which came off – and the attempt to beat the Tibetan defence system – which failed. Again there was the protracted withdrawal towards British territory, which on this occasion took Hedin back into the Kailas region and then down the Sutlej valley, past the ruins of Tsaparang and the lost kingdom of Gugé where Antonio de Andrade and his brave Jesuits had laboured fruitlessly three centuries earlier.

As always, Hedin had shared every discomfort with his men, holding back few of the *sahib*'s privileges for himself. Yet he was always alone, saving his real affections for the succession of dogs that he took with him. 'It was always more difficult to say goodbye to the dogs than to the men,' he once declared. On this last expedition his favourite was Brown Puppy, a stray found in the bazaar at Srinagar and the only

214

animal to survive Hedin's earlier journey. When Brown Puppy failed to reappear after a sandstorm Hedin missed him terribly: 'How often did it not seem to me as I lay awake at night, that the tent-cloth was raised and that my old travelling-companion crawled in and lay down in the corner? But always it was the wind that deceived me.' For some days afterwards he suffered the persistent delusion that the dog was at his heels: 'I felt the presence of an invisible dog which followed me into my tent, and among the Tibetans, and always whined and pleaded for help, and I was worried that I could give no help or consolation to my lost, wandering friend.'

From the geographical point of view the journey's main achievement was the further demarcation of the great mountain barrier north of the Tsangpo, which Hedin was now calling the Trans-Himalayan range, but it hardly justified Hedin's claim, put in a letter to Keltie from Viceregal Lodge, Simla, that as a result of this last circuit nobody could now fail to appreciate that 'these discoveries are certainly the finest and most important that were still left on earth.' Hedin was staying as a guest of Lord and Lady Minto, who had received him 'like a conqueror' and had been the guests of honour at an intimate gathering at which Hedin had given his first lecture on his travels. He was in the highest of spirits and rounded off his letter to Keltie with a triumphant flourish: 'Now goodbye, old Keltie, I must be off to Kitchener, with whom I am dining tonight quite alone.'

But old Keltie was no longer so warmly disposed towards his Swedish correspondent. Hedin had agreed to read his first paper at a meeting of the RGS early in the new year but he seemed to be in no particular hurry to return to Europe. In December Keltie wrote to him in Moscow: a curt and transparently unfriendly letter in which he made it clear that Hedin's claims were going to be contested:

You will of course in writing your paper state as precisely as possible what you claim to have done in the great trans-Himalayan range. Certain people here are inclined to be a little critical about your claim to have discovered the range . . . Also to state exactly what you mean when you

215

say that you have discovered the sources of the Brahma-putra and the Sutlej and the Indus.

I thought it well to give you a hint about these little details, which I am sure you will put in such a way as will leave no room for doubt as to what you really claim.

By now Hedin had already begun to receive rather more than hints of the hostile reception that was awaiting him. On his slow journey back to Sweden by way of Japan and the trans-Siberian railway he saw himself described in Japanese newspapers as a Russian spy, in Chinese papers as a Japanese spy and in Russian papers as an English spy. He read that a consortium of English businessmen had paid him hand-somely to find gold in Tibet, that it was only through the intervention of Frank Younghusband that he had been able to enter Shigatse, that his discoveries merely confirmed those made by an earlier traveller, a certain Mr Henry Savage Landor. Finally, when he reached Stockholm in mid-January 1909 – after an absence of nearly three and a half years – he was shown press reports of an article in the Royal Geographical Society's *Journal* that was said to reduce his discoveries to a minimum.

In fact, the original article, written by the young English mountaineer Tom Longstaff, was no more than a short letter which cast doubts on only one of Hedin's claims – his discovery of the Trans-Himalayan range – but coming hard on the heels of John Scott Keltie's letter and the attacks in the press it had a devastating effect on Hedin's already bruised ego. His first letter to Keltie after his homecoming was full of the most bitter recriminations:

I never believed that *you* of all men in the world and when I regarded you as a friend should accuse me in the very days when I return home and when this article of your friend Longstaff was published in all Swedish newspapers. The fact will always remain that the meanest and most envious attacks that have ever been made against me have come from England, the country which refused me every kind of assistance and even made the very best to make the

216

whole journey impossible, England the country to which I have given all my maps!

If the feelings you express in your last letters to me are the general feelings of the RGS I refuse to appear before you.

The letter ends abruptly. Part of the last page has been cut out with a pair of scissors, which suggests all sorts of dramatic possibilities but could have been no more than the removal of some indiscreet comment on its contents. It certainly provoked alarm and consternation at the RGS. Hedin's lecture was due to be given in only three weeks' time; the Queen's Hall had been booked for the occasion and invitations sent out. The crisis had to be averted and Hedin mollified. After conferring with the President, Major Leonard Darwin (son of Erasmus), Keltie wrote a soothing letter to Hedin. He hinted that there were certain high honours waiting to be conferred on him and that he could be sure of a most friendly reception: 'You have pictured to yourself a state of affairs in England which absolutely does not exist.' Hedin countered by demanding that he be allowed to deliver a second paper in addition to the first, to counter 'this reaction against me'. It was agreed that this would be read at a special meeting of the Society to be held after the public meeting at the Queen's Hall.

In the days leading up to Hedin's arrival in England the Secretary of the RGS continued to receive a barrage of accusations and taunts from him. 'We have had a trying time of him,' Keltie confessed in a letter to another of his correspondents in India, Major C. H. D. Ryder. He also asserted that he himself had been against the publication of Tom Longstaff's critical letter:

I considered it premature, and it was quoted in all the German and Swedish papers as indicating that the Council of the Society discredited Hedin's discoveries. Of course, it was a purely personal matter with Longstaff, but I could not persuade Hedin that it was so.

This shifting of the blame on to Tom Longstaff was hardly fair. It may have become a personal matter with him but the

217

initiative had come from Keltie. 'I don't know what you want this for,' Longstaff had written when he had first sent his criticisms of Hedin's claims in to Keltie. 'In any case not for the GJ [*Geographical Journal*] unless Hedin persists in his "discovery" claims.'

It was said of Longstaff in later years that he rather delighted in playing the role of *enfant terrible*. He was thirty-three at the time of the Sven Hedin dispute, a newly-elected and comparatively youthful Member of Council at the RGS and unquestionably more energetic than most of his fellow-Members. Once he had got the subject of Sven Hedin's claims between his teeth he found it impossible to let go, and having paid a brief visit to the holy lake after his unsuccessful attempt to climb Gurla Mandhata in 1905 he could speak with more authority than most.

He began to go back over the records of the Society and wrote to some of its older Fellows. His researches convinced him that the Swede's claims had to be challenged. 'How far are you going to let Sven Hedin go?' he asked Keltie, when the publication of his letter seemed in doubt. The Society had recently suffered a bout of exaggerated claims from returned explorers and it seemed to him that such claims should not be allowed to continue unchecked.

Longstaff was not the only Fellow to express his doubts publicly. Only two days before Hedin was due to arrive in London, Keltie received another furious tirade from Stockholm. Now Hedin's wrath was directed against Sir Thomas Holdich, one of the grandest of the grand old men of British – and Indian – geography, and author of *Tibet the Mysterious*, widely regarded as the most authoritative work on Tibet and its exploration. Holdich had dared to publish an attack on Hedin's surveying methods, the basis of his criticism being that 'neither triangulation nor topography formed any part of Sven Hedin's methods.' In contrast, a number of British explorers had done the job as it ought to have been done: 'Bower, Deasy, Rawling, Ryder and Stein (especially Stein) have all affected excellent mapping with the theodolite and plane-table in Tibet, and so far we cannot but regret that no such results are forthcoming from Sven Hedin.' The criticism was perfectly valid but in view of all the obstacles that the

British government had placed in his path, including the last-minute withdrawal of the survey team laid on for him by Lord Curzon, it was also palpably unfair. Hedin was outraged:

When I returned, not only alive, but with the finest results since Stanley discovered the Northern bend of the Congo, then they begin to ask: why did he not do this and that, it was all known before, why had he not a scientific staff, his results are quite insufficient etc etc. I should not wonder if they begin also to ask why I did not introduce mining companies to the gold fields and build up some cathedrals. I am sorry for Holdich because he has put weapons in my hands by which I can make him perfectly ridiculous.

It now looked very much as if what should have been no more than a reasoned and reasonable academic dispute was about to become an ugly – and public – brawl. The President, Secretary and Members of Council, as well as those Fellows of the RGS who were in the know, awaited Hedin's arrival with foreboding, fearing the worst.

Sven Hedin's first engagement in London was on the Saturday evening, two days before his Queen's Hall lecture. Dining as a guest of honour of the Savage Club he produced a witty, uncontroversial speech that amused and disarmed his audience. 'My geographical moral (sic) is quite different from my ordinary moral,' he declared, to laughter and applause. 'When it comes to geographical matters my moral is very very bad!' His reception helped to bolster Hedin's confidence, and when he finally came to face his audience at the Queen's Hall on the evening of 8 February 1909 he knew he would meet the same uncritical response.

Hedin entered the Queen's Hall to a storm of applause and cheering that lasted for several minutes, and continued to punctuate his lecture at appropriate moments. According to the report of the Hedin lecture carried by *The Times*, it was a capacity audience made up of 'many hundreds of male and female geographers' who reacted to what turned out to be a rather leaden account of Hedin's Tibetan travels with wild enthusiasm. For Sven Hedin it was to be 'the most precious recollection I have of the Royal Geographical Society', an

219

unqualified triumph made all the sweeter by the fact that the person whose task it was to propose the vote of thanks after his lecture was none other than Lord Morley, the Secretary of State for India, the very man who had closed the door to Tibet in Hedin's face three years earlier. It was not something that Hedin allowed him to forget, as *The Times* report noted:

> He did not love Lord Morley three years ago, when he refused him permission to enter Tibet from the Indian side (laughter). But really he had every reason to be grateful to Lord Morley for his action, for by closing the frontier on the Indian side he had kept all other explorers out of Tibet (laughter and cheers). The result was that he had been free of even the shadow of competition as an explorer of Tibet and was left quite alone with his great white patches.

Grasping Lord Morley by the hand, Sven Hedin swore eternal friendship. His audience stood and roared its approval.

It had originally been intended that the special meeting of the Society asked for by Hedin should follow straight on from the Queen's Hall lecture, but as this proved to be impractical it was arranged that the discreetly phrased 'Discussion of Geographical Problems concerning Tibet' should be held two weeks later. In the meantime, Hedin visited Oxford and Cambridge, where he received honorary doctorates from both universities.

On the evening of 23 February there assembled in the lecture room at 1 Savile Row a small but distinguished group of geographers. There were some notable absentees, including the man who in private at least had shown himself to be Hedin's chief ally, Lord Curzon, as well as the most distinguished of Hedin's critics, Sir Thomas Holdich. Having been warned of the Swede's threat to make him look 'perfectly ridiculous', Holdich may well have thought it wise to avoid a face-to-face confrontation. Instead, he sent in a short note to be read on his behalf and held his fire for a second attack on Hedin's mapping to be published in the April edition of the *Geographical Journal*.

By now Hedin had gathered enough from informal meetings and talks to know that his critics were concentrating the main force of their attacks on his 'Trans-Himalaya'. His answer was to deliver a pre-emptive strike of such strength and depth that it all but silenced the opposition. Never was his remarkable capacity for research and the marshalling of facts to support his case better shown than in his presentation of his defence. It was a virtuoso performance – and a very lengthy one – and its effect was to diminish the arguments of nearly everybody who spoke after him. He made extensive use of extracts from the writings of those who sat listening to him, finding much to agree with in what they had said and acknowledging their work in uncharacteristically generous terms. Only once, in disparaging the professional skill of a group of men who were not there to defend themselves, the Pundits, did he put a foot badly wrong.

The replies to Hedin's speech followed an unspoken but well understood order of precedence. First there was a written communication from Sir Clements Markham, an illustrious past President of the RGS who had been closely associated with the Survey of India. To the discomfiture of many of those present he described Hedin as the 'beau idéal of a Victoria Medallist', hailed him as the discoverer of the Trans-Himalayan range and declared it to be the best and most convenient name that could be adopted. This was followed by Holdich's short message, beginning bluntly, 'I do not like the name Trans-Himalaya,' and giving his reasons why.

The first speaker from the floor was Colonel Godwin-Austen, who had made his name a full half-century earlier with his surveys in the Karakoram. He too was full of praise for Sven Hedin's work. But as for Hedin's remarks about the Manasarovar outlet, he reminded the meeting of the work of the Strachey brothers in the 1840s: Richard had died a year ago but Henry, aged ninety-three, was still alive although too frail to be able to attend the meeting in person. Godwin-Austen also expressed doubts about the name 'Trans-Himalaya', which had been used loosely in a number of different ways by earlier geographers.

He was followed by another ex-Survey of India officer, Sir Henry Trotter, the man who had succeeded Montgomerie as the chief controller of the Pundits and their surveys. He took strong exception to Hedin's remarks about their journeys being 'useless for scientific purposes', and felt bound to vindicate their reputation for accurate and valuable work. He conceded that Hedin's discovery of the Brahmaputra source was 'a great triumph' but he, too, disliked the name Hedin had given to the great mountain range north of the river.

The next two speakers were both distinguished mountaineers: Sir Martin Conway had climbed in the Karakoram in the 1890s and Douglas Freshfield had explored in the Causasus and in the Kangchenjunga region of the Eastern Himalaya. Conway was prepared to credit Hedin as the man who had reduced the Trans-Himalayan range to some sort of geographical order, rather than actually discovering it. Freshfield, for some curious reason, used the opportunity to expound a theory that Tibet could be used by a hostile power as a possible launching-pad for the invasion of India.

Finally it was the turn of the younger men. First Captain Cecil Rawling, whose chief concern was to defend the survey work that Ryder and his team had accomplished during their joint Lhasa-Gartok journey of 1904. He was full of praise for Hedin's extensive exploration of the upper and northern watershed of the Brahmaputra, but wished it to be understood that Sven Hedin's 'Trans-Himalaya' was 'the range surveyed by Ryder' and 'what I will call at the present moment Ryder's mountains'. He thought Hedin's term for this range inappropriate, since 'by rights this belongs to the range lying immediately to the north of the Himalayas and between that range and the Brahmaputra.' As regards the Brahmaputra, he showed that Hedin had taken a 'too literal reading' of Ryder's and his own remarks about the Maryum La being the source, and he was able to quote chapter and verse to support his claim. He felt the whole question of Hedin's achievement here could be summed up in one sentence: 'that the principal sources of the Brahmaputra *were known* to lie in the Indo-Tibet borderline glaciers but it has *remained* for Dr Sven Hedin to survey and locate, more definitely than has ever been done before, the headwaters of the river.'

Finally Rawling touched upon the one issue which still, after half a century of dispute, had no firm definition. What exactly constituted a source? He himself defined it as 'the longest visible branch of a river system and, if there are two branches of equal length, then that which carries most water at its greatest flood'. With that definition in mind he disagreed with Hedin on his siting of the Sutlej source and supported Ryder in placing its modern source in one of the southern tributaries west of Rakas Tal, the Darma Yankti. But, as he had said, 'the whole question appears to turn on the definition of the word "source".'

Now at last it was Tom Longstaff's turn to speak. As Hedin had expected, he concentrated the main force of his attack on the 'Trans-Himalaya', opposing both Hedin's claim to its discovery and his name for it. A number of geographers from the middle of the nineteenth century onwards had described such a range north of the upper Brahmaputra or had shown it on their maps. In particular, Longstaff supported the prior claims of Pundit Nain Singh, who had discovered such a range in 1874 and whose work formed the basis of a map published in 1889, on which it appeared as the Kangri range. He drew attention to Saunders' *Memoir* accompanying the map, in which it was stated that 'the northern side of the great Tibetan trough culminates in a range that, for extent, importance and altitude may well stand alongside of the parallel ranges of the Himalaya.' As to the name, 'Trans-Himalaya' was *already* associated with the Ladakh range lying between the Indus and the Sutlej.

As far as Hedin's claims to have discovered the sources of the Indus, Sutlej and Brahmaputra were concerned, Longstaff was prepared only to allow Hedin 'the distinction of being the first traveller to reach the ultimate source of the Indus'. Having visited the upper Sutlej himself after his attempt on Gurla Mandhata he supported Henry Strachey's contention that the main source of the Sutlej would have to be sought at the head of the Darma Yankti, and as for the Brahmaputra, it was his contention that a 'party of British sportsmen' should be given the credit instead of Dr Sven Hedin.

This unexpected revelation by Longstaff provided the one dramatic moment of the evening. It was a very bold assertion to make because it struck at the heart of what Hedin regarded as his strongest claim, but Longstaff could speak with some confidence because he had among his notes a letter that

223

confirmed the bizarre account given by Thomas Webber in his memoirs. The letter was from the elusive Edmund Smyth himself, and it told how that extraordinary shooting party had made its way over an unusually high pass to reach 'a country swarming with wild yaks, mostly cows' east of Gurla Mandhata:

> The pass we crossed over the Gurla Mandhata must have been about 19,000 ft, and some of our party went 1,000 ft further up to explore, & looked down upon a lake covered with ice & snow. This was in the middle of July.

Edmund Smyth's letter had been written to Longstaff in September 1908 from his home in Haslemere, soon after Longstaff had begun to make his inquiries into Hedin's claims. Smyth was eighty-five but 'still going strong', and his brief account of the hunting party's three-week excursion was proof that Webber's story was true. What it could not show, as Longstaff had undoubtedly hoped it would, was whether or not the *shikaris* had ventured up Hedin's Kubi-Tsangpo as well as the Chemayungdung valley. Smyth himself could not provide the answer because soon after crossing the high pass he had left the main party:

> As my object was to secure some Hodsonian antellope [sic] I parted from my companions & joined them again in 8 or 10 days, & I went in the direction of the Mansorovar, but agreable [sic] to our arrangement I did not go within 6 miles of the lake & I did not attempt to cross the Marium La to the head waters of the Brahmaputra. We all returned together at the end of our 21 days to Taklahar & met with quite a friendly reception from the Tibetans.
>   It was Mr Robert Drummond who in company with a friend of his about 15 years before this had reached the Mansorovar & launched an India rubber boat on it, to the great indignation of Hindus & Tibetans alike.

With this tantalizing footnote, which tells us where he did not go but not where he went, and of the others tell us nothing, the enigmatic Edmund Smyth finally fades out of

224

geographical history, his death passing unnoted in the pages of the *Geographical Journal*.

When it came to Hedin's turn to answer his critics he reserved most of his attention and his sarcasm for Tom Longstaff. He began by challenging him directly: 'It is very comfortable and easy to sit down in your study at home and write down a lot of hypotheses; go out and try to observe the facts; it was open to everybody as well as me.' All Longstaff's arguments, he declared, were built on a foundation of useless theories put forward by different people at different times, none of whom were genuine explorers. Those who were not familiar with Tibetan exploration might be taken in by all the names, dates and figures that Longstaff had cited, but the real experts in the room would know better:

Dr Longstaff has never touched the country of which I am speaking now, that is why he has been obliged to quote half a dozen travellers and geographers who have never been in the country either. They have probably collected their information from native explorers who have never been in the country either, and who have got their wisdom from natives. Is it surprising, I ask you, that the result of this uncritical criticism is a hopeless confusion?

All this was pretty loose – and inaccurate – talk and did nothing to improve Hedin's case, but now his blood was up. As he continued to make ill-judged personal remarks much of the support that his carefully composed defence had gained him in the first half of the proceedings began to ebb away. He ended on a note of defiance: whatever they cared to write or say, neither Longstaff nor anybody else would be able to deny him his greatest achievement, as the important work that he was preparing would reveal. And whatever *they* liked to call his mountain range he would still take the liberty of calling it Trans-Himalaya – 'and the signification which is the strongest will be accepted by geographers, and will survive long after the golden inscription on your graves and mine has disappeared.'

Alas for Sven Hedin and his hopes, his great Trans-Himalaya did not stand the test of time either in name or form. Even before his death in 1952 it had become an orographical embarrassment. The definitive *Columbia Lippincott Gazetteer*, last revised in that same year, describes his Trans-Himalaya as an 'ill-defined mountain area' with 'no marked crest line or central alignment and no division by rivers'. Modern maps have split his great range into two; in the west there is the Kailas range (Kang-ti-sé Shan), in the east the Nyenchen Tanglha range.

'It was very unfair that I should have not have had the slightest idea of what Longstaff and the others were going to say,' Hedin complained to Keltie soon after the debate. But he had very little to complain about: he had dominated the proceedings almost from beginning to end; such criticisms as there had been – even those from Tom Longstaff – had always been tempered with praise; and it was generally acknowledged that apart from his lapse near the end Dr Hedin had given a brave account of himself. But it was not just Hedin's claims that had been on trial. The argument had also been one about his style, his determination to treat geographical exploration as if it were an out-and-out contest, his sheer bad manners – his pettiness in not making the customary bow to those who had gone before him – his lack of modesty in success, his crowing over others and his stress on triumph gained through suffering. All this had grated on people, especially on those whose wings had been clipped by an inflexible government. For a man who had set out to be like an Englishman, who had had the good sense to acknowledge the unrivalled virtues of English geography and English geographers, he had let the side down horribly with his crude reversion to un-British, Continental sporting ethics. He may not have cheated, exactly, but he certainly had not played the game. British geography could still applaud his romantic, fighting spirit – but never the man himself.

So Hedin left England for Germany – and still the complaints came flowing from his pen. On 15 March he was writing to Keltie from Berlin to complain about the April number of the *Geographical Journal*, loaded though it was with reports of Hedin's speeches at both the public and private meetings of the Society, arguing that they should allow him yet more space. After all the prizes that Sweden had awarded to Englishmen, surely the RGS could have made this Hedin number somewhat larger: 'But this is in perfect harmony with all the rest and I cannot and will not do anything to change your dispositions.'

John Scott Keltie did his best – 'I hope when you get home and you have cooled down you will see that you have taken a very exaggerated view of the situation' – but to no avail. Hedin was determined to believe that British geography had put him on trial for no other reason than that of jealousy of his success, because he – a 'poor Swede' – had succeeded where they had all failed:

The whole impression I have brought home from the RGS is a desperate attempt to minimise the value of the journey; they criticise a lot of unimportant things and keep absolutely silent about the great geographical questions which have been solved.

'Altogether it has been a fearful muddle,' wrote Keltie to Major Ryder in early May after Hedin had returned to Sweden, 'he has now got home and has been interviewed and has been saying very nasty things about us, and about England generally and his reception here. The real fact, I may say to you confidentally, is that Hedin was disappointed because he did not get a third medal, and, most of all, an honour from the King.' Hedin had good cause to feel disappointed in this respect. In the annual awards of the RGS made that year was the Founder's Medal for Aurel Stein for his painstaking mapping in Chinese Turkestan and the Murchison Award for Captain Rawling. A lesser award went to an Indian surveyor who had worked for Stein. For the man who had put enother 65,000 square miles of Tibet on the map and had returned with, in his own estimation, the 'finest results since Stanley discovered the northern bend of the Congo', there was nothing. British geography had moved on; it was celebrating Shackleton's return from the Antarctic and preparing for Scott's departure. Such interest as could be spared for Tibet and Himalayan exploration would be concentrated on the wholly British endeavour in the Abor hills and the hidden 'knee-bend' to the north. Afterwards there would be

227

the Great War and an almost total eclipse of interest in Tibet and Central Asia.

If there was one man in England who could understand something of Hedin's nature and his disappointment it was George Nathaniel Curzon. He too knew what it was to have great dreams and revelations and what it felt like to be dragged down by those whom he regarded as lesser men. He had shared Hedin's sense of quest and romance and could bring his own experience to bear on Hedin's sense of outrage. In April 1909 he wrote to Hedin in a spirit of encouragement, telling him that he should not allow himself to be disturbed by petty criticisms: 'Experts always like "having a fling" at rival and greater experts but neither in this country nor in India is there the faintest hesitation in recognising your splendid achievements.'

It was Lord Curzon, with the support of Lord Morley, who eventually secured for Hedin the prize that the explorer had most coveted and thought he had lost: an honorary title bestowed by the King-Emperor that made him Sir Sven Hedin and a Knight Commander of the Indian Empire. It was Curzon, too, who gave Hedin the recognition that was due to him by recording in the pages of the *Geographical Journal* the value of Hedin's work in Tibet, as he saw it, placing Hedin's discoveries in three categories of merit:

The highest ambition of a geographer is to add to the sum total of human knowledge by filling a blank space on the map; first accordingly, I should be disposed to place his filling up of that great 'white patch' of 65,000 square miles, between the Tsang-po and the Central Tibetan plateau, stretching from Gartok on the west to Shigatse on the east.

Alongside of this great discovery I would place the tracing for hundreds of miles and the assurance of a definite orographical existence to the mighty mountain palisade or series of palisades to which he has, in my opinion very appropriately, given the title of the Trans-Himalaya. This range has been surmised to exist in its entire length for many years; it has been crossed at its extremities by native surveyors. But it was reserved for Dr Hedin to trace it on

228

the spot and place it upon the map in its long, unbroken, and massive significance.

Second in order of importance I would place the discovery of the true source of the Indus. There can be no doubt that Dr Hedin is the first European traveller who has traced the main branch of this mighty river to its glacial origin.

Third, I should be inclined to place what I would call the determination, rather, perhaps, than the discovery, of the true sources of the Brahmaputra and the Sutlej. When a traveller visits or ascertains or sees something which no one has visited, ascertained, or seen or perhaps even suspected before, he discovers. When he pursues earlier investigations a few stages further, on lines already followed and accepted but not carried to their logical or geographical conclusion, he determines.

It was not enough for Sven Hedin, of course, but it was an acknowledgement of sorts from the British geographical establishment that not all his claims had been rejected out of hand. All the same, Hedin continued to feel that he had been slighted and betrayed by the Royal Geographical Society and when he got back to Stockholm in early May 1909 he at once set to work on a popular three-volume account of his Tibetan travels. With characteristic defiance, he entitled it *Trans-Himalaya*, and with equally characteristic energy he had the first two volumes ready for publication within five months. No sooner was *Trans-Himalaya* out of the way than he began working on a far more ambitious and scientific enterprise, his massive masterwork *Southern Tibet*, running to eight volumes with two additional books of maps. In it he placed not only all the results of his scientific studies in Tibet but also a comprehensive geographical history of the Kailas-Manasarovar region and the great rivers of India that had their sources there. It had become his obsession, an occupation of necessity that was to occupy him for the next decade.

Tragically, for Sven Hedin, the same obsessive desire for approbation that had driven him from England drove him into the arms of Germany, where he found a welcome among a people who could appreciate him not only for what he was but also for his unmistakable victory over the British. With

229

the outbreak of war his paranoia over Russia's political ambitions led him to actively support Kaiser Wilhelm II and the German war effort. Asked by Sir Douglas Freshfield, now President of the Royal Geographical Society, in November 1914 whether he wished to repudiate an article he had written for a German newspaper supporting the Kaiser, Hedin replied that no one but himself was responsible for his political views. Accordingly, in March 1915 he was informed by the President that since he had actively identified himself with the King's enemies a motion had been proposed and carried that 'his name be removed from the list of Honorary Corresponding Members of the Society'. Thus Sven Hedin was, in effect, stripped of his Fellowship of the RGS and would never be reinstated.

Hedin's answer to this sorry act contained all that was best in his nature; it was a brave, proud, generous and ironical reply that gave him the last word – and perhaps the last, strained laugh:

> I congratulate you on this noble and chivalrous deed and I congratulate myself thus to have obtained the political liberty which I believed could be claimed even by a member of the RGS. I beg you to present to the Council my hearty thanks for the 17 years during which I had the honour of belonging to the most renowned and the greatest of all the Geographical Societies in the world. My name has been removed but [with] the deep and warm regard I have always felt for British geographers and British geographical work [I] will always remain an invisible member of the RGS.

Hedin's exit speech finally brought to an end the controversy that he himself had provoked. It also marked the conclusion, as far as the West was concerned, of that ancient geographical puzzle, the happy enigma built round a mountain, a lake and the sources of four great rivers. Kailas-Manasarovar and its attendant streams was allowed to revert to its former obscurity, its mysteries – to all intents – resolved. It became once more an essentially oriental concern.

Shunned by his own countrymen for his enthusiastic

230

support for Adolf Hitler and his cause in the Second World War, Hedin died all but forgotten in November 1952. Only with his death and his obituaries did a hint of the old controversy and the geographical mysteries that had provoked it flare briefly into life again. By a sad irony the year of Hedin's death also saw the return of Chinese rule to Tibet and with it the old Manchu xenophobia, resulting in the building of an ice-curtain along its frontiers that even Hedin would have found impossible to surmount But after three decades that ice-curtain seems at last to be melting and there is even talk of pilgrims from India and Bhotia traders from Milam and elsewhere once more being allowed to cross the high passes into South-West Tibet. With luck and the passing of years we may yet witness the entry of other foreigners, peling from the West, with a chance to follow – at least part of the way – the footsteps of other, earlier Pilgrims.

Postscript. In September 1981 the first Indian pilgrims to be allowed to visit Kailas-Manasarovar for over two decades crossed the Lipu Lekh pass into Tibet. Leading the first party of twenty pilgrims was S. C. Rawat, a grandson of 'A-K', the Pundit explorer Kishen Singh.

Postscript to 2003 edition

Since this book was first published in 1982 a mass of new source material has become accessible to scholars outside Tibet. This has transformed our understanding of Tibet's early history and culture – and makes nonsense of what I have written about the Bon religion and its roots in far Western Tibet in the first chapter of this book. It turns out that the Kailas region has a far more astonishing early history than that set down in these pages – one that is too important and complex to be squeezed into a few pages of revised edition. A full account, in what really amounts to a combined prequel and sequel to *A Mountain in Tibet*, can be found in my book *The Search for Shangri-La: A Journey into Tibetan History*, first published by Little Brown in 1999 and now available in paperback from Abacus.

Charles Allen, Somerset, May 2002

Glossary

To attempt a rational or scholarly approach to the spelling of Asian words, particularly with regard to Tibetan, is to enter a linguistic minefield. For obvious historical reasons I have avoided pinyin, and have kept to basic contemporary usage.

(A) = Assamese
(B) = Bhotia
(H) = Hindustani or Urdu

(N) = Nepali
(S) = Sanskrit
(T) = Tibetan

basha (H) – thatch hut
Bashahr – former hill-state on Tibetan border, now part of Himachal Pradesh; thus *Bashahri* – inhabitant of Bashahr
bashi (Arab) – caravan leader
Bhagirathi – traditional source-river of the Ganga, named after the sage Bhagirath
Bhot (H) – Indian borderland of northern Garhwal and Kumaon, inhabited principally by Bhotias, semi-nomadic peoples of mixed Indo-Tibetan stock
bibi (H) – orig. high-class lady but later used to signify kept woman
BNI – Bengal Native Infantry
Bodhisattva (S) – one qualified to attain Buddhahood but who delays it to preach the Law
Bon-Po (T) – animistic religion of Tibet, predating Buddhism
Bot (T) – Tibet, also Bod, Bod-yul
Brahma (S) – the Creator, father of gods and men, first of the Hindu Trinity; thus Brahmaputra – son of Brahma. See also Tsangpo
burrhel – Blue Wild Sheep, a species of mountain goat
bursat (H) – monsoon; thus *chota bursat* – little monsoon, that precedes the *burra bursat* – great monsoon

Chang Tang – northern plain, northern region of Tibetan plateau with an average elevation of 16,000 ft, sometimes Jang Tang.
chapri (A) – sand bank with vegetation
chela (H) – disciple
chema (T) – sand, as in Chemayungdung
chho (T) – lake; also *tso*
chhu (T) – water, river

Chief Pundit – code-name for Pundit Nain Singh Rawat, also 'The Pundit'

chir (H) – long-needled pine, *pinus longifolia*, growing between 4000 and 9000 ft

chit (H) – letter or note

choga (T) – thick homespun coat worn by Tibetan nomads

chorten (T) – small temple containing religious images

chowhur (B) – see *yak*

chumi (T) – spring, thus *Chumik Ganga*

CSI – Companion of the Order of the Star of India

Dalai Lama (Mongolian) – former sovereign and spiritual leader of Tibet, known to Tibetans as *Gyalpo Rinpoche*, leader of the Gelugpa sect

damaru (H) – small double-headed shamanistic drum

dandi (H) – open sedan chair

dao (A) – sword used by Assamese hill tribes

Deba (T) – senior monk, more correctly *Drapo*

Demchog (T) – four-faced Tibetan deity representing Supreme Bliss, identified with Shiva and residing on Kang Rinpoche; also Demchhok, Shamvara, Dhampala

deo (S) – god, *deva*; thus *Mahadeo* – great god (Shiva)

deodar (S) – tree of god, species of large Himalayan pine, *cedrus deodara*, found between 600 and 11,000 ft

Devi (S) – Goddess, specifically Shiva's consort, also Gauri, Parvati, Durga, Kali

dhura (B) – long; thus Unta Dhura, the long pass north of Milam

dim-dam (A) – stinging fly found in E. Assam and Burma, formerly known as *dam-dim or dam-doom*

dopka (T) – dweller of black tent, Tibetan nomad

Dorje Phangmo (T) – consort of Demchog, red in colour, identified with Durga (see Devi); also Tseringma, Vajra-Varahi

dwar (H) – gate, thus Hardwar – gate of Hari

dzong (T) – fort or residence of *Dzongpon*, district governor; also *jong*

feringhi – European, derived from Frank

Ganga Mai (H) – Mother Ganga or Ganges, daughter of the Himalayas

Garhwal – former Himalayan district bordering on Tibet, divided in 1816 into British and Tehri-Garhwal, inhabited mostly by Garhwalis

Gartok (T) – high fort, capital of Ngari province of Western Tibet, administered by Garpon or Viceroy. Gardzong, the winter seat, is forty miles downstream from Gartok, the summer seat.

233

Gaumukh (H) – Cow's Mouth, traditional source of Ganga at the base of the Gangotri Glacier

ghat (H) – river of mountain crossing, steps leading down to water's edge; also *ghati*

gompa (T) – monastery or lamasery, also *gonpa*

goral (H) – Himalayan chamois, *nemorhalus goral*

Gugé – ancient kingdom centred on upper Sutlej, its capital at Tsaparang, its royal temple and monastery at Totling, destroyed in seventeenth century and abandoned

Gurkha (N) – Nepalese soldier, originally from hill-fort of Gorkha

guru (S) – teacher of philosophy

Har – Shiva; thus Hardwar, gate of Shiva

Hari – Vishnu; thus Hardwar, gate of Vishnu

havildar (H) – sergeant

Himalaya (S) – abode of snow (*him*); also *Himavant*

Hundes (B) – Tibet; also Undes, thus *Hunyia* – Tibetan

Indus – originally Sindhu, the Lion River, 1800 miles long with its source north of Mount Kailas, traditionally at the Senge-Khambab, Lion-Mouth

Indra (S) – king of gods, Vedic god of rain and storm

jagir (H) – grant of land from government from which the owner draws rent

jampan (H) – large covered litter of palanquin, formerly *jampuan*

Jemadar (H) – senior sergeant

Jerko La – pass between Indus and Sutlej basins, elevation 16,300 ft

John Company – East India Company, also known as the Honourable Company

kadakh (T) – ceremonial white scarf

Kailas – lit. spire, 22,028-ft mountain peak in S.W. Tibet believed by Hindus to be physical manifestation of Meru and Shiva's paradise. See Kang Rinpoche

Kali – black goddess, see Devi

kang (T) – ice, snow; also *gang*, thus *kangri* – snow peak;

Kang Rinpoche – jewel of chief of snows, Tibetan name for Kailas, believed by Tibetans to be physical manifestation of Tisé

khola (N) – river

kiang (T) – Tibetan wild ass

Kumaon – former Himalayan province west of Nepal and east of British Garhwal

kund (S) – pool or lake, thus Brahmakund

Kungribingri – up and down, pass from Milam to Tibet, elevation 18,300 ft

la (T) – pass, hill
lama (T) – superior person, thus priest or teacher
Lanchen-Khambab (T) – Elephant-Mouth, source or upper reaches of the Sutlej river
lapcha (T) – cairn of stones, surmounted with prayer-flags; also *laptche*
lingam (S) – phallic symbol, the form in which Shiva is most commonly worshipped
Lipu Lekh – border pass leading from Garbyang to Taklakar, elevation 16,750 ft

Mahabharata – epic poem assembled about 400 BC but describing events that took place a thousand years earlier in N. India
Mahadeva – the great god, Shiva
Mana, La – border pass between Mana and Tsaparang, elevation 17,900 ft
Manasarovar (S) – Manasa-sarovara – formed in the mind (of Brahma), celebrated in the Manasa Khanda and puranas as the holiest of lakes; also Mapham Tso
mandala (S) – symbolic microcosm for meditation; see *yantra*
mani (T) – the *mantra Om Mane Padme Hum*, thus *mani*-cylinder or prayer-wheel containing *mantra*, and *mani*-walls on which inscribed *mani*-stones are placed
mantra (S) – mystic formula or incantation
Mapchhu-Khambab – Peacock-Mouth, source or upper reaches of the Karnali river
Mapham Tso (T) – unconquerable lake, see Manasarovar
Marathas – Hindu peasant-warriors of Deccan and Western Ghats
Marchhas (B) – Bhotias living in upper Alaknanda and Dhauli Ganga valleys
Maryum La (T) – pass dividing provinces of Ngari and Tsang; also *Mayum, Mariam,* elevation 16,900 ft
mela (H) – fair, festival; thus Magh Mela – early spring festival at Hardwar and *Kumbh Mela* held every twelve years at several sites beside the Ganga
Meru (S) – Sumeru, mythical world-pillar, world-lotus or cosmic navel, on which is sited Swarga – heaven, also known as Tisé to Tibetans. Manifest as Kailas or Kang Rinpoche
Milarepa – Tibetan yogi of twelfth century, known also as Jetsun, Milarspa

mithun (A) – form of Indian bison, domesticated and reared only for status
morang (Abor) – tribal long-house
munshi (H) – language teacher or interpreter

Ngari (T) – province of Western Tibet, capital at Gartok
nirvana (S) – salvation, ultimate absorption into the absolute
Niti La – border pass leading from Niti to upper Sutlej, elevation 16,630 ft
nor (T) – lake, thus Tengri Nor
nyen (T) – Great Tibetan Sheep, *Ovis Ammon*; also *nyan*

obo (T) – cairn, more correctly *lapcha*
Om (S) – *mantra*, mystic symbol and sound of the universe

padma (T) – lotus, thus Padmasambava, Indian founder of Tibetan Buddhism in the eighth century AD
pahar (H) – hill, mountain; thus *pahari* – hill-man
palki (H) – palanquin
Panchen Lama (T) – spiritual co-leader of Tibet, living at Tashilunpo monastery, also known as Tashi Lama
parbat (H) – mountain; thus Kailas *Parbat*, Mount Kailas; *Parvati* (the Mountaineer) – Devi
parikarama (S) – circuit of object of devotion made by devotee
pashmin (Kashmiri) – long-haired goat of Kashmir and Tibet
peling (T) – European
Po (T) – Tibet, thus Tsang-Po, great river of Tibet
posa (A) – annual grant of government funds
prayag (S) – sacred confluence, as in Deoprayag
puja (S) – act of worship; thus *pujari* – priest
pundit (H) – learned man, religious teacher (sometimes *pandit*); also title given to the surveyor-spies trained by the Survey of India
purana (S) – old, thus *Puranas*, eighteen sacred texts written between 200 BC and AD 800, of which the *Vishnu Purana* is the best known
Purang (T) – ancient kingdom in S.W. Tibet, now a district, with its capital at Taklakar

Raj (H) – kingdom, but generally understood to refer to period of British crown rule from 1858–1947
Rajput (H) – martial Hindu caste, originally from Rajputana – land of kings
rakshas (S) – demon
Rakas Tal – lake of demons, known to Tibetans as Langak Tso, Rawan Hrad

236

Ramayana (S) – oldest Sanskrit epic, probably compiled about 500 BC
Rawat (B) – clan name for Bhotias of Johar; see Shokpas
ri (T) – peak; thus *kangri* – snowpeak;
Rinpoche (T) – jewel, blessed; thus *Gyalpo Rinpoche* – blessed leader
rishi (S) – sage; thus Rishikesh – abode of sages

sadhu (S) – ascetic, holy man
Sakya Muni (T) – Buddha
sal (H) – plains hardwood, *shorea robusta*
sambur (H) – large deer, found throughout India
sanyasi (S) – ascetic
semal (H) – plains tree, *bombax hepta phyllum*
Senge-Khambab (T) – Lion-Mouth, source or upper reaches of the
  Indus
Shaiva – See Shiva
shakti (H) – female creative energy released in conjunction with male
  principle, Shiva. See *tantra*
shikar (H) – hunting; thus *shikari* – hunter
Shiva (S) – (also Siva) destroyer and transformer, third god of the
  Hindu trinity, evolved from Rudra, also manifest as Mahadeva,
  Nilkantha, Kedareshwar, most often worshipped in form of *lingam*,
  residing on Kailas; thus *Shaiva* – follower of Shiva
Shivling – Shiva's lingam, 21,468-ft peak near Gaumukh
Shokpas (B) – Bhotias of Johar, also known as *Rawats* or *Shokas*
sirdar (H) – honorific title of chief, often given to leader of working
  men
Siwalik (S) – abode of Shiva, first range of the Himalayan foothills
  bordering on UP
sola topee (H) – pith helmet made from sola plant fibre
stupa (S) – Buddhist monument in the form of a microcosmic mound
swastika (H) – talisman or mark of spiritual strength, good luck

tal (H) – lake, as in Rakas Tal
Tamchok-Khambab (T) – Horse-Mouth, source or upper reaches of the
  Tsang-po-Brahmaputra
tang (T) – plain, plateau, as in Chang Tang
tantra (H) – mystical cult associated with Shiva-Shakti
tasam (T) – staging-post for changing horses; thus the Tasam
  highway from Lhasa to Leh, and *Tarjum* – official in charge
Tashi Lama (T) – see Panchen Lama
terai (H) – belt of formerly thick jungle south of Himalayan ranges
thugee (H) – secret cult of Kali involving murder prevalent in N.
  India until about 1845

237

Tisé (T) – peak, world-pillar, Tibetan version of Meru, also Ri-Rab, made manifest as Kang Rinpoche

tsampa (T) – parched barley flour, staple food of Tibet

Tsangpo (Tsang-Po) (T) – great river of Tibet, upper course of Brahmaputra river

tso (T) – lake, as in Mapham Tso; also *tsho*

Unta Dhura (B) – pass leading north from Milam to Kungribingri pass, elevation 17,590 ft

UP – Uttar Pradesh, formerly United Provinces, originally comprising Rohilkand, Budelkand, Oude and Doab, first absorbed by stages into the East India Company's Bengal Presidency, then North-West Provinces

Vaisnova – See Vishnu

Vishnu – preserver and creator, second god in the Hindu trinity after Brahma, also manifest as Badrinath, Krishna, Hari, Rama; thus *Vaisnava* – follower of Vishnu

Vedic – first 'Aryan' form of Hindu religion, being principally nature-worship

yab-yum (T) – male-female principles or deities of tantric Buddhism

yak (T) – Tibetan ox, *bos grunniens*, found domesticated and wild (*dong*) and cross-bred with cattle; also *Chowhur* (B), *Banchowr* (H)

yankti (B) – river

yantra (S) – mystic instrument for meditation and *tantric* exercises; see *mandala*

yatra (H) – journey to holy places; thus *yatri* – pilgrim

yin-yang (Chinese) – female-male polar forces of Taoist philosophy

yoni (H) – female sexual principle; see *lingam*

Notes and Sources

My use of *Ganga* for the more familiar (to Westerners) Graeco-Roman *Ganges* may irritate some readers, but if 650 million Indians prefer to call this most sacred of rivers the Ganga then the least Westerners can do is to follow suit.

Scholars may be disappointed at the absence of numbers in the text and footnotes, but not, I think, the general reader. The following notes give the main sources for each chapter.

Anyone embarking on a more detailed study of the subject would do well to start with Sven Hedin's *Southern Tibet* (vols I–III) and Col. R. H. Phillimore's *Records of the Survey of India* (vols I–IV), both prodigious works of scholarship, and my more or less constant companions over the last four years. Hedin's work is much more than a chronicle of his own travels and discoveries, being also a wide-ranging survey from remote antiquity to his own time of lake Manasarovar, the sources of the great Indian rivers and the Trans-Himalayan range. All the same, these three volumes represent the case for Sven Hedin's defence and should be read with caution. Phillimore's *Records* – the fruit of two decades of painstaking research after his retirement from the Survey of India – provide as accurate and comprehensive a history of the Survey up to 1860 as one could ever hope to find. For a pilgrim's view of Kailas-Manasarovar that combines the esoteric with the scholarly point of view there is Swami Pranavananda's *Exploration in Tibet* (1955), based on the Swami's many pilgrimages to the area made between 1928 and 1947. For those seeking a more up-to-date and possibly definitive view on the sources of the Indus, Brahmaputra, Sutlej and Karnali his book has all the answers. Readers searching for a higher plane would do well to consult the German-Bolivian 'Lama Anagarika Govinda's' *The Way of the White Clouds* (1966).

ABBREVIATIONS
AR   Asiatic(k) Researches
BL   British Library
GJ   Geographical Journal
IOLR   India Office Library and Records
JASB   Journal of the Asiatic Society of Bengal
JRAS   Journal of the Royal Asiatic Society
RGS   Royal Geographical Society

PROLOGUE
GJ CXIX (1955); The Times 26 November 1952.

CHAPTER 1
For the geography and geology of the Himalayas and Tibet, see: B. C. Law(ed.), Mountains and Rivers of India (1968). A. Gansser and H. Heim, Geology of Central Himalaya (1958); Thron der Götter (1938) (also private correspondence). D. N. Wadia, 'The Himalaya Moutains', Himalayan Journal 26 (1965–6). S. G. Burrard and H. H. Haydon, A Sketch of the Geography and Geology of the Himalayan Mountains and Tibet (revised 1934). Prof. K. Mason, The Abode of Snow (1955)

For the Himalayas, Kailas-Manasarovar and the Indian rivers in antiquity see: Hedin, Southern Tibet. E. T. Atkinson, The Himalayan Districts of the North-Western Provinces vols I–II (1882). J. Dowson, A Classical Dictionary of Hindu Mythology and Religion (1913). K. S. Fonia, Uttarakhand (1978). Eric Newby, Ganga (1974). Hindu and Tibetan sources as stated in the narrative. Translations from the Puranas are H. H. Wilson's. See also AR VI (1807), and AR X (1810).

For Hindu and Buddhist religion see especially: W. Y. Evans-Wentz, Tibetan Yoga and Secret Doctrines (1935). Govinda, op. cit,. and The Foundations of Tibetan Mysticism (1960). Philip Rawson, Tantra, and Indian Cult of Ecstasy (1973). W. Y. Evans-Wentz, Milarepa – Tibet's Great Yogi (1928). H. Hoffman, The Religions of Tibet (1955). E. B. Havell, The Himalayas in Indian Art (1934). E. Stoll, Ti-sé, Der Heilige Berg in Tibet, G. Helvetica 21 (1966). G. Tucci, Il Manasarovar, Lage Sacro del Tibet, Vie Italia e Mondo, vol. III (1936).

CHAPTER 2
For European views of Mogul India, see: Niccolo Manuchi, Storia di Mogor ed. W. Irvine (1908). S. Purchas, Purchas his Pilgrimes (1625). Sir W. Foster, The Embassy of Sir Thomas Roe to India (1926).

For the story of the Jesuit explorers, see: John MacGregor, Tibet: A Chronicle of Exploration (1970). C. Wessels, SJ, Early Jesuit Travellers in Central Asia (1924). Carlo Puini, Il Tibet, SGI Memorie X (1904). Filippo de Filippi, An Account of Tibet – the Travels of Ippolito Desideri

(1931). Father Hosten, *JASB* (1912), Memoirs of the ASB, vol. III (1914).

For a moving picture of Tsaparang as it is now, see Govinda.

Still the best account of that exciting period (for the British) at the turn of the eighteenth and nineteenth centuries is Philip Woodruff's *The Men Who Ruled India*, vol. I (1954). M. Gray and J. Garrett's *European Adventurers of Northern India* (1929), provides a vivid account of the activities or mercenaries like Hearsey. Col. H. Pearce, *The Hearseys: Five Generations of an Anglo-Indian Family* (1905) is an inaccurate and dull account of a lively family (John Hearsey is currently engaged in writing a new history of the Hearsey family in India).

For exploration and surveys see: Phillimore, vols I and II. James Rennell, *Memoir of A Map of Hindustan* (1793). Capt. F. Raper, 'Narrative of a Survey with the Purpose of Discovering the Source of the River Ganges', *AR* XI(1810). Major H. Y. Hearsey, *Account of a Tour to the Sources of the Ganges* (1808), BL 26653. J. B. Fraser, *Journal of a Tour Through Part of the Snowy Mountains of the Himala Mountains and to the Sources of the River Jumma and Ganges* (1820). *AR* vols VIII, XI, XII, XIV; *GJ* vol. XXXI (1851). Emily Eden, *Up the Country* (1866).

CHAPTER 4

The best account of Moorcroft's extraordinary travels to date is given in John Keay's *Where Men and Mountains Meet* (1977). Dr Garry Alder has a biography in preparation. See also: W. Moorcroft, 'A Journey to Lake Manasarova in Undes, A Province of Little Tibet', *AR* XII (1816). Hyder Jung Hearsey, 'A Tour to Eastern Tatary' (MS in the possession of John Hearsey). Col. H. Pearce, 'Moorcroft and Hearsey's Visit to Lake Manasarovar', *GJ* XXVI (1905); *London Asiatic Journal* XVIII, Phillimore, vol. II. Hedin, vols I and II. There are several accounts of the Anglo-Nepalese War of 1814-16, including John Pemble, *The Invasion of Nepal* (1962).

Richard Wilcox's narrative is contained in his 'Memoir of a Survey of Assam and the Neighbouring Countries, Executed in 1825-6-7-8', *AR* XVII. James Burlton's MS Journal is in the Records of the Survey of India. See also: H. T. von Klaproth, *Magazin Asiatique* (1825-6). V. Elwin, *India's North-East Frontier in the Nineteenth Century* (1959). L. W. Shakespear, *History of Upper Assam* (1914). Sir R. Reid, *History of the Frontier Areas of Assam* (1942). R. M. Lahiri, *The Annexation of Assam* (1955). Phillimore, vol. III. Hedin, vol. II.

CHAPTER 6

For accounts of the Strachey and Schlagintweit brothers' visits to Manasarovar see: Atkinson, op cit. H. Strachey, 'On the Physical Geography of Western Tibet', *GJ* XXIII (1853). R. Strachey, 'Narrative of a Journey to Manasarovar', *GJ* XV (1900); Notebook, Eur. Mss 2331, IOLR (1848); *JASB* XVI–XIX (1848–9), Letters RGS. Schlagintweit, *Result of the Schlagintweit Mission to India* (1862) RGS Map Room.

For Smyth's journey of 1862 see T. L. Webber, *Forests of Upper India* (1902). Gen. G. MacIntyre, *Hindu Koh: Wanderings and Wild Sports On and Beyond the Himalayas* (1889).

For the Pundits see: K. Mason, op, cit., 'Great Figures in Nineteenth Century Exploration, *JRCAS* (1956); 'Kishen Singh and the Indian Explorers', *GJ* (Dec. 1923). Indra Singh Rawat, *Indian Explorers in the Nineteenth Century* (1973). Col. T. G. Montgomerie, 'Report on a Route Survey made by Pundit *——, from Nepal to Lhasa and thence through the Upper Valley of the Brahmaputra to its Source', *GJ* XXXVIII (1868), XXXIX (1869). C. Markham, *A Memoir on the Indian Surveys* (1878), Survey of India Records, VIII, VIX. Gerald Morgan, 'Myth and Reality in the Great Game', *Asian Affairs* (Feb. 1973).

CHAPTER 7

Shakespear, op. cit. Reid, op. cit. H. E. Richardson, *Tibetan Précis* (1942). E. T. Dalton, *Descriptive Ethnology of Bengal* (1872). Sgt-Major G. Carter's *Diary* of 1858, Eur. Mss. E.262 IOLR.

For Nain Singh Rawat's last journey see: Rawat, op, cit., Survey of India Records vol. VIII. Capt. H. Trotter, 'Account of the Pundit's Journey in Great Tibet from Leh in Ladadkh to Lhasa and his Return to India via Assam', *GJ* XLVII (1877).

For Kinthup's story see 'Explorations on the Tsangpo in 1880–4', *GJ* XXXVIII (1911). L. A. Waddell, 'The Falls of the San-Pu', *GJ* (1885); *Among the Himalayas* (1899). Proceedings RGS 1885–6. Survey of India Records IX. Sarat Chandra Das, 'Note of the Identity of the Great Tsang-Po', *JASB* (1898).

For Needham and exploration of the Dihong see: St J. F. Michell, *Report on the N.E. Frontier of India* (1883). J. F. Needham, *Report of a Trip into the Abor Hills* (1884); *Report of a Visit paid to the Abor Villages of Padu and Kumku* (1885); *Excursion in the Abor Hills*. RGS Suppl. Papers vol. II (1887–9); RGS Letters. W. R. Little, *Report on the Abor Expedition* (1894).

For the Abor Campaign see: Angus Hamilton, *In Abor Jungle* (1913). Lt-Col. A. B. Lindsay, 'Expedition Against the Abors', *Army Review*, IV (1913); private letters belonging to Sir Martin Lindsay.

For European attempts to explore the Tsangpo gorge see: Capt. C. G. Rawling, *The Great Plateau* (1905); *GJ* XXXIII (1909). Major C. H. D. Ryder, *GJ* XXVI (1905), XXXII (1909). F. M. Bailey, *China-Tibet-Assam: A Journey* (1945); *No Passport to Tibet* (1937); *Reports on an Exploration on the North-East Frontier* (1913, with Capt. H. T. Morshead). Arthur Swinson, *Beyond the Frontiers* (1971). Sir F. Younghusband, *The Epic of Mount Everest* (1926).

For Curzon see: David Dilks, *Curzon in India*, vols I and II (1970).

CHAPTER 8
Ekai Kawaguchi's story is told in *Three Years in Tibet* (1909); Henry Savage Landor's in *In the Forbidden Land*, vols I and II (1898), *Nepal and Tibet* (1905), *Everywhere* (1924). For the other side of the story see T. Longstaff, *This My Voyage* (1950), MS The Manasarovar-Sutlej Problem (1908), and other papers owned by Mrs C. Longstaff, Letters RGS. See also Hedin, II and III.

CHAPTERS 9 and 10
Sven Hedin has yet to find a biographer who can write about him dispassionately. Dr Rutger Essen's *Sven Hedin, Ein Grosses Leben* (1956) fills a few gaps. Hedin himself left almost too much about himself – see: Letters, Sven Hedin Institute; *Life and Letters* (in Swedish, 1964); *My Life as an Explorer* (for children) (1926); *A Conquest of Tibet* (1935); *Trans-Himalaya*, vols I–III (1913) *Through Asia* (1899); *Central Asia and Tibet* (1903); *Adventures in Tibet* (1904). The article on his discoveries that he had failed to sell to the *Geographical Journal* was eventually bought by *Harper's Monthly* and published in Aug.–Sept. 1908. See also Sir F. Younghusband, *The Heart of a Continent* (1890); *India and Tibet* (1910); Letters RGS; and every edition of the *Geographical Journal* from Sept. 1908 to May 1909. For the last word see Pranavananda, op. cit., and the *Columbia Lippincott Gazetteer* (1952).

Index

Hedin, Sven Anders—*contd.*
 213, 215–30 in Shigatse,
 202–3
 on Silk Route, 192
 and Smyth/Webber
 expedition, 129–30, 131–3,
 224–5
 Southern Tibet, 131, 229
 and Sutlej, 204, 207, 209,
 223, 229
 and Takla Makan, 193–5
 to Tarim basin and China,
 195
 Tibet, last visit to, 213–14
 and Trans-Himalayan range,
 179, 205, 215, 216, 221–2,
 223, 225–6, 228
 and Tsango/Brahmaputra,
 129, 131–4, 199–202,
 203–6, 211, 222, 223,
 229
 and Younghusband,
 Younghusband Mission,
 160, 192, 198–200
Herbert, Captain James, 73–4,
 95, 118
Herodotus, 142
Himalayas, 17–18, 23–4
 exploration of, 13–15, 33–4
 and passim
 height of, 57, 58, 96
 in Hindu myth, 19–20, 20–1
 pilgrimage to, 20–1, 24–5
 rivers flowing from, or
 through, *see* rivers and
 world mountain, *see*
 mountain
Hindus, Hinduism, 12, 19–21,
 32, 124
Hiru Dham Singh, 120
Hodgson, Henry, 130–4
Hodgson, Captain John, 61,
 67–73, 75, 95, 96–7, 103,
 115, 116, 118

Holdich, Sir Thomas, 218, 220 ,
horse-mouth river, *see*
 Tamchok-Khambab
Hughes, Thomas, 125
Humboldt, Baron, 124
Hurruck Dao, 79, 89
Hwang Ho, river, 30

India
 British in, 14–15, 55, 98, 145,
 155
 Survey of, 57–8, 59, 67, 119,
 135–7, 140, 154
Indra, 18
Indus (*see also* rivers, four) in
 Chinese cosmography, 30
 exploration of, 14, 27, 40
 Desideri, 48, 50–1; Rennell,
 57; Moorcroft and Hearsey,
 84–5; Pundits, 140–3;
 Hedin, 204, 206, 210–11,
 223, 229
Irrawaddy, river, 40, 99, 103,
 107, 112, 113, 148–9
Isa, Mohamed, 201–2, 204

Jacquemont, Victor, 80–1
Jaintia hills, 99
Java, 22
Jerko La, 48, 49
Jesuits, 34–5, 39–41; *see also*
 Andrade; Desideri
Johar valley, 120
Joseph (servant of Andrade), 40
Juliana, Donna, 41

Kailas, Mount, 12–13
 in Chinese cosmography,
 30–2
 circumambulation of, 25–6,
 50, 187–8, 208–10
 descriptions of, 25–6, 123–4,
 208
 exploration of, 13; Desideri,

Now you can order superb titles directly from Abacus

☐ Plain Tales from the Raj	Charles Allen	£8.99
☐ Tales from the South China Seas	Charles Allen	£9.99
☐ Soldier Sahibs	Charles Allen	£9.99

The prices shown above are correct at time of going to press. However, the publishers reserve the right to increase prices on covers from those previously advertised, without further notice.

───────────────── ⟨ABACUS⟩ ─────────────────

Please allow for postage and packing: **Free UK delivery.**
Europe: add 25% of retail price; Rest of World: 45% of retail price.

To order any of the above or any other Abacus titles, please call our credit card orderline or fill in this coupon and send/fax it to:

Abacus, PO Box 121, Kettering, Northants NN14 4ZQ
Fax: 01832 733076   Tel: 01832 737527
Email: aspenhouse@FSBDial.co.uk

☐ I enclose a UK bank cheque made payable to Abacus for £ . . . .
☐ Please charge £ . . . . . . to my Visa/Access/Mastercard/Eurocard

[ ][ ][ ][ ][ ][ ][ ][ ][ ][ ][ ][ ][ ][ ][ ][ ][ ][ ]

Expiry Date [ ][ ][ ][ ]   Switch Issue No. [ ][ ]

NAME (BLOCK LETTERS please) . . . .

ADDRESS . . . .

. . . .

. . . .

Postcode . . . . Telephone . . . .

Signature . . . .

Please allow 28 days for delivery within the UK. Offer subject to price and availability.

Please do not send any further mailings from companies carefully selected by Abacus ☐